# SCHOOL IMPROVEMENT
# *for* ALL

## A **How-To Guide**
## for **Doing** the **Right** Work

**Sharon V. Kramer**
**Sarah Schuhl**

Solution Tree | Press  a division of
Solution Tree

555 North Morton Street
Bloomington, IN 47404
800.733.6786 (toll free) / 812.336.7700
FAX: 812.336.7790

email: info@SolutionTree.com
SolutionTree.com

Visit **go.SolutionTree.com/PLCbooks** to download the free reproducibles in this book.

Printed in the United States of America

21 20 19 18 17          1 2 3 4 5

Library of Congress Cataloging-in-Publication Data

Names: Kramer, Sharon V., author. | Schuhl, Sarah, author.
Title: School improvement for all : a how-to guide for doing the right work /
  Sharon V. Kramer and Sarah Schuhl.
Description: Bloomington, IN : Solution Tree Press, [2017] | Includes
  bibliographical references and index.
Identifiers: LCCN 2017005335 | ISBN 9781943874828 (perfect bound)
Subjects: LCSH: School improvement programs--United States. | School
  management and organization--United States. | Educational change--United
  States.
Classification: LCC LB2822.82 .K72 2017 | DDC 371.2/07--dc23 LC record available at https://lccn.loc.gov/2017005335

**Solution Tree**
Jeffrey C. Jones, CEO
Edmund M. Ackerman, President

**Solution Tree Press**
*President and Publisher:* Douglas M. Rife
*Editorial Director:* Sarah Payne-Mills
*Managing Production Editor:* Caroline Weiss
*Senior Production Editor:* Suzanne Kraszewski
*Senior Editor:* Amy Rubenstein
*Copy Editor:* Miranda Addonizio
*Proofreader:* Evie Madsen
*Text and Cover Designer:* Laura Cox
*Editorial Assistants:* Jessi Finn and Kendra Slayton

*We dedicate this book to the tireless work of educators striving to improve the learning of each and every student. Because of you, lives are being saved and doors of opportunity continue to be opened.*

# Acknowledgments

This book stands on the shoulders of many leaders and pioneers in our education community. None are as impactful as Richard DuFour, who not only wrote prolifically about the work that matters most to students but also made that work come alive in his experiences as principal and superintendent at Adlai E. Stevenson High School. He, Robert Eaker, and Rebecca DuFour, the founders of Professional Learning Communities at Work™, have had an everlasting influence on our work and the work of countless others across the world. We are eternally grateful for the opportunity to learn from them. We share a special bond with Rick, Bob, and Becky that we cherish.

We are also fortunate to have the passionate support of Jeff Jones, the chief executive officer of Solution Tree, and the entire Solution Tree family. We are especially indebted to Douglas Rife, president and publisher of Solution Tree Press, for his encouragement along the way and Suzanne Kraszewski, our editor, for her attention to detail. Shannon Ritz, Claudia Wheatley, and countless others at Solution Tree support us each and every day.

In addition, our colleagues and friends—fellow Solution Tree associates who we have had the privilege of working alongside for years—have challenged us to grow in so many ways. They work endlessly on behalf of students and travel across the world often missing time with their families to spread the message that *all students can learn.*

Finally, this book could not have been written without the endless work of the educators in schools across the United States that have invited us on their continuous-improvement journeys. We learn so much from them as they work through the challenges and struggles schools that serve at-risk populations face. Their tireless focus on students is what keeps us going. This book is really their story.

Last, but not least, we have had the good fortune of coauthoring this book and are grateful to our families for their support. Continuous improvement for all is our passion. We believe all students should have the same options and opportunities that we want for our own children and grandchildren. This book represents our contribution to *learning for all.*

Solution Tree Press would like to thank the following reviewers:

Janel Keating
Superintendent
White River School District
Buckley, Washington

Barbara Phillips
Director of Data, Accountability, and Continuous Improvement
Windsor Central School District
Windsor, New York

Karen Branscombe Power
Educational Consultant
Moncton, New Brunswick
Canada

Jeanne Spiller
Assistant Superintendent for Teaching and Learning
Kildeer Countryside Community Consolidated School District 96
Buffalo Grove, Illinois

Mona Toncheff
Educational Consultant
Phoenix, Arizona

Megann Tresemer
Curriculum Professional Development Leader
Cedar Falls Community School District
Cedar Falls, Iowa

Mary White
Director of Elementary Programs and School Improvement
Martin County School District
Stuart, Florida

Visit **go.SolutionTree.com/PLCbooks** to download the free reproducibles in this book.

# Table of Contents

# About the Authors

**Sharon V. Kramer, PhD,** knows firsthand the demands and rewards of working in a professional learning community (PLC). As a leader in the field, she emphasizes the importance of creating and using quality assessments as a continual part of the learning process. Sharon served as assistant superintendent for curriculum and instruction of Kildeer Countryside Community Consolidated School District 96 in Illinois. In this position, she ensured all students were prepared to enter Adlai E. Stevenson High School, a model PLC started and formerly led by Richard DuFour. A seasoned educator, Sharon has taught in elementary and middle school classrooms and served as principal, director of elementary education, and university professor.

In addition to her PLC experience, Sharon has completed assessment training by Rick Stiggins, Steve Chappuis, Larry Ainsworth, and the Center for Performance Assessment (now the Leadership and Learning Center). She has presented a variety of assessment workshops at institutes and summits and for state departments of education. Sharon has also worked with school districts across the United States to determine their power standards and develop assessments. She has been a Comprehensive School Reform consultant to schools that have received grant funding to implement PLC as their whole-school reform model, and her customized PLC coaching academies have empowered school and district leadership teams across the United States.

Sharon has presented at state and national conferences sponsored by Learning Forward, National Association for Gifted Children, American Federation of Teachers, and California State University. She has been instrumental in facilitating professional development initiatives focused on standards-based learning and teaching, improved understanding and utilization of assessment data, interventions and differentiation that meet the needs of all learners, and strengthened efforts to ensure K–12 literacy.

Sharon earned a doctorate in educational leadership and policy studies from Loyola University Chicago.

To learn more about Sharon's work, follow @DrKramer1 on Twitter.

**Sarah Schuhl, MS,** is a consultant specializing in PLC, common formative and summative assessments, school improvement, and mathematics. She has been a secondary mathematics teacher, high school instructional coach, and K–12 mathematics specialist for more than twenty years.

Sarah was instrumental in the creation of a PLC in the Centennial School District in Oregon, helping teachers make large gains in student achievement. She earned the Centennial School District Triple C Award in 2012.

In addition to her work in Oregon, Sarah has worked with other districts throughout the United States to implement PLCs and create common assessments. Her practical approach includes working with teachers and administrators to implement assessments for learning, analyze data, collectively respond to student learning, and map standards. She is a consultant and coach in many schools, including those targeted for school improvement.

Sarah also works with districts as a consultant and coach to implement the Common Core State Standards for mathematics or independent state mathematics standards for K–12. Her work includes short- and long-term professional development focused on implementing content standards, Standards for Mathematical Practice or state process standards, and assessment, including formative assessment and an understanding of current state assessment practices. Her book, *Engage in the Mathematical Practices: Strategies to Build Numeracy and Literacy With K–5 Learners,* focuses on strategies to use when designing lessons that develop the habits of mind in students necessary for them to effectively learn mathematics.

Previously, Sarah served as a member and chair of the National Council of Teachers of Mathematics (NCTM) editorial panel for the journal *Mathematics Teacher.* Her work with the Oregon Department of Education includes designing mathematics assessment items, test specifications and blueprints, and rubrics for achievement-level descriptors. She has also contributed as a writer to a middle school mathematics series and an elementary mathematics intervention program.

Sarah earned a bachelor of science in mathematics from Eastern Oregon University and a master of science in mathematics education from Portland State University.

To book Sharon V. Kramer or Sarah Schuhl for professional development, contact pd@SolutionTree.com.

# Introduction

To aptly describe the state of education, one might paraphrase a familiar quote from the works of Charles Dickens (1859): it is the best of times and the worst of times (Eaker & Keating, 2011; Marzano, 2003). At this moment, the United States is experiencing the highest graduation rate in its history, according to data from the U.S. Department of Education's National Center for Education Statistics (NCES, 2016b). The high school graduation rate reached 82 percent in 2013–2014, the highest level since states adopted a uniform way of calculating graduation rates in 2010 (NCES, 2016b). More students than ever before are succeeding in rigorous curriculum, with Advanced Placement (AP) program participation at an all-time high (College Board, 2014). Perhaps even more important, there is evidence that students with low socioeconomic status have greater access to such opportunities. Schools are encouraging more students to participate in AP classes, making access to rigorous courses possible for all students who want to learn. From 2003 to 2013, the number of students who have taken AP courses nearly doubled, and the number of low-income students taking AP classes more than quadrupled from 58,489 to 275,864 (College Board, 2014). According to the College Board (2014), more students earned qualifying scores of 3, 4, or 5 than took exams in 2003.

In addition, the National Assessment of Education Progress (NAEP) reports increases in student achievement in reading and mathematics from 1990 (Nation's Report Card, 2015). Since 1990, NAEP has administered assessments to fourth- and eighth-grade students. In 2015, students had an average score in mathematics of 240 points at fourth grade and 282 points at eighth grade on scales of 0–500 points. Scores for both grades were higher than those from the earliest mathematics assessments in 1990 by 27 points at fourth grade and 20 points at eighth grade (Nation's Report Card, 2015). Reading achievement levels have risen slowly since 1992 with increases in fourth grade of 6 points from 217 to 223 and at eighth grade an increase of 5 points from 260 to 265 (Nation's Report Card, 2015). In addition, on the first NAEP Technology and Engineering Test, eighth-grade girls scored higher on average than eighth-grade boys (Zubrzycki, 2016), indicating the closing of the achievement gap for females.

The encouraging news continues with the improving results of the Trends in International Mathematics and Science Study (TIMSS). This is an assessment administered to approximately four thousand students in sixty-three countries. The results indicate that U.S. students have improved their scores from 1995 to 2015 in fourth grade from 518 to 539 and in eighth grade from 492 to 518 (International Association for the Evaluation of Educational Achievement [IEA], 2015a). In addition, in 2015, on the fourth-grade science assessment, U.S. students scored an all-time high of 546, and in eighth grade a new high of 230 (IEA, 2015b).

So, with all of this good news, how is it *also* the worst of times? Unfortunately, although the trends on the NAEP show growth for U.S. students from the start of the assessment through 2015, in reality, fourth-grade mathematics reached a high in 2013 of 242 and dropped 2 points in 2015; eighth-grade mathematics scores reached a high in 2013 of 285 and dropped 3 points in 2015. Similarly, eighth-grade reading scores reached a high in 2013 of 268 and dropped 3 points in 2015. Only fourth-grade reading achieved a high in 2015, increasing by 1 point over the results in 2013 (Nation's Report Card, 2015). Additionally, on the TIMSS assessments, fourth-grade mathematic dropped from a high of 541 in 2011 to 539 in 2015, while eighth-grade mathematics and fourth- and eighth-grade science showed growth in the same time period (IEA, 2015a, 2015b). The Programme for International Student Assessment (PISA), given to fifteen-year-olds, shows that U.S. students have declined in both mathematics and reading scores: from 483 in 2003 to 470 in 2015 for mathematics and 504 in 2003 to 497 in 2015 for reading (NCES, 2016c).

Furthermore, although more students are graduating, according to state listings noting priority schools most in need of improvement, too many schools still do not meet needed growth targets or the equivalent of adequate yearly progress (AYP) defined by No Child Left Behind. Additionally, half of U.S. high school dropouts come from about 15 percent of high schools. Unfortunately, there are few examples to date of such low-performing schools producing substantial and sustained achievement gains (Kutash, Nico, Gorin, Rahmatullah, & Tallant, 2010).

The gap in standardized test scores between affluent and low-income students has grown about 40 percent since the 1960s, and the imbalance between rich and poor students in college completion, the single most important predictor of success in the workforce, has grown 50 percent since the late 1980s (Greenstone, Looney, Patashnik, & Yu, 2013). Additionally, while the dropout rates of high school students are decreasing, there is a significantly larger percentage of students who drop out and are from families in the lowest quartile of family income—11.6 percent in 2014 compared to an overall rate of 6.5 percent (NCES, 2015). Education is the most powerful tool for helping students of poverty (Greenstone et al., 2013). Yet the numbers of students from low-income families who enter college after high school is unchanged in comparison to those from high-income families:

> The immediate college enrollment rate for high school completers increased from 60 percent in 1990 to 68 percent in 2014. The rate in 2014 for those from high-income families (81 percent) was nearly 29 percentage points higher than the rate for those from low-income families (52 percent). The 2014 gap between those from high- and low-income families did not measurably differ from the corresponding gap in 1990. (NCES, 2016b)

To complicate matters further, the neediest schools experience the most difficulty in attracting and retaining leaders and teachers. A study of Texas administrative data concludes that principal-retention rates are related to both student achievement and student poverty levels, with higher turnover among low-achieving, disadvantaged schools (Fuller & Young, 2009). In addition, these schools lose more than half of their teaching staff every five years (Allensworth, Ponisciak, & Mazzeo, 2009; Hemphill & Nauer, 2009, as cited in Le Floch, Garcia, & Barbour, 2016). The constant change of principals and teachers eliminates the consistent focused efforts necessary to improve schools.

Policymakers and education leaders have sought to improve America's low-performing schools. The U.S. government has made substantial investments in the form of School Improvement Grants (SIG) and Race to the Top (RTT) grants. However, the current systems and reform efforts are not working. Even considering the increase in graduation rates, approximately 20 percent of students who enter high school will drop out. In the 48 percent of U.S. schools that need improvement, the number of high school dropouts is much greater (Kutash et al., 2010). Schools can predict which students are at risk of dropping out by as early as first grade and identify these students with accuracy by third grade (American Psychological Association, 2012; Sparks, 2013).

Unfortunately, there are serious implications for students who do not succeed in school. In the United States, dropouts are three times more likely to be unemployed and therefore more likely to live in poverty with an estimated annual salary of $20,241 (Breslow, 2012). They will earn thirty-three cents for every dollar a college graduate earns. This is the highest discrepancy in the world (Organisation for Economic Co-operation and Development, 2011; U.S. Census Bureau, 2006). Also of concern is the fact that dropouts are more prone to ill health and are four times more likely to be uninsured or underinsured. The most astonishing statistic is that the life expectancy for dropouts is an average of ten and a half fewer years for women and thirteen fewer years for men than those with a high school diploma (Tavernise, 2012).

These alarming facts describe the urgency that failing schools face every day. The question is not *should* our schools improve, but *how?* The greatest challenge to school improvement is the overwhelming perception that no matter what teachers and administrators do, there seems to be no way out of failing results. Each year brings more state and federal mandates and sanctions to respond to with little hope of making a real difference for students. Failing schools want and need improvement—now!

So why haven't all the initiatives and reforms produced appreciable results that schools have sustained over time? Because "successful and sustainable improvement can never be done *to or even for* teachers. It can only be achieved *by and with* them" (Hargreaves & Fullan, 2012, p. 45). The missing element in all of these efforts is teachers and administrators. They are the only ones who can and do improve schools. Real school improvement occurs when a school harnesses the power within and focuses its efforts on higher levels of learning for all students. No amount of outside pressure will make schools improve; they only do so when the adults who work directly with the students decide it is their job to ensure all students learn at high levels. Helping students learn requires a collaborative and collective effort. Teachers and administrators must be ready to implement any necessary changes so that students can reach proficiency and beyond. Everyone focuses on evidence of student learning, every day, in every classroom—not just before administering a test.

## School Improvement for All

The processes we detail in this book harness the power within a school or district to achieve high levels of learning for all students. It does not require years of workshops and professional development before teachers can do the actual work. It requires learning through action—for a staff to roll up their sleeves and start the work immediately. If a patient comes into the emergency room with difficulty breathing, the nurses and doctors do not take the patient's temperature; they perform immediate triage to save the patient's life. Failing schools need a triage plan—an immediate course of action to put a halt to the continual-failure cycle.

First and most important, Professional Learning Communities at Work™ (PLC at Work) is the foundation for *School Improvement for All*. When a school operates as a PLC, real improvement becomes much more possible. Schools that embrace the three big ideas of a PLC as described by founders Richard DuFour, Robert Eaker, and Rebecca DuFour (DuFour, DuFour, Eaker, Many, & Mattos, 2016) understand the following.

1. The school's purpose is to ensure high levels of learning for *all* students. Therefore, there is a laser-sharp focus on student learning. In order to ensure high levels of learning, teachers must work together.

2. Only collaborative efforts will improve learning. No one person has all of the knowledge, skill, stamina, and patience to meet all student needs. Teachers have to hold hands and cross the street together because student needs are too great and the consequences of failure too dire to go it alone.

3. Schools must focus on results. Every teacher comes to school with good intentions, but if those good intentions do not materialize into greater learning for students, it doesn't matter. In the end, the proof is in the tangible results.

The schools and districts featured on AllThingsPLCs (www.allthingsplc.info) are examples of the PLC continuous-improvement cycle in action. Although each of their stories is unique, these schools have demonstrated evidence of effectiveness of PLC implementation that has resulted in higher levels of learning for all students.

How does *School Improvement for All* address the focus of PLCs that want to create the necessary environment for success for all students? The most distinct way is to use school-improvement efforts to target specific needs—determining the triage plan. Within a PLC, teachers must drive their work with a collaborative audit or needs-assessment process that takes a 360-degree view of a school's policies, practices, processes, and procedures in light of their effect on student achievement. The focus on data is relentless. The process is a true problem-solving model that leaves no stone unturned in the quest to ensure that all students learn at high levels. The true measure of success in schools that use *School Improvement for All* as a guide is that more students are learning at proficient or above-proficient levels on typical assessments from the school, district, state or province, or nation. This requires that teachers and administrators exert a focused, cohesive, and consistent effort over time; it demands a commitment from everyone to be *all in for student success*.

Although we recognize that all schools can and should improve, this book specifically supports schools and districts that are currently at risk or in danger of being designated in need of improvement by state or federal guidelines. It is also geared to support schools that have made few or no achievement gains over a number of years—in other words, schools with data that have flatlined. These schools are frustrated by their lack of progress and feel as if they have exhausted all of their options to improve, so triage is in order.

## Achieve Improvement

It turns out that superhuman powers are not a requirement for school improvement. School improvement is possible no matter the school's size; students' demographics, poverty levels, and achievement levels; or the amount of resources the staff and students have.

Figure I.1 shows the key features of *School Improvement for All*. At the center are the students, focusing on their unique needs as 21st century learners. These students are growing up in a world that has changed drastically from the one that the majority of educators experienced as students. Students in the 21st century are poised to be active participants in their own learning. Teachers must focus on preparing them for the possibilities of their future, not our past.

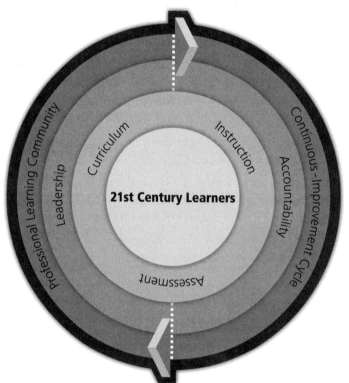

**Figure I.1: *School Improvement for All* features.**

To prepare students for their future, we must consider the question, What is the work that matters most? Teacher teams must do that work to yield increased learning for students. We know very well how hard teachers work on behalf of their students. They very often give up personal time to prepare lessons and activities. We are not suggesting that teachers need to work harder or longer; teachers already work hard enough. But it is important to engage in the right work—the work that yields better results. This means deeply understanding the standards they expect students to know and do, developing an assessment system that supports learning, aligning instructional practices to the cognitive complexity of the learning expectations, and providing interventions and extensions based on the data teams collect as part of the ongoing improvement cycle.

The next ring in figure I.1 is leadership and accountability. All members of the school and district staff should share these responsibilities. Everyone serves in a leadership capacity and is accountable for ensuring that all students learn at high levels. Leadership includes creating and nurturing a culture of success. Culture is not the principal's sole responsibility; everyone has a role in defining and shaping the school's culture. Administrators engage their staff in charting the course that leads to student learning. This requires that everyone embrace accountability—not shy away from it. Students need to be accountable for their learning, teachers accountable to their students, and administrators accountable to teachers and students. Leadership for learning is not a solo act; it is shared and widely dispersed.

The outer ring in figure I.1 contains the foundation of school improvement: a continuous improvement cycle based in the big ideas that all students can succeed, staff must work in a collaborative culture, and they must focus on results. These big ideas form the basis for the PLC process (DuFour et al., 2016), and schools that reculture themselves to become PLCs have successfully improved student learning. For example, see Sanger Unified School District under the See the Evidence webpage on AllThingsPLC (www.allthingsplc.info/evidence). (Visit **go.SolutionTree .com/PLCbooks** to access live links to the websites mentioned in this book.)

In the PLC continuous-improvement model, SMART goals (goals that are strategic and specific, measurable, attainable, results oriented, and time bound; Conzemius & O'Neill, 2013) and data drive the work of the entire organization. Schools work on sustaining their efforts from the beginning instead of waiting until they realize better results and only then asking how to sustain them. Sustainability begins with developing highly effective and efficient collaborative teams that engage in the right work, and schools can ensure they thrive by establishing the processes and protocols that represent the way the educators work together (DuFour et al., 2016). School improvement should never depend on who will do the work, but rather on how educators work together to achieve success for all students.

## About This Book

We designed this book to further describe the elements of the PLC continuous-improvement cycle shown in figure I.1. The chapters answer the how-to questions of implementation by providing templates and protocols that any school or district can use to improve student learning.

Each chapter culminates with an opportunity for schools and teams to reflect on their current reality and determine actions that will increase student learning. A rubric guides the reflection process. Finally, questions to consider when doing the work in each chapter allow for collaborative team discussions to further target improvement efforts.

### Chapter 1: Charting a Course Focused on Learning

This chapter outlines the actions necessary to chart a course focused on improved student learning. It demonstrates a model of leadership that is shared and widely dispersed to engage all stakeholders in the school-improvement process. The chapter also includes a collaborative audit, called a *needs assessment*, that helps teachers get at the root causes of stalled improvement and plan how to improve.

### Chapter 2: Transforming Culture and Structures

In our experience, creating a culture of success is the number one challenge in underperforming schools. This chapter details specific and targeted ways to move schools from a fixed mindset to a growth mindset and outlines the differences between toxic and healthy cultures. It shows how staff within schools can envision the desired culture and determine a plan to get there.

### Chapter 3: Focusing on 21st Century Learners

Students in 21st century classrooms face higher expectations for learning than ever before. To improve, schools and teachers must first answer the question, Who are our learners and what are their needs? To ensure high levels of learning for all students, teachers must focus on what each student needs. This chapter describes how to shift the focus to the individual needs of 21st century learners.

### Chapter 4: Establishing a Common Guaranteed and Viable Curriculum

All improvement efforts begin by asking, "What is it that students need to know and be able to do?" the first of four critical questions of a PLC (DuFour et al., 2016). The answer to this question cannot be up to each individual teacher. Collaborative teams of teachers work together to determine priority standards, unpack them into learning targets, and develop a common curriculum map that paces student learning. This chapter walks teachers through the rationale and process for developing a guaranteed and viable curriculum.

### Chapter 5: Creating and Using Common Assessments

Common formative and summative assessments are the lynchpin around which student learning revolves. Using timely and specific data on student learning drives instruction on a daily basis and helps students reflect on their learning. This chapter lays out the steps to developing common assessments. These are a crucial part of a system that ensures more learning and aligns with the requirements of the state and national assessments. When done well, this aligned system has predictive value for the high-stakes assessments.

### Chapter 6: Planning Meaningful and Effective Instruction

This chapter demonstrates how to plan effective instruction using the proficiency and curriculum maps that we establish in the two previous chapters. It describes the necessary shifts in instruction to meet the demands of increased rigor. We discuss the process of responding to student learning within core instruction (first-best instruction), as a collaborative team and as a school. We also outline the process of analyzing data and student work in a PLC that results in a targeted, effective response to student learning.

### Chapter 7: Embracing Accountability

A continual focus on data is the key to school improvement. There is so much to learn from even the most negative data. This chapter takes a broad look at data sources that are extremely helpful in the school-improvement process. It reinforces the need for regular data review cycles in a PLC, which are necessary to monitor progress along the journey. These data reviews promote authentic ways to measure growth and celebrate small successes of both collaborative teams and students. The only way to reverse a cycle of failure is to celebrate small wins.

## Follow the Path Ahead

We acknowledge that all schools are in need of improvement, but some more than others. We believe that if all students can learn, all schools can become models that others emulate. Our intent with this book is to further that cause for every school or district on an improvement journey.

CHAPTER 1

# Charting a Course Focused on Learning

*Indeed, there are virtually no documented instances of troubled schools being turned around without intervention by a powerful leader. Many other factors may contribute to such turnarounds, but leadership is the catalyst.*

*—Kenneth Leithwood, Karen Seashore Louis,*
*Stephen Anderson, and Kyla Wahlstrom*

It was October at Grant High School when the newly assigned principal realized that 204 of the 264 seniors were not on track to graduate that year. Most of them had not passed the state end-of-year assessment or had failed required courses. As Sharon, the school-improvement coach for the PLC at Work process (DuFour et al., 2016), met with the new principal, it was evident that immediate action was necessary. No student should spend an entire year in school with absolutely no hope of graduating. Sharon and the principal created a spreadsheet to show the current status of each student and each student's relevant information. The spreadsheet included courses completed, passing of required assessments, days absent, discipline referrals, tardies, and other pertinent data. The principal assembled a team consisting of the principal, assistant principals, counselors, registrar, team leaders, and the coach. The team discussed each failing student to determine his or her most appropriate pathway to graduation—for example, course recovery, night school, GED completion, and alternative options like blended schools or online school.

It became painfully clear that to meet the needs of these seniors, the entire master schedule, student schedules, and even teacher assignments would need to change. Many staff members complained and reminded the principal that schedules were only changed at the beginning of each semester—not in October. The principal met with teachers individually, in teams, and as a whole faculty to discuss the dire need for the changes. She told the stories of specific students to further demonstrate this need. She asked her staff members to put aside their own concerns because the consequences of not earning a high school diploma would be life altering.

She then met with each student and his or her parents to discuss the pathway to graduation that was most appropriate. As the principal and staff agreed on an individual plan for each student, they revised schedules and made appropriate placements.

The school year ended with all but seven students graduating through either the standard pathway or an alternative route. On graduation day, the teachers led the processional in caps and gowns. The student speaker at graduation thanked the teachers and administration and proclaimed, "You believed in me when I did not believe in myself."

Without the strong leadership of a student-centered principal, this story would have a very different ending. She understood that her priority was to be an advocate for her students no matter how difficult or how many obstacles stood in the way. She was willing to take up the cause with students, parents, teachers, counselors, and even the district office. When the school-improvement coach asked if it was worth all the trouble and effort, the principal answered with a resounding, "Yes! This was the right thing to do, and I would do it again without question" (T. Sanders, personal communication, October 2012).

School leadership matters. Strong school leadership is associated with higher student achievement levels (Branch, Hanushek, & Rivkin, 2013). It is second only to teaching itself among school-related factors that impact student learning. Principals can either support or inhibit the learning of both adults and students.

## Determine Vision Versus Reality

All too often the challenges facing a school in urgent need of improvement are numerous and varied. Determining where to start can be overwhelming; yet changes are critical to achieving student success. It takes a focused and intentional leader to create the effective leadership structures necessary to move teachers, students, parents, and community members toward a collective vision of teaching and learning. The goal is to become the effective school that leaders envision rather than settling for a less impactful alternative. A leader cannot simply impose new policies and procedures and expect better results.

In part, leading the task of turning around student achievement can be daunting because it requires second-order change. *First-order change* is doing more or less of what one is already doing, such as changing bus procedures to ensure a more orderly process or moving teachers of the same course or grade level to closer proximity with each other in the hope of increasing collaboration. First-order change is always reversible. It consists of adjusting the existing structure and seeks to restore balance or homeostasis. It is nontransformational and does not often require new learning. First-order change is change without making a real difference.

Conversely, *second-order change* is doing something significantly or fundamentally different from what one has done before. The process is usually irreversible. Once it has begun, it becomes undesirable to return to the former way of doing or being. It requires a new way of seeing things and is transformational. Table 1.1 shows examples that demonstrate the difference between first-order change and second-order change. First-order changes are usually strategies, while second-order change requires a shift in deeper philosophical beliefs. Second-order change requires new learning and results in creating a different story about the school. It shifts the culture to a more desired state. It is absolutely essential that underperforming schools understand second-order change. Table 1.1 describes a first-order change or change in strategy, such as creating smaller classes. This change will not result in more learning (or second-order change) unless the teaching philosophy shifts from whole-class to individual learning while establishing new relationships.

Table 1.1: First-Order Change and Corresponding Second-Order Change

| First-Order Change (Strategies) | Second-Order Change (Philosophies and Beliefs) |
| --- | --- |
| Smaller classes | New relationships and teaching philosophies (from whole-group instruction to an individualized approach to learning) |
| Site-based management | Collaborative ownership (from "This is *my* classroom" to "This is *our* school") |
| Ninety-minute teaching blocks | Extended teaching and learning opportunities to ensure all students learn (from doing more of the same type of instruction to varying instructional strategies) |
| Small learning communities (such as freshman academies or houses) | New interactions and relationships (from students being isolated to creating a system of support) |
| Teaching teams with common planning time | Collaborative teams focused on curriculum, instruction, and assessment (from spending team time planning lessons to focusing on student learning) |

*Source: Adapted from Fouts, 2003.*

With a clear understanding of the second-order change required, schools can move from a reality of false promises from too many strategy changes to philosophical and belief shifts in a system that actually improves learning. It takes an effective leader to manage this type of complex change and better the lives of students.

## Start Now

Principals and other administrators in underperforming schools are clearly not managing second-order change. Principals must understand how to lead this type of change; not impose change. So, what are the high-leverage leadership actions that support the change process? Leadership for change must include these four specific tasks.

1. Form a team capable of leading change.

2. Develop urgency and a collective vision for change.

3. Develop collective commitments that lead to action.

4. Clarify and communicate expectations for collaborative teams.

### Form a Team Capable of Leading Change

To be a leader is not a position or a title; it means one takes action and models behaviors. The most powerful and effective role the principal assumes is that of lead learner, not expert or "all-knowing one." Leadership that gets real results is collaborative; it's a process that involves building a school leadership team, a *guiding coalition* (DuFour et al., 2016), to lead the school-improvement transformation in what we can almost guarantee to be tumultuous work. The role of the leadership team is not the same as traditional leadership teams. Traditional leadership teams operate as communication vehicles between teachers and administration. The teachers typically bring up concerns or issues that they have heard about or are experiencing and want the principal to address. The principal uses this time to communicate information most often related to the operation of the building. The team rarely, if ever, spends this time discussing data or related topics. In contrast, the leadership team has the responsibility of leading the change process by focusing on learning. The members of this team are cheerleaders and problem solvers who are hungry for data that fuel school improvement.

The single most important task a principal can do to ensure high levels of learning for students and adults is to build a leadership team. We use the term *school learning team* because in schools in need of improvement, this team works to gain a deeper learning and understanding of the work. This team comprises administrators and team leaders from every teacher team. The group functions as a collaborative team and models the teaming process for the entire school. Leaders should never delegate selection of leadership team members to the teachers themselves or choose membership based on seniority. This is the leader's opportunity to grow the leadership in his or her school. The leader's responsibility is to create a strong team with members who have complementary strengths. It should include a balance of individuals who possess one or more of the following qualities.

- An eagerness to promote change

- Expertise relevant to the tasks at hand

- High credibility with all stakeholders

- Proven leadership skills

Use figure 1.1 (page 10) as a protocol to determine which teachers have these characteristics.

| Use the characteristics in each section to determine the most effective members of the leadership team. | |
|---|---|
| **Eagerness to Promote Change**<br><br>List individuals who are committed to school improvement. | **Expertise**<br><br>List individuals who have demonstrated knowledge and experience that will support school improvement. |
| **Credibility**<br><br>List individuals who are influential among the other staff members. | **Leadership Skills**<br><br>List individuals who are proven leaders in the school. |

*Source: Adapted from Buffum, Mattos, and Weber (2014) and Kotter (1996).*

**Figure 1.1: Leadership team selection protocol.**

*Visit **go.SolutionTree.com/PLCbooks** for a free reproducible version of this figure.*

These characteristics positively impact how the team will engage in the work and ultimately how much progress it will make along the way. Use the chart to list names of individuals who possess the stated qualities. Some names may appear in more than one category. Eliminate anyone who does not possess any of these qualities. It's possible that a current team leader or department chair may not be a good fit for the leadership team. Be aware that those on the leadership team are not always staff members who eagerly agree with one another or the principal. It is also important to include support staff representatives as a part of the leadership team. Everyone must be *all in for student success!*

It is not enough to simply create a leadership team; as DuFour et al. (2016) note, this team must engage in the right work. Its primary responsibility is to coordinate the school's collective efforts across grade levels, departments, and subjects. The leadership team meetings focus primarily on these PLC tasks.

- Build and support the school's mission of *learning for all.*

- Model the collaborative team process by using norms, agendas, meeting records, and so on.

- Create a master schedule that provides time for team collaboration, core instruction, intervention, and remediation.

- Coordinate staff and other resources to support core instruction and interventions.

- Articulate essential learning outcomes across grade levels and subjects.
- Ensure all students have access to grade-level or course-specific core instruction.
- Continually monitor schoolwide evidence of student learning.
- Support the work of collaborative grade-level and content teams.
- Problem solve school-improvement strategies to support increased student learning.
- Celebrate small wins along the journey with the entire staff.

The leadership team must operate as a model for all of the other collaborative teams in the school. The members should meet biweekly, or even more frequently, and provide meeting agendas and minutes to all staff members for their continued learning and understanding.

The first step in the modeling process is to set norms for adult behavior. *Norms* are the standards of behavior that members of the team agree to follow so that meetings are effective and efficient (Mattos et al., 2016). Team members can think of norms as the commitments they make to each other about how they will accomplish working together. As DuFour et al. (2016) note, there are procedural norms such as meeting times, attendance policies, punctuality expectations, shared responsibility for the work, and the need for follow through. In addition, there are behavioral expectations that address how a team will handle disagreements or make a team decision. The team must define, clarify, and describe a process for consensus decision making. The team should also establish an accountability norm that specifically states how the team will respond if any member violates the norms. The administrator is not the norm monitor; instead, the team designates a monitor and uses a nonverbal signal to indicate violations in an effort to monitor them. It is best for teams to handle norm violations themselves. Principals should meet with the entire team rather than individual members if norm violations are a persistent problem.

At the start and end of every meeting, the team reviews these norms, which describe how the team will function. Some typical team norms include but are not limited to the following.

- Procedural norms:
  - ‣ Start on time and end on time.
  - ‣ Be engaged.
  - ‣ Come prepared.
  - ‣ Be present—no cell phones, email, texting, and so on.
- Behavioral norms:
  - ‣ Focus on only those things we have control over.
  - ‣ Talk about students as if their parents are in the room.
  - ‣ Assume good intentions.
  - ‣ Focus on solutions rather than problems.
  - ‣ Use data and information to make decisions.
  - ‣ No parking lot meetings. Discuss concerns at the meeting, not elsewhere.
  - ‣ Respect the consensus of the group. Consensus means we will agree with the clear will of the group and enact the decision collectively after hearing each opinion and having a public *fist to five* vote (DuFour et al., 2016).
- Accountability norm:
  - ‣ The norm monitor designated for each team meeting (chosen on a rotating basis) signals any norm violations with team member input.

Every member of the leadership team must model norms at the meetings he or she leads. This means collaborative teacher team meetings as well as faculty meetings. Norms help every group to function as a high-performing team rather than simply a collection or group of people.

## Develop Urgency and a Collective Vision for Change

Every journey of improvement starts with the *why* before the *how*. This means that a school must examine the current reality and confront the brutal facts before it can take any meaningful action (Collins, 2001; DuFour et al., 2016). This is an especially difficult task for underperforming schools because they often have extremely negative or stagnant data. They must be willing to look at the good, the bad, and the ugly, no matter how uncomfortable that may be.

To determine each school's urgent and targeted needs for improvement, we use a needs-assessment protocol (much like an audit) based on the work of DuFour et al. (2016). An unbiased coach from outside the school usually administers the assessment, taking a 360-degree view of all of the school's policies, practices, procedures, and structures in light of their effect on student learning. The coach gathers evidence and summarizes the needs-assessment results. This protocol creates a safe environment for the coach, principal, and leadership team to engage in the difficult conversations that allow them to develop specific action steps for improvement. The protocol includes interviews with small focus groups of stakeholders and a review of all related data and information from which the coach, in collaboration with leadership, develops an actionable plan. The leader's job is to frame the challenge or challenges that are getting in the way of improvement in student learning without placing blame. This process requires a fearless inventory of the entire organization that paints a data picture of the school landscape. See the data-collection and focus-group protocols in figures 1.2 and 1.3 (pages 12–16).

| School Improvement for All *Data Collection Protocol* | |
| --- | --- |
| Provide the following school and student demographic data as available. | |
| Number of students in the school | |
| Gender (by number) | Male: _____   Female: _____ |
| Average class size | |
| Absentee rate (daily average) | |
| Ethnicity subgroup percentages | |
| Free and reduced lunch percentages | |
| Dropout rate | |
| Special needs subgroup percentages | |
| Mobility rate | |
| Honors and AP status percentage | |
| English learner percentage | |
| **Staff Demographics** | |
| Number of teachers | |
| Number of administrators | |
| Number of paraprofessionals | |
| Years of experience (average years by grade level) | |

| Absentee rate (daily average) | |
|---|---|
| Gender | Male: _____ Female: _____ |
| Retirement projections (the number of staff retiring in the next five years) | |
| Ethnicity subgroup percentages | |

| **School Demographics** |
|---|
| History of the school (describe briefly): |
| Safety and crime concerns: |
| Discipline referrals (year to date, monthly, average, and breakout of types of incidences by frequency): |
| Turnover rates of principals, teachers, and staff: |
| Special strengths and qualities of the school: |
| Programs offered, including academic, extracurricular, athletics, and so on: |
| Community support (describe briefly): |

| **Community Demographics** |
|---|
| Location and history (describe briefly): |
| Types of employers: |

**Figure 1.2: Data-collection protocol.**

continued →

| Population trends: |
| --- |
| Projection of growth: |
| Economic base: |
| Community and business involvement with school: |
| Other information: |

### *Student Learning Data*

(Attach student learning data as needed.)

| Indicator | Current Year | Previous Year |
| --- | --- | --- |
| Percentage of students reading at grade level | Percentage proficient or advanced | Percentage proficient or advanced |
| State test results for reading, English, and writing (by grade level or course) | Percentage proficient or advanced | Percentage proficient or advanced |
| State test results for mathematics (by grade level or course) | Percentage proficient or advanced | Percentage proficient or advanced |
| Gap-analysis state assessment results for reading, English, and writing by subgroups | Percentage proficient or advanced | Percentage proficient or advanced |
| Gap-analysis state assessment results for mathematics by subgroups | Percentage proficient or advanced | Percentage proficient or advanced |
| District, benchmark, and interim assessment results | Percentage proficient or advanced | Percentage proficient or advanced |

| Percentage of students failing courses for reading, English, and writing by course or grade level | Percentage of course or grade failures | Percentage of course or grade failures |
|---|---|---|
| Percentage of students failing courses for mathematics by course or grade level | Percentage of course or grade failures | Percentage of course or grade failures |
| High school graduation rate | | |
| Other achievement indicators (ACT, SAT, WorkKeys, course recovery, ACT Aspire, English learner assessments, and so on) | | |

*Visit **go.SolutionTree.com/PLCbooks** for a free reproducible version of this figure.*

| *Focus-Group Questions* |
|---|
| **Student Focus-Group Questions** |
| • How does your school celebrate student success? <br> • Do you feel safe at school? Why or why not? <br> • How is the attendance at your school? Do your classmates make coming to school a priority? <br> • What could teachers and staff do to help you do better at school? <br> • Is the school preparing you for middle school, high school, or career and college expectations? <br> • What opportunities do you have to provide input on how the school could better help and support you? <br> • How does the school involve your family in what is happening in your learning? <br> • How do the teachers show you that they care about you and encourage you to be your best? <br> • What would make this a better school? |
| **Parent Focus-Group Questions** |
| • Do you believe that the teachers at your child's school help your child to succeed in reading and English language arts? In mathematics? Why or why not? <br> • Do you believe that your child is going to be prepared for the next level of learning in school? Do you believe your child will graduate? Why do you think so? <br> • Do you see yourself as part of the school community? Why or why not? <br> • How does the school solicit your input for improvement? <br> • How does the school celebrate success? <br> • What suggestions or concerns do you have that could help this school do a better job of preparing students for the future? |

**Figure 1.3: Focus-group protocol.**

continued →

| Teacher Focus-Group Questions |
|---|
| • How does the school celebrate success for students? For teachers? For the school as a whole? |
| • Has the school identified what it expects students to know and be able to do with learning targets for each subject? If not all subjects, what subjects are completed? Is this aligned with state standards and testing requirements? |
| • How do teams use a teaching calendar to ensure mastery in time for the state assessment? Does it include time for reteaching? |
| • Do teacher teams administer common formative assessments? If so, how do they use the data? |
| • Have teacher teams agreed on what proficiency looks like for each assessment? Do students know how to become proficient on each standard? |
| • What intervention schedules and programs are in place to support students when they have not learned the standards and learning targets the first time? |
| • How do teachers provide input in improving the school? |
| • What suggestions or concerns do you have that could help this school improve to better prepare students for the future? |

*Visit **go.SolutionTree.com/PLCbooks** for a free reproducible version of this figure.*

Leadership consists of both pressure and support. A leader must create more pressure for change than there is resistance to change or nothing will change. Second-order or lasting change will only occur if the leader is willing to frame the challenges that block improvement efforts. When schools try to improve without a clear understanding of the root causes of the issues and problems they face, their progress is slow and minimal. A school cannot continue to treat the symptoms of the problem without understanding the underlying causes. The audit or needs assessment helps teams analyze these root causes and leads to actionable steps to improvement. A graphic organizer for determining root causes and solutions appears in chapter 2 (page 27). The end result of the collaborative conversations within the assessment is a shared definition of the current reality as advocated by DuFour et al. (2016). It answers the *why* of school improvement before the *how*.

Once teams understand the current reality, the next step is to create a shared vision for change. A shared vision answers the question, What do we want to become? (DuFour et al., 2016). Without a clear and compelling vision, organizations have no direction. To use a navigational system for directions, we must first decide on the destination—otherwise the GPS just tells us the current location. If a school does not have a clear understanding of where it is headed, it may vaguely hope for better results year after year, but has no clear goal.

A school's vision describes a compelling picture of a preferred future that inspires action throughout an organization (DuFour et al., 2016). The process for creating a shared vision for change asks each staff member to envision the ideal school in just a few sentences. Leaders can accomplish this by asking staff to write a headline that will appear in the newspaper five years from now about their school. What will they write on the front page of the newspaper? (See figure 1.4.) The leadership team collects these headlines to look for commonalities and themes. The team then drafts a vision statement to share with the entire staff for input and revision. After all voices have weighed in, the team reaches consensus for final approval of the vision.

---

**Headline News**

Five years from now, what will the front page of the newspaper say about our school because of our collective focus on student learning? Write the story's headline.

---

What are the key points in this article?

1.




2.




3.

---

**Figure 1.4: Shared-vision protocol.**

*Visit **go.SolutionTree.com/PLCbooks** for a free reproducible version of this figure.*

## Develop Collective Commitments That Lead to Action

Unfortunately, creating a vision statement does nothing to improve learning. Each staff member in the school must commit to action. Without cohesive, focused effort to further the vision, the statement is nothing more than a picture on the wall. Every staff member asks, "How must we behave to reach our vision? What must I do to ensure we will get there? What must happen to make the words and phrases in the vision come alive? How will we live our vision every day?" In other words, What if we really meant it?

Truly living the vision for improvement requires *collective commitments*: "the specific attitudes and behaviors people within the organization pledge to demonstrate" (Mattos et al., 2016, p. 24). These statements begin with the words, *We will* . . . . The process of developing collective commitments begins by the principal asking each staff member to answer the question, What actions, if we collectively committed to them, would lead our school closer to achieving our vision than anything else? The learning team collects and reviews these statements to determine commonalities and themes and then sends them to the entire staff for a final consensus. Figure 1.5 (page 18) is an example of collective commitments that the Mason Crest Elementary staff members made.

---

***Mason Crest Elementary Staff Collective Commitments***

**2015–2016**

In order to honor and advance our shared purpose, vision, and goals, we pledge to honor the following collective commitments. We will:

- Identify and teach the agreed-upon essential standards and break them down into learning outcomes (written in student-friendly language), adhere to the curriculum pacing established by the team, and help our students discover what they can do with that knowledge.

- Create both common formative and summative assessments and administer them according to the team's agreed-upon time line.

- Use the results from our common assessments to improve our individual and collective practice and to meet the extension and intervention needs of our students.

- Contribute to an effective system of intervention and extension while providing enrichment opportunities to all.

- Be positive, contributing members of the schoolwide team as we work interdependently using common language to achieve shared goals and demonstrate mutual accountability.

- Engage in open and frequent two-way communication among all stakeholders, provide families with ongoing information about their children, and offer specific ideas and materials to help families become full partners in the ongoing education of their children.

- Embrace shared responsibilities and help others grow in their leadership responsibilities.

- Contribute to a culture of celebration by acknowledging the efforts and achievements of our students and colleagues as we continually strive for even greater success.

- Agree to common behavioral expectations, model and teach that behavior, and consistently reinforce our expectations.

- Consider all points of view and come to our work each day as the best versions of ourselves.

- Honor the individual and unique qualities of our students and at the same time not use their uniqueness to label them.

---

*Source: Mason Crest Elementary, Annandale, Virginia. Used with permission.*

**Figure 1.5: Collective commitments example from Mason Crest Elementary.**

The staff review and revise these commitments each and every school year. Staff members hold each other accountable for keeping these promises. The principal and administrators must also be willing to make commitments by identifying the specific actions they will take to support the staff's collective efforts to reach the vision. (See figure 1.6 for an example.) As the principal and administrators share these commitments with the staff, they align the sense of urgency for improvement with real actions. People begin to believe that reaching the vision is possible. This internal accountability is what harnesses the power within a school to increase student learning.

*Collective Commitments From Mason Crest Elementary Administrators*

**2015–2016**

In order to create the school we have described in our shared vision, we make the following commitments. We pledge that we will:

- Promote and protect our shared mission, vision, collective commitments, and goals, and keep them at the forefront of all decisions and actions. In doing so, we will confront staff whose actions are incongruent with our shared purpose and priorities and attempt to buffer the staff from competing initiatives so they can devote their full energies to the PLC process.

- Build shared knowledge around the term *collaborative team* and the various structures these teams can take.

- Support collaborative teams by providing them with sufficient time to meet, clear direction regarding the work to be done, ongoing feedback, and the training and resources necessary to help them succeed at what they are being asked to do.

- Provide all teams with the Program of Studies and ensure the specialists working with the teams facilitate dialogue to promote a deep understanding of essential standards and learning outcomes.

- Build shared knowledge around team-developed common formative assessments and provide training that will enable teams to easily and effectively disaggregate data to—
  - ➤ Better meet the intervention and extension needs of individual students
  - ➤ Inform and improve practice of individual members of the team
  - ➤ Improve the team's collective ability to achieve its SMART goals

- Provide examples of systems of intervention, extension, and enrichment and work with staff to create effective systems for Mason Crest.

- Help staff understand the definition of and their roles as team members.

- Model open communication by sharing important information in a timely manner.

- Create opportunities for leadership throughout the staff based on individual expertise and interest.

- Model, encourage, and plan for celebration as a part of our culture, and approach initial efforts that do not achieve the intended results as opportunities to begin again more intelligently rather than as failures.

*Source: Mason Crest Elementary, Annandale, Virginia. Used with permission.*

**Figure 1.6: Administrative collective commitments example from Mason Crest Elementary.**

In order to realize the vision, the school creates goals with short- and long-term action steps. These are learning goals that focus on increasing student achievement. Goals help monitor progress along the way. They are "measurable milestones that leaders use to assess progress in advancing toward a vision" (Mattos et al., 2016, p. 25). They structure the work in a manner that gets real results. Without goals, schools simply hope for better results, and when they achieve them, it is usually a surprise; the school has no real understanding of how it improved. No one has ownership. They cannot clearly explain the antecedents of excellence to continue or enhance. Schoolwide goals state the priorities and are the benchmarks that teams monitor throughout the year. Figure 1.7 (page 20) contains examples of schoolwide goals for both high school and elementary school (DuFour et al., 2016, pp. 44, 45).

| High School Goals |
| --- |
| • Reduce the failure rate. |
| • Increase the percentage of students pursuing and succeeding in the most rigorous curriculum in each program. |
| • Increase student achievement on local, state, and national high-stakes assessments. |
| • Increase the percentage of graduates who experience success in postsecondary learning. |
| **Elementary School Goals** |
| • Improve student achievement in language arts in each grade level as measured by performance on local, district, state, and national assessments. |
| • Improve student achievement in mathematics in each grade level as measured by performance on local, district, state, and national assessments. |

*Source: DuFour et al., 2016, pp. 44, 45.*

**Figure 1.7: Schoolwide goal examples.**

Based on the schoolwide goals, each collaborative team of teachers creates a SMART goal that describes the greatest area of need for that grade level or content area. It uses data to determine the current reality and achievement levels. Using the current data, the team projects an increase in learning. This is usually a school-year goal that fulfills the SMART criteria (Conzemius & O'Neill, 2013).

- **S**trategic and specific
- **M**easurable
- **A**ttainable
- **R**esults oriented
- **T**ime bound

A goal is strategic and specific when it addresses a targeted need that teachers have identified by analyzing several data points. Teachers determine SMART goals by determining the gap between the current reality and proficiency. In addition, using data ensures that the goal is measurable. The gap between current performance and proficiency can be large and difficult to reach. Therefore, teachers should write goals with high expectations in mind and require some stretch to get there, but at the same time, they must be attainable. SMART goals are results oriented, not a to-do list of activities or a process. This means that a results-oriented goal includes a measurable focus on some aspect of student learning. We show the difference between process goals and results goals in table 1.2.

**Table 1.2: Process Versus Results Goals**

| Process Goals | Results Goals |
| --- | --- |
| Implement an integrated mathematics and science curriculum. | Reduce the failure of mathematics and science students by at least 20 percent. |
| Develop a balanced literacy program for primary students. | Increase the number of students who are reading on grade level by the end of third grade from 67 percent to at least 87 percent. |
| Adopt a zero-tolerance policy toward violence. | Eliminate violent behavioral incidences. |

Finally, SMART goals are time bound; there is a specific time frame to successfully achieve the goal. Examples of team SMART goals include the following.

- By spring 2017, the percentage of fifth-grade students meeting or exceeding grade-level proficiency on the reading state assessment will increase from 40 percent to at least 85 percent.

- By spring 2017, the percentage of ninth-grade algebra 1 students meeting or exceeding proficiency on the state end-of-instruction assessment will increase from 60 percent to at least 87 percent.

- By spring 2017, the number of second-grade students solving two-step word problems will increase from 27 percent (pretest) to at least 80 percent (post-test).

Teams develop SMART goals by examining data to determine program goals (goals focused on improving student learning in a grade-level subject or course) and cohort goals (goals for the same group of students over time). Teams review the data from the previous year to decide how they will improve their results in the upcoming school year. As collaborative teams focus on program-improvement goals, they should expect to get better results every year because they are learning more about what works and what needs improvement in instruction, curriculum, and assessment practices. Then the teams *graduate the data to the next grade level or course* to allow the teachers to review the results of their incoming students. Teams review the students' data over time, as they progress through the grades, to determine if these cohort groups are continuing to grow across grade levels. The cohort data also provide more information to successive teachers as to who the new learners will be and what they may need.

The teams then chunk these yearly team goals into short-term checkpoints. Teams use common formative and summative assessments to determine if they are making progress toward achieving the end goal. (See chapter 5, page 79.) The results of these collaboratively developed and scored assessments determine instructional revisions and interventions for students along the way. This increases student learning and informs instruction in unit-by-unit cycles. Through this process of monitoring the short-term goals, students and teachers are able to celebrate successes and check progress closely to meet individual student needs and get them to proficiency. (See chapter 7, page 137, for more information on using SMART goals for accountability purposes.)

## Clarify and Communicate Expectations for Collaborative Teams

As Rebecca DuFour often states in her PLC staff development presentations, "Clarity precedes competence." Every educator comes to work wanting to do a good job, but if he or she doesn't know what a good job looks like, it will ultimately lead to confusion and frustration. Collaborative teacher teams must engage in the right work that improves student achievement. The role of the principal and the leadership team is to clarify and communicate exactly what the right work looks like, sounds like, and feels like for all staff members. Increasing the capacity of any organization begins by building shared knowledge.

All school-improvement efforts designed to increase student learning consist of the following five essential elements as described by Richard DuFour in his PLC at Work keynote presentations (DuFour, 2016).

1. All teachers must work on a collaborative team. No one works in isolation.

2. Teachers implement a guaranteed and viable curriculum—a curriculum that contains the most important or essential knowledge and skills students need with time to learn them—on a unit-by-unit basis (Marzano, 2003).

3. Teams monitor student learning in an ongoing assessment process that includes team-developed common formative assessments.

4. Teams use the results of common assessments to improve individual practice, build team capacity to achieve goals, and intervene in or extend student learning.

5. The school provides a system of teacher, team, and schoolwide interventions and extensions.

Principals create a loose-tight culture by explicitly communicating (tight) what everyone will do and giving the teachers and collaborative teams the autonomy (loose) to determine how they will get there (DuFour et al., 2016). These five tight elements will increase student learning. We discuss them in further detail throughout this book.

Collaboration is the key to learning for all. It is the "engine that fuels the school improvement process" (Mattos et al., 2016, p. 37). As a part of the collaborative teaming process, teams take collective responsibility for student learning. "Team members work interdependently to achieve common goals for which they are mutually accountable" (Mattos et al., p. 37). Teachers begin to refer to students as *our* students, not just *my* students or the students in time-block five. No one individual has all of the knowledge, skill, patience, or insights to meet the needs of all students. It is through collaborative efforts that options and opportunities grow for the students each teacher serves. This process is as much about adult learning as it is about student learning. Student learning will not increase if the capacity of the teachers to deliver specific lessons and implement best practices does not also increase. In fact, "teachers and students go hand-in-hand as learners—or they don't go at all" (Barth, 2001, p. 23).

Just being a member of a team isn't enough. Collaborative teams must engage in the right work. The principal and leadership team must define, clarify, and communicate what that work looks like. The four critical questions of a PLC (DuFour et al., 2016) that teams answer on a unit-by-unit basis embody the right work. This is applicable for all schools, no matter if they are involved in the PLC process or not.

1. What do we want students to know and be able to do?
2. How will we know if they learned it?
3. What will we do if they don't learn it?
4. What will we do for those who have already learned the concept?

Principals need to provide and protect the time for collaborative team meetings during the school day. It is impossible for teams to answer these four questions without the necessary time it takes to discuss each one. Leaders need to structure school schedules so that teams of teachers meet regularly (almost daily) during the regular school day to engage in this work. Scheduling reflects a school's priorities. If collaboration is a priority, and it should be, then the schedule will reflect the time necessary to actually do the work of the team. Sample school schedules with collaborative team time are accessible at AllThingsPLC under Tools and Resources (www.allthingsplc.info /tools-resources).

It is not enough to tell teams that they must answer the four critical questions of a PLC on a unit-by-unit basis; it is also important to describe the work teams would engage in during this process. The best way to describe, clarify, and monitor the tasks of teams is to delineate the products that they would create from answering the four questions. For example, the team products for question one (What do we want students to know and be able to do?) are the essential or priority standards for this unit, the standards unpacked into learning targets, and descriptions of proficient, above proficient, and below. Figure 1.8 outlines the tasks of collaborative teams, products, and time lines for each of the four questions.

| *Collaborative Team Tasks and Products* | | |
| --- | --- | --- |
| **Short-Term and Long-Term Goals** | | |
| **Defined Tasks** | **Completion Date** | **Products and Artifacts** |
| Create and monitor team norms. | | Norms |
| Establish protocols: roles, agenda building, record keeping, consensus, and so on. | | Protocols |
| Establish team SMART goals. | | SMART goals |
| Continually monitor progress on SMART goals using summative and common formative assessments. | | SMART goal action plan |
| Celebrate success (frequent small wins along the way)! | | Celebration sheet |

| *PLC Critical Question One* | | |
|---|---|---|
| **What do we expect students to know and be able to do?** | | |
| **Defined Tasks** | **Completion Date** | **Products and Artifacts** |
| Review state standards and align curriculum. | | Curriculum documents |
| Identify the essential standards for each grade level and subject area using endurance, leverage, and readiness criteria. | | List of essential grade-level or content-specific standards |
| Vertically align essential standards, looking for gaps and redundancies. | | Aligned curriculum guides |
| Pace the curriculum, emphasizing when to teach the learning targets. | | Pacing guide or course sequence |
| *PLC Critical Question Two* | | |
| **How will we know if students have learned it?** | | |
| Unwrap each of the essential standards into learning targets (determine learning progression). | | Unwrapped essential standards with learning targets |
| Map each standard, indicating the summative and formative assessments. | | Assessment map for each essential standard |
| Develop common formative assessments for each learning target. | | Common formative assessments |
| Determine proficiency levels. | | Rationale |
| Develop grading rubric or scoring guide. | | Rubric or written criteria |
| Write learning targets in student-friendly language by engaging students in the process. | | Student-friendly targets |
| Create and share anchor papers with students, demonstrating strong and weak work (collaboratively score student work). | | Anchor papers |
| Analyze assessment results. | | Item analysis with data team protocol |
| *PLC Critical Question Three* | | |
| **How will we respond if students have not learned?** | | |
| Identify systematic responses for students who are failing. | | Remediation strategies |
| Create interventions for students who fail to meet learning targets on common formative assessments. | | Intervention strategies |
| Identify students in need of interventions by essential standard or learning target and specific need. | | List of students with specific data |
| Group students for instruction by specific essential standard or learning target. | | Student groupings by standard, learning target, or need |
| Evaluate the progress of students after interventions. | | Monitoring tool |

**Figure 1.8: The work of collaborative teams.**

continued ➡

| PLC Critical Question Four<br>How will we respond if students have already learned? | | |
|---|---|---|
| **Defined Tasks** | **Completion Date** | **Products and Artifacts** |
| Identify systematic responses for students who have already mastered the essential standards. | | Student groupings by standard, learning target, or need |
| Identify students who demonstrate proficiency and above on common formative assessments. | | List of students with specific data |
| Create extension activities for students who demonstrate proficiency and above. | | Extension activities |
| Evaluate student progress after the extension activity. | | Monitoring tool |

*Sources: DuFour et al., 2010; Kramer, 2015.*

*Visit **go.SolutionTree.com/PLCbooks** for a free reproducible version of this figure.*

As teams answer question one (What do we expect students to know and be able to do?), they create and implement the guaranteed and viable curriculum on a unit-by-unit basis. Teams answer question two (How will we know if students have learned it?) as they develop common formative assessments to monitor learning. Teams address question three (How will we respond if students have not learned?) as they examine data from common assessments for the purposes of intervening with students. Teams answer question four (How will we respond if students have already learned?) as they develop extension questions and activities that align to the learning targets in the unit. Students extend their learning while others may need extra time and support to learn. As teams answer these targeted and specific questions, they create the products of collaboration that improve schools. The administration and leadership team monitor these actions in an effort to support collaborative teams in the process. We will discuss how to answer these questions in the ensuing chapters.

Finally, clarifying and communicating expectations is never a one-time event; it is an ongoing process of building shared knowledge as an entire staff, in team meetings, and one conversation at a time. It requires different levels of support for different groups of people. No one way will work for the entire staff. The important point is that the principal and learning team must speak with one voice. Everyone must communicate the same clear, consistent message over and over again. As each year begins, the principal, leadership team, and collaborative teams revisit and further clarify their expectations. This is the continuous-improvement cycle in action.

As we previously stated, leadership for learning is a combination of exerting pressure and providing support. Principals practice reciprocal accountability in both their words and actions (Elmore, 2004). This means that whenever a leader holds others accountable for completing a task or goal, the leader is accountable for providing the resources necessary for success. The leadership team is the vehicle for modeling the expectations and providing the supports necessary so that every team can experience success. If the goal is highly effective and efficient collaborative teams, the question becomes, What will they need to perform at this level? It is certain they will need sufficient time to meet, clear direction regarding the work to be done, ongoing feedback, and training and resources necessary to help them succeed at what they are being asked to do. Leadership for learning develops people and harnesses the power within the organization to increase student learning.

The key to charting a course focused on learning is to create a common vision together and commit to each other to act and hold each other accountable for engaging in that work. Leaders demonstrate what they value by those things they choose to monitor, celebrate, and confront (DuFour et al., 2016). Choose the most important factors presented in this chapter that will improve student achievement at your school based on your current reality and needs. Be willing to address an obvious problem and hold people accountable for the collective commitments and core practices that are essential to improved results. What you permit, you promote. Be intentional and purposeful in promoting the right work.

## Reflect and Take Action

The rubric in figure 1.9 shows levels in charting a course focused on learning. Look at the rubric to determine staff strengths and next steps to plan the actions necessary to improve learning.

|  | Level 1<br>Beginning | Level 2<br>Attempting | Level 3<br>Practicing | Level 4<br>Embracing |
|---|---|---|---|---|
| **Leadership Team** | Team contains volunteer teachers and staff.<br><br>Team focuses on every issue and may spend more time on complaints and ideas for first-order change than student learning.<br><br>Team creates an agenda but does not always follow it and operates using procedural norms. | Team contains previously designated leaders or rotating leaders.<br><br>Team leads the work of school improvement, but may be focused on first-order change.<br><br>Team creates agendas for meetings in advance of the meetings and operates using norms. | Team contains teachers with characteristics including change agent, expert, credible, and leader.<br><br>Team models and leads the work of school improvement.<br><br>Team creates agendas, shares meeting minutes, and operates using norms. | Team contains teachers with characteristics, including change agent, expert, credible, and leader, and re-evaluates members each year with entrance and exit interviews.<br><br>Team models, monitors with feedback, and leads the work of school improvement.<br><br>Team creates agendas and shares minutes electronically while using norms. |
| **Vision and Action** | Team looks at data related to student achievement and demographics.<br><br>A vision statement exists, though the team seldom, if ever, references or addresses it.<br><br>The team has only loosely agreed on collective commitments and has not written them down. It is focused on goals and not results. | Teams gather and analyze data related to demographics and student learning.<br><br>The team has established a vision and written it down for each adult in the school. Some staff members work toward it.<br><br>The team has established collective commitments or goals. | Teams gather and analyze a full picture of data to determine the root issues to address to improve learning.<br><br>The team has established a vision, which compels those in the building to reach it.<br><br>The team has established collective commitments and goals. | Teams gather and analyze data from all stakeholders routinely and in a location that leadership can easily access.<br><br>The team has established a vision and all in the community work toward achieving it.<br><br>The team has established collective commitments and goals and routinely reviews and updates them as necessary. |

**Figure 1.9: Chart a course focused on learning rubric.**

continued →

| | Level 1 Beginning | Level 2 Attempting | Level 3 Practicing | Level 4 Embracing |
|---|---|---|---|---|
| Leading the Right Work | Teachers wait to be told what to do (and will do it) but are not clear about what is tight and loose in the work of school improvement. Teacher teams are clear about and address some of the four critical questions of a PLC. | The work of collaborative teams is all designated as tight and teams are on rigid schedules of what to address and when, but may not be clear about why. Teacher teams comply with addressing the four critical questions of a PLC but are still unclear about why. | The principal and teachers are clear about what is tight and what is loose in the work of school improvement. Teachers work to address the four critical questions of a PLC in collaborative teams, using data to determine student learning. | The principal, teachers, and staff are clear about what is tight and loose in the work of school improvement and focus on student learning. Teachers work in collaborative teams to improve student learning using the four critical questions of a PLC and monitor that journey continually. |

Visit **go.SolutionTree.com/PLCbooks** for a free reproducible version of this figure.

Once teams have reached agreement about their current status, they should use figure 1.10 to determine the next steps focused on learning.

| Action | Team-Level Rating | Next Steps |
|---|---|---|
| Forming a leadership team | | |
| Developing vision and action | | |
| Leading the right work | | |

**Figure 1.10: Chart a course focused on learning reflection and action plan.**

Visit **go.SolutionTree.com/PLCbooks** for a free reproducible version of this figure.

## Collaborative Team Questions to Consider

- How can your school build a leadership structure that focuses on learning?
- How will you engage teachers as leaders?
- What products of collaboration will you monitor? How will you provide meaningful feedback?
- How will you support the work of teams?
- What structures exist to lead and support the work of teams?
- What is your compelling vision?
- What steps will you take to make sure that your vision lives beyond the paper it is written on?
- How will you turn your collective commitments into actions?
- What process will you use to create, monitor, and celebrate SMART goals throughout the year?

CHAPTER 2

# Transforming Culture and Structures

The greatest challenge to school improvement is the overwhelming perception that no matter what the teachers and administrators do, there seems to be no way out of failing results. With some of the lowest annual student-achievement results, there is a perception among staff that students' poverty and low skills, as well as disengaged families, are more potent than any teacher's impact, which leads to a sense of futility. Teachers often feel deflated by a sense that their best efforts are ineffective and unappreciated by students, families, or the system in which they work.

—*Sharon V. Kramer*

Sharon entered Washington Middle School just as students were starting to arrive, lining up to start their school day by walking through metal detectors while security staff searched their backpacks. As she watched the students enter, she was struck by how many of them looked down and avoided eye contact with others. So far, Sharon had witnessed little laughter or joy in the eyes of staff or students. Unfortunately, this scene plays out daily in schools that have repeatedly experienced failure. Missing is the joy and passion for learning of teachers and students alike, replaced instead by a feeling of compliance and hopelessness. Students are acutely aware when they attend a school that ranks as low or underperforming. They often come to school with a "Why try?" attitude of defeat.

No amount of structural or technical change can overcome a feeling that failure defines us. Only a shift in culture can defeat this feeling. In PLCs, this is called *reculturing* (DuFour et al., 2016). Often schools attempt to fix problems related to failure by adopting a new curriculum or textbooks, revising the schedule, or implementing a new discipline program—all first-order changes. While these types of structural changes may be necessary, they alone are never enough to overcome a culture of failure. "Structural change that is not supported by cultural change will eventually be overwhelmed by the culture, for it is in the culture that any organization finds meaning and stability" (Schlechty, 2001, p. 52).

School culture is "the set of norms, values, and beliefs, rituals, ceremonies, symbols, and stories that make up the 'persona' of the school" (Peterson, 2002, p. 10). It manifests itself in the stories the staff and administrators tell about their work, the students, and the school or district. Staff members in underperforming schools are often frustrated by students' lack of progress. Unfortunately, a highly frustrated staff is also a highly unproductive staff. The constant feeling of having no control saps their energy. This leads to a toxic culture that permeates the entire school. Teaching and learning do not flourish in a toxic environment. Second-order change is necessary to reculture the school.

## Determine Vision Versus Reality

A toxic or dysfunctional culture promotes the belief that student success is based on students' level of concern, attentiveness, prior knowledge, and willingness to comply with the demands of the school (Muhammad, 2009). In other words, schools with toxic cultures deflect blame from the school to the students. The stories teachers tell often reflect their frustration and shift blame to students or parents. Negativity replaces optimism among staff and students, leading to increased absenteeism. Both from our experiences and those of Anthony Muhammad, in schools with a toxic or dysfunctional culture, it is not uncommon for teacher absenteeism to be higher than student absenteeism (Muhammad, 2009).

Often principals in underperforming schools inherit toxic cultures and staff division. In this scenario, principals regularly shift their focus to maintaining order in an attempt to support staff. This negative culture for teaching and learning creates an almost impossible learning environment. The following six familiar stories illustrate the most common characteristics of toxic cultures.

1. **Our students and parents have changed:** In the past, our school had high-achieving students. Our scores were great and we were considered one of the best schools to attend. Then the students and parents changed. Now the students refuse to do their homework and the parents are unresponsive and uninvolved. Many of the students in our classes do not even speak English. We have a high rate of special education students who are too far behind to ever catch up. If only the students and parents were different, achievement would increase.

2. **Teachers are independent contractors who share a common hallway:** I have been teaching in this school for over twenty years. I get pretty good results every year. I truly understand my curriculum expectations and teach it the way I believe it should be taught. Academic freedom and autonomy are the only ways to increase student achievement. My colleagues and I rarely meet because it is a waste of time. I get more done when I do things by myself. If the students don't learn in my class, it is because they did not put forth the effort necessary to get the job done. I have a life after work and other important commitments. I put my time in and the students need to do the same.

3. **Students rule:** Discipline is a mess here. The administration is very lax; administrators do not fully enforce the rules. They allow students to do whatever they want. Even when you call an administrator to the classroom for assistance, he or she rarely comes. When an administrator does show up, it takes a long time. The other teachers do not have the same expectations and standards for student behavior. This affects my class because the students can get away with being tardy or not listening in other classes. The students are out of control. They are more cohesive than the staff. How does the administration expect me to teach in this environment?

4. **Cliques and subcultures are the norm:** All schools have subcultures, but in our school there is a definite "in crowd" and "out crowd." The principal has his favorites and if he likes you, you can do anything you want. It is difficult to know whom you can trust. Some people tell the administration everything just to get in good with them. There is a really negative group of teachers who scream the loudest for what they want. The principal is afraid that they will complain to the district, union, or board members, so that group usually gets its way. It is best to lay low and share as little information and as few ideas as possible with others. At least that is what I tell all of the new teachers when they arrive. It is the only way to survive here.

5. **Power seekers control everything:** Power can be both positive and negative. In our school, negative power seekers control everything. No matter what I want to do, I have to check with them to make sure they approve before I can proceed. Otherwise, it becomes a union issue usually concerning working conditions. For instance, they believe that if I decide to tutor after school, everyone will be required to do the same. That, they say, is a change in working conditions. So I had to stop tutoring even if it was on my own time and exactly what my students needed. This is a hard place to work because of the negative

people who are in control of everything! Some people thrive on negative power and a constant attempt to stir up negative feelings. No one is really here for the students.

6. **Negative stories become reality:** In our school we never celebrate the good things that teachers do. It would be great if someone appreciated all of our hard work. When we do try to celebrate individual teacher accomplishments, teachers are usually embarrassed by it. No one wants to be singled out in front of the entire school. Those who are not recognized are resentful and talk about it afterward. Now we only celebrate personal events like weddings, the birth of babies and grandchildren, anniversaries, and so on. Social interactions among the staff are nonexistent. Even when we try to do something together, almost no one shows up. Instead, teachers meet in their small private groups to talk about poor student performance, parent apathy, and the lack of district support.

Each of these scenarios shows a toxic culture—cultures that are difficult to change. Terrence E. Deal and Kent D. Peterson (2016) note, "When a school is mired in a noxious past and dysfunctional present it is hard to envision a more promising future" (p. 190).

In contrast, a healthy culture is a school in which educators have an unwavering belief in the ability of all students to achieve success, and they pass that belief on to others in overt and covert ways (Muhammad, 2009). Their actions support the belief that all students can learn at high levels. The entire school staff takes collective ownership of the ability of all students to successfully learn at high levels. Educators create policies and procedures and adopt practices that support their belief in these abilities.

We base the healthy culture we describe on the findings of the effective schools research of Ron Edmonds, Larry Lezotte, Wilbur Brookover, Michael Rutter, and others, who have discovered that all students can learn and schools control the factors that ensure students master the core curriculum (Lezotte & Snyder, 2011). Teachers in a healthy culture know that they possess both the skill and the will to make a difference for the students they serve (Muhammad & Hollie, 2011). They seek out the tools they need to increase student success. Teachers understand that they cannot do this alone, so they work collaboratively with others to accomplish their goal of universal student achievement.

Robert J. Marzano (2003) concludes, "An analysis of research conducted over a thirty-five-year period demonstrates that schools that are highly effective produce results that almost entirely overcome the effects of student backgrounds" (p. 7). Teachers and administrators have within their control the ability to ensure all students learn at high levels. Their efforts are more powerful than the obstacles of poverty or learning in a second language. Despite the fact that students come to school with differing levels of prior knowledge, preparation, and support at home, educators can still influence them to ensure high levels of learning for all. In a healthy culture, teachers believe they are making a difference in the learning and lives of their students.

## Start Now

To move from a toxic or negative culture to a healthy culture requires a shift in mindset for the staff. The movement from a fixed mindset to a growth mindset transforms the culture and breathes new life into a school (Dweck, 2006). We can demonstrate the difference between a fixed mindset and a growth mindset with this simple question that any teacher may ask his or her students: "Mary scored 100 percent on her paper. Why do you think she scored 100 percent?" Too often, the students' response is predictable: because she is smart. This implies that Mary is smart but others may not be. This also indicates that there is just so much smart to go around and some people get it while others are not as fortunate. A fixed mindset says that no matter how much effort and preparation a student puts forth, the outcome will not change.

On the other hand, a growth mindset is a belief that with focused effort and preparation, anyone can earn the same score as Mary. It encourages self-efficacy and confidence in the abilities of all students. It promotes pathways to learning rather than highlighting a dead end. Students become partners in learning because they believe that they can achieve at high levels. Teachers work together to become more aware of exactly what each student has learned in an effort to support students in reaching the desired outcomes.

In a healthy culture, educators understand that teaching is much more than a job, profession, or even a noble calling; it is the moral imperative to prepare future generations. Educators believe that the same expectations and desires they hold for the future of their own children and grandchildren are the norm for the students who they serve. This moral imperative underpins their efforts and drives each instructional decision.

## Assess Culture

According to Muhammad (2009, 2015), there are three key components to a healthy culture: (1) commitment, (2) reflection, and (3) prescription. Commitment to the belief that all students can and will learn is essential. In order to achieve this student success, teachers must also commit to school goals. The second component is teachers' willingness to reflect on their practice by analyzing data to confront the facts in a nonjudgmental way. This is a problem-solving process, not a chance to play the blame game. The third component, prescription, is how teachers actually accomplish the work. Teachers realize that alone, it is difficult for them to meet their students' diverse needs. They work in collaborative teams to draw on each other's experience, knowledge, insights, ideas, and strengths. Each team member commits to engage in those practices that yield the greatest results for all students. They are willing to learn new ways to reach the academic diversity that exists in every classroom.

What indicates a healthy school culture? Is there a continuum that describes the cultural shifts or pathways to a healthy culture? What are the necessary steps to shape a culture that supports student learning? There are seven indicators of a healthy culture according to Muhammad and Peterson (2012). These indicators appear on a continuum that ranges from no implementation to exemplary implementation (Muhammad & Peterson, 2012).

1. The school culture supports a safe, orderly, and equitable learning environment.

2. The school creates experiences that foster the belief that all students can learn at high levels.

3. Teachers hold high expectations for all students academically and behaviorally, and this is evidenced in their practice.

4. The school has established traditions and experiences that reinforce high academic and behavioral expectations.

5. Teachers communicate regularly with families about individual student progress.

6. There is evidence that student achievement is publicly celebrated (such as displays of student work, assemblies, and so on).

7. The school provides support for the physical, cultural, socioeconomic, and intellectual needs of all students which are reflected in a commitment to equity and appreciation of diversity.

The leadership team can assess school culture both formally and informally. Formal methods include using a rubric or continuum that describes the seven indicators of a healthy culture. An outside person trained in assessing culture examines the culture with new eyes, completes the rubric or continuum, and offers suggestions for improvement. This is an unbiased assessment, with no connections to the staff or administration, that sheds light on the current reality of the school.

The leadership team can also gather information using informal methods, including asking questions that cause teachers to reflect on their policies, practices, strategies, and procedures in light of their effect on student learning. This can present an alternative mindset and is most effective on an individual basis or with small groups of teachers, parents, or students. During this process, the leadership team can collect new data and at the same time any new ideas that emerge. Questions to stimulate discussion with teachers appear in figure 2.1. The leadership team can analyze the responses first as part of the problem-solving process and later share them with staff.

1. At this school, how do teachers support one another? Given the academic diversity in our school, is it really possible to work effectively and efficiently independent of your team? How can we collaborate to make a real difference for our students?

2. What rituals and routines do you employ in your classroom and hallways to make sure that the school has a safe and orderly environment? Are these your own strategies or an agreed-upon collective effort of your team and the school?

3. How and when do you celebrate student successes or progress toward proficiency on the priority outcomes? Is there a need for more celebration and recognition on a schoolwide basis?

4. Do you feel appreciated? If so, by whom—parents, students, the administration, colleagues, the district?

5. What do people say and think about the school? What are the stories people tell about the school? Is this an accurate perception? Why or why not?

6. How are new teachers welcomed into the school? How are they supported and mentored and by whom?

7. Are there cliques and subgroups in the school? Is this helpful or hurtful to our efforts to improve?

8. What aspirations do you have for our students? What do others wish for in service to students?

9. How can we improve student achievement? What indicators are most important to monitor?

**Figure 2.1: Staff questions to assess culture.**

*Visit **go.SolutionTree.com/PLCbooks** for a free reproducible version of this figure.*

A healthy culture depends on intentional and purposeful actions by staff members schoolwide. One might compare it to maintaining a healthy relationship or marriage. Both must be cultivated, promoted, and respected on a continual basis. A healthy school culture is not a destination but an ongoing process of developing and sustaining mindsets that support and enhance student learning. It requires the firm belief that all students can learn—that all really means *all*.

## Transform Culture

It is up to school leaders, principals, and teachers to identify, shape, support, and maintain a strong, positive, student-focused culture. Leaders need to analyze the culture daily and assess the effectiveness of cultural elements and shape them by reinforcing the positive and transforming the negative. The first step in transforming the culture and mindset of a school is to adopt three core principles that guide the work and set the tone for school improvement (David & Talbert, 2013).

1. Do not blame the students.

2. Learning is required, not optional.

3. Hope is not a strategy for success.

Internalizing these three simple tenets will begin the shift from a toxic culture to a healthy culture.

First of all, there is no one person or factor to blame for failing schools, least of all the students. The issue of failing schools is complex and difficult to tackle because of the multiple interacting factors that all play a role in the problem. In addition, placing blame distracts from the problem solving that must take place to determine the root cause of failure. Instead of blaming students, the staff should examine and analyze their own practices to find better ways to meet the needs of the students in their classrooms. Often school staff members react by trying to use the same practices on today's students that worked when they were in school. Educators need to prepare their students for the future, not the past. This requires that they closely examine curriculum, instruction, and assessment. A "this is the way we always have done it" attitude will not turn around failing schools.

*Learning is required, not optional* is the mantra of improving schools. School should not be a place where students "sit and get" all day long; it must be a place where students work harder than the adults on a regular basis. Educators must make learning a requirement, not just a wish or a hope. In a PLC, students cannot opt out of learning. Teachers must provide tasks and assignments that are authentic and worthy of the time that students will spend to complete them. Then, educators institute a system of privileges to make sure students complete the required work to learn. Students who choose not to learn lose privileges, such as eating lunch with friends, until they complete the necessary assignments and demonstrate their learning.

Finally, the principle *hope is not a strategy* requires all staff members to use data to make important instructional decisions. In too many instances, teachers follow the curriculum and hope that the results will be different on the high-stakes assessments. However, data represent the only real, concrete evidence of student learning. Teachers need to rely on these data from frequent common formative and summative assessments to guide instruction and determine the individual learning needs of their students (see chapter 5, page 79). It is only when teachers have data to support student learning that they can expect better results. Hope alone will not be sufficient to measure and ensure student progress.

Continually working within these core principles sets the stage for cultural transformation. Moving from placing blame to determining solutions, however, is not easy. Consider using staff meetings and leadership team meetings to identify a current issue, recognize root causes, and problem solve to figure out what the adults in the school can do as a strategy to improve learning. One useful method is to use a fishbone diagram, which examines attributes associated with a topic; a concept map; or another graphic organizer like the one in figure 2.2 as a protocol to channel problem solving. Notice in figure 2.2 the teachers initially blame the students for the issue; then the team works through questions to address the root causes in order to problem solve the issue with factors the teachers can control. Teams may need help from administrators, instructional coaches, or outside stakeholders to create the necessary questions to solve the issue. We've left the answers column blank as these will vary in regard to the team, though we share possible actions a team may commit to as result of the protocol. This exercise will show teams how to turn an issue into questions that teams can address to lead to actions toward a solution.

| Issue to Address | |
| --- | --- |
| Too many students are failing algebra 1. | |
| **Data to Support Claim** | **Reasons This Issue Exists** |
| For the second semester:<br>• 44 percent failed in 2015–2016<br>• 46 percent failed in 2014–2015<br>• 48 percent failed in 2013–2014<br>(About 450 students are in algebra 1 each year.) | (Quick brainstorm as a team)<br>• Students not doing homework<br>• Students not retaking exams<br>• Students not trying in class or coming in for help<br>• Students not ready for algebra 1 in the first place<br>• Students not coming to class |

| Examine Each Reason | Identify Questions to Address to Find a Solution | Answers |
|---|---|---|
| Homework | • How many students failed due to homework?<br><br>• Why are students not doing homework?<br><br>• How many students failed homework but passed tests?<br><br>• How do teachers assign homework?<br><br>• How do teachers use homework in class for learning?<br><br>• What portion of a student's grade depends on homework? | |
| Exam retakes | • When are retake opportunities available?<br><br>• Why are students not retaking exams?<br><br>• What must students do prior to retaking an exam?<br><br>• How do teachers tell students when and how to retake an exam? | |
| Not trying or getting help | • How many students are not trying? Why?<br><br>(Examine trends in students' behaviors, instructional practices, and classroom expectations.)<br><br>• When can students get additional help? Is it optional or mandatory? Can they get help during the school day? | |
| Not ready | • How many students would benefit from intervention or remediation?<br><br>• How can students get the intervention or remediation they need during the school day?<br><br>• What skills do students need to be successful? | |
| Attendance | • Why are students late or not coming to class?<br><br>• How many students failed due to attendance? | |

**Figure 2.2: Issue-to-solution graphic organizer.**

continued →

> ### *Action Steps Toward a Solution*
>
> - Assign meaningful and focused homework (about twenty minutes of work—it might be one word problem or eight to ten questions).
> - Align homework to the lesson and assessment learning target.
> - Have students share their strategies or solutions to the homework at the start of class in learning groups while two students share their answers at the board (no longer than five to eight minutes of class).
> - Provide answers to the homework so students can use them as formative feedback.
> - Determine a time for retaking exams during the school day.
> - Determine schoolwide intervention and remediation time in addition to core instruction to use flexibly with students as needed.
> - Re-examine grading practices as a team to be sure each teacher is calculating grades the same way with a heavy emphasis on common unit assessments.
> - Examine instructional practices during lessons with the goal of having students try and work with one another to learn as classroom community members.
> - Work with counselors and the attendance secretary to assist students who are chronically absent.

*Visit **go.SolutionTree.com/PLCbooks** for a free reproducible version of this figure.*

During this work, outside research and expertise can be a powerful resource to focus discussions beyond the opinions of those on staff. Teams can use articles to answer questions formed in the issue-to-solution graphic organizer or to move staff toward fulfilling the mission and vision of the school. Use protocols when reading articles. For example, have teachers identify one thing they agree with and one thing they argue against in the research, and then hold small-group discussions before sharing these discussions on poster paper with the entire staff. Conclude by asking the staff what they would like to do based on what they've read and have them commit to an action.

Kerry Patterson, Joseph Grenny, David Maxfield, Ron McMillan, and Al Switzler (2008) contend that the greatest persuader is personal experience and that it is the "gold standard of change" (p. 57). They suggest site visits to other similar schools that are making an intentional difference in student learning. This practice prevents the justification of blaming the students. As we'll discuss further, leaders must focus on stories of specific student successes rather than just on test results. Many principals show photographs of students and describe their journeys to achievement. This shows that the change is a defining moment for each student—he or she is not just a number.

When the entire staff makes a conscious commitment to these core values, conversations and behaviors begin to change. But this alone will not shift the culture—it only sets the stage for the real work. The principal and the leadership team must ask themselves and others continually, "How will this program, curriculum, or activity help us reach our vision for success? Are we making progress toward our goals? What data do we have that indicate progress? What is getting in the way of achieving our vision for success?" As staff reflect on these questions, the mission, vision, collective commitments, and goals (as discussed in chapter 1, page 7) come alive. Together, they move from just words to actions.

## Recognize Symbols and Artifacts

Symbols and artifacts communicate meaning and define the culture. Consider for a moment the meaning attached to a school logo. When a teacher or administrator sees the logo on letterhead, a website, a sweatshirt, or the sign at the front of the school, what feelings does it evoke? What does a student feel? What might a parent or community member feel? The emotions that symbols and artifacts elicit among the school community contribute to its current and desired cultures. There are many positive and negative emotions attached to symbols. How can the logo become a representation of pride, success, learning, and safety?

A school's culture is reflected in what people see and hear throughout the school. As a visitor enters the school, what is the first thing he or she sees? If it's the law enforcement office, this gives a vivid impression of the school's culture. If a person instead sees artifacts of student learning and is greeted by a friendly, helpful person, he or she will get a very different sense of the culture. The entryway to a school can symbolize its purpose by reinforcing its core values. It is important to model the shared mission and vision in overt ways. Symbols and artifacts are important in demonstrating in a very visual manner the mission, vision, and commitments that the school and it educators are making to ensure high levels of learning for all students. In one urban high school in Oklahoma, people who enter the building immediately see a sign that reads, "Learning is required." This clearly sends a message that describes the mission of the school to all who enter.

In addition, displaying student work in the hallways and other public places reinforces the meaning and purpose of hard work. If a school only displays trophies from major athletic accomplishments, it is in fact sending a clear message regarding what it values. In effect, this may unintentionally devalue academic achievements. A school should recognize all aspects of student growth and accomplishment in meaningful ways throughout the school.

Honoring the past with historical artifacts of school accomplishments supports a sense of commitment to the values of the school and community it serves. It honors the alumni and future graduates. It recounts the successes and connects the past, present, and future for students, staff, and parents. Alternately, at a high school, recognizing students who will soon be attending a college, university, or apprenticeship program the next fall shows students the possibilities available to them.

Teachers and leaders should consider taking a field trip around the campus and look at the walls as if they are new to the building, visitors. What is important to the adults and students in the school? Use figure 2.3 to document findings and discuss them as leaders, a leadership team, or as an entire staff.

| Symbol and Artifact Walk | | |
|---|---|---|
| 1. Walk around your school and observe the symbols and artifacts contributing to its story. Document your findings in the following section. | | |
| **Location** | **What Do You See?** | **What Do You Hear?** |
| School entryway | | |
| Main office | | |
| Hallways | | |
| Traditional classrooms | | |
| Library | | |
| Cafeteria | | |
| Bus drop-off area | | |
| Computer lab | | |
| Other: _____ | | |
| Other: _____ | | |

**Figure 2.3: Symbol and artifact walk recording sheet.**

continued →

| 2. What percentage of visual images supports or reflects the following items? | | | |
|---|---|---|---|
| **Academic Learning** | **Arts** | **Sports or Activities** | **Behavior Expectations** |
|  |  |  |  |

| 3. What contributes to your vision of culture and what needs to be changed? | |
|---|---|
| **What Positive Symbols and Artifacts Should Remain?** | **What Symbol and Artifact Modifications Do You Suggest?** |
|  |  |

*Visit **go.SolutionTree.com/PLCbooks** for a free reproducible version of this figure.*

Along with walking the school to determine what visitors see and hear, also consider what staff members feel on a daily basis. What does this reveal about the culture? What should the school keep? What should the school change? Transforming a culture is an ongoing journey.

### Celebrate

The single best way to drive the shift in culture is to celebrate small and big wins every day—not just during a monthly assembly or at the end of the school year (DuFour et al., 2016). Periodic celebrations are important and necessary but usually are not sufficient to turn the tide in a failing school.

Ongoing, authentic celebrations that tell stories of success embed purpose and meaning in a school. Celebration stories that describe gains in student achievement and attendance and reductions in discipline referrals help a new, more positive culture emerge. Celebrations of results can include gains on standardized tests, AP participation and scores, improved grade distribution, reduced failure rates, reduction in suspensions, and higher levels of parent satisfaction. But celebrations can also recognize more students turning in homework, fewer tardies, an increase in proficient scores on common assessments, an increase in the books students have read, fewer students in need of interventions, students improving their scores on unit tests, more students exceeding expectations, and so on. The most effective celebrations encompass large and small wins. More important than anything is timing. Celebrate often and early.

Celebrating staff members is equally important. Schools can recognize individuals for acts of kindness toward each other and for going above and beyond to ensure students are successful. Adlai E. Stevenson High School District 125 in Lincolnshire, Illinois, surveys its students annually, asking them which teacher has had the greatest impact on their lives. As students describe the impact the teachers have made, inspiring stories of teacher heroes emerge. The school shares these stories during a schoolwide ceremony each year to celebrate teachers. Teachers do not often fully realize their actual impact on students' lives because the tangible results of their work do not show up until much later in life. This is a powerful way to celebrate the work of teachers in the moment.

Since collaborative teams are the engine that drives school improvement in a PLC (DuFour et al., 2016), it is also important to celebrate their work. These celebrations occur in two ways. The first is a celebration of gains or progress toward goals. Another equally important celebration of teams is to recognize them for lessons learned. If a team tried a novel way to reach its goal and it did not work exactly as planned, the school should celebrate its efforts as well. It is true that one often learns more from something that did not go well than from something that worked exactly as planned. In this way, instead of punishing mistakes as failures, schools see mistakes as opportunities to learn and grow for both students and educators.

Celebrations act as an antidote to constant change. They indicate what an organization values. They shape the stories that the people in a school tell themselves and others about their school, students, teachers, parents, and administration. Stories can feed the cycle of failure or describe a culture of success. Everyone has a story, negative or positive. It is important in an underperforming school to tell the story of success and progress.

## Examine Rituals

Rituals in the context of school play an enormous role in culture building. *Rituals* consist of a series of actions and behaviors a group regularly and invariably follows. As people perform rituals over and over again, they become traditions, and traditions are culture in action. Schools with healthy cultures have a strong core sense of tradition. Some may have a special way in which school begins and ends. Others begin the year with celebrating students by showing pictures of those who have shown progress or achieved success both academically and in extracurricular areas. These students represent the values of the school and the vision for the future. One school in Arizona begins the year by engaging all staff members in a pledge to be "All in for All Kids." Another school has a new school year party to celebrate the beginning of the opportunity to make a difference in students' lives. Yet another school district begins the year with skits that reveal the goals for the upcoming year in a comedic manner. The district-level staff members perform the skits in full costume and the entire staff looks forward to the themed performance each year.

End-of-year traditions are also important to establish a positive culture. Some schools end the year by reviewing all the funny events. Staff members have an opportunity to laugh and mark the end of the year by celebrating themselves. New teachers receive recognition for surviving their first year. Celebration also occurs for teachers who have earned permanent employment status. These traditions are an opportunity to look back on accomplishments and reflect on the work of the year.

Graduation is another celebration that uses rituals to enhance the positive culture of the school. There are high schools that invite all of the teachers in the district, from kindergarten through twelfth grade, to the ceremony. The teachers wear caps and gowns with the appropriate collars to indicate their level and types of degrees. The graduation processional begins with all teachers marching in prior to the entrance of students. This indicates the impact every teacher has had on the students. In another school district, the graduates go back to their elementary and middle schools wearing their caps and gowns to get high fives from the students. The younger students are in awe as the graduates proceed through the school. It is an incredible celebration of learning for even the youngest students. One final graduation ritual includes inviting the kindergarten class to the high school ceremony to walk across the stage. The district implemented this tradition to allow the youngest students and their parents envision their future.

Figure 2.4 (page 38) is a tool for school personnel to use to identify school rituals that have become traditions as well as new rituals to begin on the journey to a healthy and effective culture for student learning.

The special traditions a school establishes showcase the culture and relationships among administrators, teachers, and students. They contribute to the optimism that can be part of the difficult work of having all students learn at high levels.

| List your current traditions. Circle those that promote a healthy culture. | List any rituals you would like to begin to further a healthy culture. |
|---|---|
| | |

Figure 2.4: Traditions past and future.

*Visit **go.SolutionTree.com/PLCbooks** for a free reproducible version of this figure.*

### Get the Right People on the Bus

In his book *Good to Great*, Jim Collins (2001) emphasizes the need to get the right people on the bus and make sure that they are in the right seats. DuFour, DuFour, Eaker, Many, and Mattos (2016) also emphasize the importance of the right people in the right positions within a PLC. What this means is that healthy cultures begin by hiring the right people. Principals need to seek out teachers with a clear sense of purpose who can connect with the students they serve. The right people for this job must be able to motivate and inspire students to believe in themselves. Teachers who are excited about working in collaboration with others and are willing to accept responsibility for student learning are best suited for the work of improving schools. Once the right people are on board, it is time to intentionally build a healthy culture by telling the story of the school and the positive impact that each individual will make on the lives of the students.

Shaping school culture is more important than ever because of the national and international focus on more rigorous curriculum standards, assessments, and accountability. Aligning curriculum, instruction, and assessment is essential to ensuring high levels of learning for all students. But in the absence of a culture that supports and values these structural changes, the efforts of staff to improve learning usually fail. Breaking the cycle of failure is a daunting task but not impossible; establishing a healthy culture is the key. Culture is intangible, but essential. Anyone can walk into a school and know immediately whether he or she wants to be there or not. The same thing goes for the students and staff. The following statement exemplifies the best way to transform the culture and turn a failing school around:

> The vital task ahead is not one of adding more structure and standardization to schools or ramping up an already over-hyped testing agenda, it is more a matter of reviving the spirit, bringing back the joy and love of learning, and celebrating the majesty of teaching that once held sway before the constant top-down battering snuffed out the story and soul of what it means on a deeper level to teach and to learn. There is something magical or enchanting about the warm rapture of learning and gift of teaching that touch places in us where little else can reach. (Deal & Peterson, 2016, p. 19)

# Reflect and Take Action

The rubric in figure 2.5 shows levels of transforming to a healthy and productive culture. Look at the rubric to determine staff strengths and next steps to achieve the culture necessary to improve learning.

| | Level 1 Beginning | Level 2 Attempting | Level 3 Practicing | Level 4 Embracing |
|---|---|---|---|---|
| **Awareness and Beliefs** | Staff members can articulate aspects of the school's culture but may not have the larger picture.<br><br>Few staff members believe in and practice the three school-improvement principles: (1) do not blame the students, (2) learning is required, not optional, and (3) hope is not a strategy. | Staff members understand the school's current culture and recognize any changes that they need to make.<br><br>Most staff members believe in and practice the three school improvement principles: (1) do not blame the students, (2) learning is required, not optional, and (3) hope is not a strategy. | Staff members understand the school's current culture and are working to make the necessary changes to create a healthy culture tied to student learning.<br><br>All staff members believe in and practice the three school improvement principles: (1) do not blame the students, (2) learning is required, not optional, and (3) hope is not a strategy. | Staff members understand the school's current culture and are successfully making the necessary changes to create a healthy culture tied to student learning.<br><br>Staff members believe in and practice the three school improvement principles and hold each other accountable for them daily. |
| **Symbols and Artifacts** | Some of the symbols and artifacts in and around the school promote a healthy culture focused on learning.<br><br>Little of what people on campus see, hear, and feel contributes to a healthy culture. | Many of the symbols and artifacts in and around the school promote a healthy culture focused on learning.<br><br>Much of what people on campus see, hear, and feel contributes to a healthy culture. | The symbols and artifacts in and around the school promote a healthy culture focused on learning.<br><br>What people on campus see, hear, and feel contributes to a healthy culture. | Teachers and leaders continually update the symbols and artifacts in and around the school; they always reflect a healthy culture focused on learning.<br><br>Adults and students work to have conversations and learning experiences all day in every school space that contribute to a healthy culture. |
| **Celebrations and Rituals** | The school celebrates some student successes in a public manner.<br><br>A few traditions promote a culture focused on learning. | The school celebrates teacher or student successes in a public manner.<br><br>Most traditions promote a culture focused on learning. | The school celebrates teacher and student successes in a meaningful and authentic way.<br><br>Established traditions promote a culture focused on learning. | The school celebrates teacher and student successes and focused work in a meaningful and authentic way.<br><br>Established traditions and newly created rituals further promote a culture focused on learning. |

**Figure 2.5: Culture rubric.**

*Visit **go.SolutionTree.com/PLCbooks** for a free reproducible version of this figure.*

Once teams have reached agreement about the current status, they should use figure 2.6 (page 40) to determine the next steps to strengthen practice in working to transform culture.

| Action | Team-Level Rating | Next Steps |
|---|---|---|
| Awareness and beliefs | | |
| Symbols and artifacts | | |
| Celebrations and rituals | | |

**Figure 2.6: Transforming culture reflection and action plan.**

*Visit* **go.SolutionTree.com/PLCbooks** *for a free reproducible version of this figure.*

## Collaborative Team Questions to Consider

- What three words currently describe your school?
- When do you most appreciate working in your school?
- What do you see, hear, and feel as you walk through school during the school day?
- What was your best lesson? Why?
- When did someone on staff show you kindness? How?
- What do you appreciate about the school every day you enter the building?
- What frustrates you related to work each day?
- What would a visitor see on your hallway bulletin boards and showcases? How do these items promote student learning?
- What would a visitor hear in the public spaces or classrooms of your school?
- What are your favorite traditions? Why? How do they promote student learning?
- How do you celebrate your work and the work of your collaborative team?
- How do you celebrate and recognize the work of your students?

## CHAPTER 3

# Focusing on 21st Century Learners

> For more than a century, the industrial model of education did a fantastic job of preparing students for careers. Those careers are no longer relevant in today's changing world. . . . Instead of preparing students for an industrialized world, the education system is now being tasked with preparing all learners to be college and career ready to compete globally with peers.
>
> —*Eric C. Sheninger*

The meeting to review student achievement data and determine the greatest areas of need at Madison Middle School began with each content team presenting their data. As Sharon looked at the information and listened to the teachers explain the data, she was excited to see that there were more students proficient in eighth-grade mathematics than in any other subject or grade level. She asked the team, "What do you believe is the reason for these good results?" The teachers quickly explained that at Madison they identify students for pre-AP or honors mathematics classes, and that these students do really well and help the school's scores. Sharon probed a little more and asked how many of the students not in pre-AP or honors classes were proficient. The answer was astonishing: three students. It was apparent at this school that pre-AP students were much more successful than those who the teachers had not identified as such. Sharon asked a follow-up question, "What if all students were labeled pre-AP or honors—would that make a difference?" The curriculum and assessment are the same despite the labels. The only difference between the two groups appeared to be the instruction and the belief that students would or would not be proficient.

Scenarios like this are common in low-performing schools; labels and classifications define how well or poorly a student achieves. In addition, students of color, from poverty, and from second-language homes are often over-represented in low-performing classes and are seldom enrolled in honors courses (Burris & Welner, 2005). Corbett C. Burris, former principal of South Side High School in Rockville Centre, New York, and Kevin G. Welner (2005), an assistant professor at the University of Colorado Boulder, looked at the effect of slower paced classes with reduced levels of rigor on student achievement. Their findings indicate that slower classes and their reduced expectations perpetuate low achievement. Burris and Welner (2005) state, "Achievement follows from opportunities—opportunities that tracking denies. When all students were taught the high-track curriculum, achievement rose for all groups of students" (p. 598).

In 2010, the Noyce Foundation conducted a study of algebra 1 placement guidelines that nine San Francisco Bay Area school districts used for students who had previously taken algebra 1 in eighth grade (Waterman, 2010). It finds the guidelines were heavily influenced by subjective factors such as teacher recommendations without more objective assessment measures. When assessment measures were used, the study finds, nearly 65 percent of students who had taken algebra 1 in eighth grade were forced to repeat the course as freshmen. Of those, 42 percent scored proficient in eighth grade on the Mathematics Assessment Resource Service (MARS) assessment for algebra and 60 percent scored proficient or advanced on the California State Test in algebra. Therefore, students were not identified appropriately. Furthermore, the majority of students held back were Latino or African American, which eventually resulted in the Silicon Valley Community Foundation hiring lawyers who determined the school districts were acting illegally with these inequities and needed to revise their guidelines for placement (Lawyers' Committee for Civil Rights of the San Francisco Bay Area, 2013). Students held back from the opportunity to enroll in geometry as freshmen will, without additional summer school time or doubling of mathematics courses in a year, be unable to enroll in AP calculus by their senior year. The student-learning decisions that adults make, though perhaps unintentional, impact the future success of the students they serve.

Gaps in achievement are a major equity concern and occur as a direct result of eliminating opportunities for success. Any student with a label is at risk of losing the opportunity to learn. Special education students have historically been taught below grade-level standards and then tested on grade-level standards (Smith, 2014). The result is predictable, yet schools continue this practice and even blame this population of students for negatively impacting their overall scores. Students cannot successfully meet standards if educators have not given them the opportunity to learn the tested curriculum.

In addition, the skills of the 21st century are remarkably different than ever before. Success now lies in one's ability to create solutions to problems, collaborate with others to meet a goal, communicate effectively, and develop unique ideas that can change things for the better (Partnership for 21st Century Learning, 2007). In other words, we can no longer prepare students for our past; we must prepare them for their future—a future of careers and opportunities that have not yet even been invented. "We are currently preparing students for jobs that don't yet exist using technologies that haven't yet been invented in order to solve problems we don't even know we have" (Melsa, 2007). So how do educators respond, especially in underperforming schools where students often have deficit skill levels?

## Determine Vision Versus Reality

Students in today's classrooms, 21st century learners, have never experienced life without the Internet and technology. They live in a world of selfies and describe their experiences through sharing pictures, video, and music rather than written notes, letters, or phone calls. They seek immediate feedback at all times and are diverse in their experiences, backgrounds, interests, income, ethnicity, religion, and gender, to name a few. As teachers work to improve learning, it is critical to know who 21st century learners are and what they need to be successful.

### Believe All Students Can Learn

The process of preparing students for their future begins when teachers believe they can reach and teach all students they serve. In our PLC coaching work, we often hear educators say, "All kids can learn." It is one thing to say all students can learn; however, it is far different to say, "I can get all kids in my classroom to learn," and really mean *all*. Teachers have to believe that they have the knowledge, skills, patience, and strategies to teach all students. In Kathryn Bell McKenzie and Linda Skrla's (2011) book *Using Equity Audits in the Classroom to Reach and Teach All Students*, the authors suggest that teachers have a zone of self-efficacy that includes the students they feel confident teaching or who they believe are easy to teach. A simple way to test this theory is to (1) have teachers review their class lists and mark the students they feel are easy to teach and then (2) mark the students they find difficult to teach using a different color highlighter. (See figure 3.1.) As teachers look at the completed lists, they indicate the characteristics of each group. The students who are easy to teach fall in the teacher's zone of self-efficacy. Teachers should take a critical look at the characteristics of each group to determine what makes some students more difficult for them to teach than others. What new strategies and assistance do teams and teachers need to effectively teach *all* students?

---

**Teaching All Students**

1. Highlight all the students on your class roster who you feel are easy to teach.

2. Highlight, using another color, all the students on your class roster who you feel are difficult to teach.

3. Use the following section to describe the characteristics that make some students easy for you to teach and others more difficult to teach.

| Characteristics of Students Who Are Easy for Me to Teach | Characteristics of Students Who Are Difficult for Me to Teach |
|---|---|
| | |

4. Looking at your list for reasons why some students are more difficult to teach, determine the learning experiences you need to feel more successful reaching all students.

**What I Need to Learn to Teach All Students**

Figure 3.1: Protocol to build self-efficacy for teaching all students.

*Visit **go.SolutionTree.com/PLCbooks** for a free reproducible version of this figure.*

Working in collaborative teams strengthens teachers' self-efficacy. No matter how effective a teacher may be, his or her individual knowledge, activities, and strategies can limit students. The options and opportunities for students grow exponentially when a teacher works on a collaborative team. Teachers grow in their ability to learn and acquire strategies to meet the needs of all learners, even those who are not easy to teach or out of the teachers' comfort zone. Collaboration makes it possible for individual teachers to meet the diverse needs of all students.

Building relationships with students is the first priority in being able to teach them and also contributes to the positive culture of the school as we discussed in chapter 2 (page 27). It has been said that in order to teach them, you have to reach them first (Sprenger, 2005). This means without strong relationships with students, teaching is difficult and learning is almost impossible. Teachers build positive relationships with students by taking a step back to examine their own feelings, thoughts, and beliefs about students and then determining their strengths in teaching and admitting that they may need help to reach all students. All teachers should consider sitting in the seat of one or more of their students to imagine how he or she experiences learning in their classrooms. What are they pleased with? What would they like to change in that student's learning environment? How can their colleagues provide help and support as they work to reach all students? Collaborative teams are the vehicle to improve teaching and learning. As teachers work together to address the learning needs of each student, they strategize and share ways to improve teaching and relationships with students.

## Understand the Skills of the 21st Century

Sometimes schools face the reality of simply trying to navigate and survive the diverse needs of students, rather than embracing the vision of celebrating them and using their diversities to strengthen the learning of everyone. As teachers look for increasingly better ways to meet the diverse needs of students, the demands of the 21st century have a definite impact.

Historically, schools taught students rote procedures for reading, writing, and computing. Now, however, these skills do not even make the list of requirements for college and career readiness. Instead, the Partnership for 21st Century Learning (2007) identifies the four Cs, critical competencies for students to learn so they may adapt to the careers and skills they will need for an unknown future. These skills are (1) communication, (2) collaboration, (3) critical thinking, and (4) creativity.

### Communication

Communication includes the ability to engage in technical reading and writing, speaking, and listening skills necessary for productive group work. This requires students to effectively analyze and process the overwhelming amount of information in their lives. Students must be able to discern which information sources are accurate and which are not. In addition, students need to understand how to use and leverage the information effectively.

### Collaboration

Collaboration is when people work together, interdependently, to reach a common goal. It involves capitalizing on each team member's strengths, talents, expertise, and skills to work for the greater purpose of accomplishing the goal. Generally, modern thinking has accepted that collaboration is essential to achieve effective results, such as teacher collaboration for school improvement. In addition, since the mid-2000s, it has become increasingly clear that collaboration is not only important, but also necessary for students. Not only does it increase learning, but it also simulates and models college and career expectations. It is difficult to find workplaces where employees work in isolation. Collaborative skills are essential because people must respond to diverse perspectives, summarize points of agreement and disagreement, and qualify and justify their own views by making connections in light of evidence and reasoning.

### Critical Thinking

Critical thinking requires the ability to look at problems in a new way and to link learning across subject areas. According to the National Education Association (n.d.):

> Successful problem solving in the 21st century requires us to work effectively and creatively with computers, with vast amounts of information, with ambiguous situations, and with other people from a variety of backgrounds. (p. 9)

The need for critical thinking is evident in English language arts state standards, which ask students to analyze relationships between primary and secondary sources on the same topic or delineate and evaluate the argument and specific claims in a text, assessing whether the reasoning is sound and the evidence is relevant and sufficient. Critical thinking is also evident in mathematics state standards, which expect students to prove theorems about parallelograms or apply geometric methods to solve design problems.

### Creativity

The final C is creativity. Creativity is the process of trying new approaches to accomplish a task, invent new products, and innovate with already established concepts and new technologies. It is the ability to integrate ideas to solve complex problems in ways that people have not tried before. English language arts state standards incorporate creativity expectations as students use technology to produce, publish, and update individual or shared writing products. In addition, the standards expect students to synthesize information from a range of sources such as texts, experiments, simulations, and video clips into a coherent understanding of a process, phenomenon, or concept. They most often involve resolving conflicting information. In mathematics, students must construct a function to model a linear relationship between quantities or make formal geometric constructions with a variety of tools and methods. In science, students use engineering standards to design experiments and develop inquiry-based questions to answer.

In order for students to learn the four Cs, they must not only learn content but also the process skills and standards in each subject area. This affects not only what teachers teach but also how students will engage in the work or activities. Students who sit in rows do not have an opportunity to collaborate. Activities that do not allow for accountable talk or reciprocal teaching will not help students communicate their ideas or reasoning. Questions with one correct answer will not afford students the opportunity to think critically. Finally, students cannot explore their creativity if all of their work is either right or wrong. Daniel Pink (as cited in National Education Association, n.d.) states:

> The future belongs to a very different kind of person with a very different kind of mind—creators and empathizers, pattern recognizers and meaning makers. These people . . . will now reap society's richest rewards and share its greatest joys. (p. 24)

It is obvious from examining the 21st century skills and the examples of standards related to them that expectations for student achievement are more rigorous than ever before and encompass more than just content and knowledge.

Developing positive relationships with all students is a prerequisite for their learning, but relationships alone will not prepare students for their future. Meaningful and relevant student learning also requires curriculum, assessment, and instruction that align to the rigorous standards for learning. According to the International Center for Leadership in Education (as cited in Daggett, 2014), it is necessary to increase the rigor and relevance of curriculum, assessment, and instruction to effectively teach and for students to learn the current standards. This was evident as Sharon worked with a team of tenth-grade English teachers in Oklahoma City.

The team was very frustrated as members reviewed their benchmark data. One of the teachers said, "We just don't get it. We taught author's point of view, but according to these results, the students did not get it at all! The students did well on our common formative assessments. It just doesn't make sense."

Sharon suggested the team compare the questions from the team common assessment to the questions on point of view on the district benchmark assessment. As the team reviewed the assessment items on each test, it became evident that the level of rigor on the common assessment was much lower than on the benchmark assessment. Questions on point of view on the formative assessment included *What is the point of view of the author in the passage?* In comparison, a benchmark item asked, *How does the point of view affect the tone of the passage?* These are two very different questions that require different thinking levels (see the section on depth of knowledge [DOK] question levels in chapter 5, page 79, for further information). If teachers deliver instruction at a less-rigorous level, then students will not be able to answer a more sophisticated benchmark question. The English team decided to review its standards and determine the thinking level or rigor of each standard, then compare the rigor of the standard to the assessment items on their common formative assessments.

In addition to ensuring that the curriculum, assessment, and instructional practices meet the cognitive demand of the standards, teachers must see that students must know why skills, concepts, processes, and information are important. In other words, they should answer the question of why the learning is relevant and why students need to learn it. In the past, students memorized an enormous amount of factual information. Simply memorizing will not help students because standards now expect them to assimilate and synthesize information from a variety of sources. Students must be able to apply what they learn in predictable and unpredictable or novel situations. Real-world and interdisciplinary applications are the norm with the more rigorous standards of today. Table 3.1 (page 46) compares 20th century thinking to 21st century thinking. These shifts are already evident in our schools. So the question still remains: How do educators respond—especially in underperforming schools where students often have deficit skill levels?

Table 3.1: Old School Versus New School

| 20th Century Thinking | 21st Century Thinking |
|---|---|
| Is time based | Is outcome based |
| Is textbook driven | Is research driven |
| Is passive | Is active |
| Is teacher centered | Is student centered |
| Features facts and memorization | Features higher-order thinking |
| Features isolation | Features collaboration |
| Uses fragmented curriculum | Uses integrated curriculum |
| Uses print | Uses multimedia |
| Uses printed assessments | Uses dynamic forms of assessment—printed and online |

The challenge becomes how to teach all students at high levels of rigor to meet the demands of learning required in the 21st century. Though we are already nearly two decades into the 21st century, too many students sitting in classrooms are still learning only content, without the process skills necessary to ensure opportunities in the future. Chapter 6 (page 113) addresses more instructional strategies for 21st century learners. Here we focus on meeting the needs of the 21st century learner at the heart of the process outlined in this book.

## Start Now

One of the greatest challenges that teachers face daily is responding to academic diversity, which is often pronounced, in their classrooms. To effectively address it, school-improvement efforts must focus on grade-level standards and both remediation and interventions. Students may be as many as two to three years below grade level in reading or mathematics. These students are at a huge disadvantage because they are struggling to keep up in their current grade level without many of the necessary prerequisite skills. Often in the traditional teach-and-test cycle, these students understand some of what teachers are trying to teach them, but not all of the important skills and concepts. To complicate matters, after giving the assessment, the teacher needs to move on to finish the required curriculum. As they do so, they try to spend time reteaching the concepts that students did not learn. This traditional approach is not only difficult for teachers to manage and pace, it is also damaging to students. Consider this: What is the likelihood that the students who failed to learn the first time would be able to relearn the essential standards from the previous unit while simultaneously keeping up in the next unit? The answer is not likely. These students fall into a cycle of remediation that is impossible to escape. As the year progresses, they get farther and farther behind. When this happens over multiple years, students give up.

John Hattie's (2009) *Visible Learning* is a synthesis of over eight hundred meta-analyses relating to achievement. It comprises over fifty thousand individual studies representing the achievement of over eighty million students worldwide. He measures his findings on a barometer of influence in four categories ranging from a reverse effect to the zone of desired effects. He uses a mean of 0.42 as the effect size of all educational actions, or the hinge point of real differences. Typical teacher effect over a grade level or year is 0.30, less than the hinge point. What actions more greatly influence and improve student learning that land above the hinge point of 0.42? Using this barometer, it is easy to see the initiatives and interventions that are associated with the most gains in student achievement as well as those that may not be as effective. The meta-analysis of studies related to teacher response to student learning through interventions had a barometer rating of 1.09—at the high end of desired effects. Response to learning had a larger effect size than poverty and other indicators that are usually associated with poor achievement. In other words, response to learning or interventions and remediation are more powerful than the negative effects of poverty.

## Address Student Needs With Classroom Intervention and Remediation

Most students in underperforming schools need intervention to keep up with the grade-level or course curriculum as well as remediation to learn the most important prerequisite skills and concepts. *Intervention* is short-term, specific help to ensure students learn the current standards and learning targets on a unit-by-unit basis. *Remediation* requires an individual plan to fill the specific gaps in a student's learning while keeping up with the grade-level curriculum.

Teachers use interventions in different ways while working to ensure the learning of all students. While introducing a new concept, for example, teachers check for understanding on a continual basis. When there are students who do not understand the learning target of the lesson, the teacher may bring a small group together to re-engage them in the learning. The teacher may also intervene and correct student misconceptions by using formative feedback from peers during the lesson as students work together to learn through a purposeful task. These types of interventions in first-best instruction (see chapter 6, page 113) are the most effective way to keep students in the curriculum on a unit-by-unit basis. The sooner the intervention or re-engagement of the learning takes place after first presenting it, the more learning occurs. This is *prevention before intervention.*

Another opportunity for intervention occurs after collaborative teams administer a common formative assessment. As the team reviews the data and examines student responses, members form student groups across a grade level or content area. These groups consist of students with similar errors and misconceptions. Teachers can share students to re-engage, they can share the planning of the activities for each group, or both. This is yet another opportunity to intervene while still in the unit of instruction. Remediation begins when a team moves on to the next unit and has a group of students who have not learned the concepts in the previous unit. It is far easier to intervene on multiplication of fractions while still teaching the fractions unit than when the class has moved on to the geometry unit.

Improving schools must develop a plan for remediation that does not take students out of direct instruction of essential standards. Schedules should include a time for remediation and an individual student-learning plan based on diagnosing the most specific skills each student will need. It is impossible to reteach all of the concepts that students have missed over a two- or three-year period. As a collaborative team, teachers must select the most important concepts that have leverage and direct implications for students as they learn the current grade-level curriculum. (See the section on priority standards in chapter 4, page 55.) So any plan for remediation needs to include only those skills that will accelerate learning in a focused and efficient manner. For example, when students receive remediation for mathematics skills, the instruction too often focuses solely on learning or memorizing addition or multiplication facts. Although mathematics fluency is important, conceptual understanding precedes a student's ability to fluently and efficiently apply operations. Students may need to learn how to compose and decompose numbers to develop flexibility, which they can then apply to mathematics facts. For example, a student can realize that he or she may think of 7 + 8 as 7 + 3 + 5 or 10 + 5, which is 15, without having to memorize every sum. Students struggling with mathematics facts can use models and base-ten pieces to develop an understanding of operations with rational numbers to simultaneously learn grade-level content while receiving remediation for mathematics fluency. Students may also need to work on understanding that there is more than one way to solve a mathematics problem.

As schools engage in interventions and remediation plans, the most common missteps occur because collaborative teams do not determine specifically what the deficit really is. (See figure 3.2, page 48.) This usually is a direct result of not clearly understanding the learning target, which in turn means that teachers are unable to articulate it to the student accurately or cannot clarify their understanding of the target with one another to build shared knowledge. They must target intervention and remediation to a specific deficit. Teams determine interventions by standard, by specific learning target, and by student by need (see learning targets in chapter 4, page 55). As students work on the specific targeted area, teachers should provide immediate feedback in relation to the target. This is the best way to move the learning forward.

| Answer the following questions as a collaborative team to begin planning for effective intervention during first-best instruction and remediation in a unit. |
| --- |
| 1.  Which content standards will students learn in this unit? |
| 2.  Which process standards will students learn in this unit? |
| 3.  What will students have to know and be able to do to be proficient with the learning expectations in this unit? |
| 4.  What common misconceptions do you anticipate students will demonstrate as they learn in first-best instruction? |
| 5.  How will you intervene when students demonstrate these misconceptions to ensure learning? |
| 6.  What prerequisite skills do students need to know to access the standards in the unit? |
| 7.  How will your team remediate students who have not yet learned the required prerequisite skills for this unit? |

**Figure 3.2: Unit intervention and remediation planning.**

*Visit go.SolutionTree.com/PLCbooks for a free reproducible version of this figure.*

Schools cannot fulfill their mission of high levels of learning for all students if they fail to focus on what each student needs to get there. When it comes to intervention and remediation, it takes a shift from *all* to *each* to improve student learning.

## Address Student Needs With a Schoolwide Focus on Student Learning

In addition to the content and process standards students must learn in grade-level units, there are universal skills and strategies that teachers can consistently address vertically—through multiple grade levels and across courses. For example, in most underperforming schools, vocabulary development is a schoolwide, universal need for all students. The vocabulary gap between students from different socioeconomic groups has been widening. Students who live in poverty have as much as a thirty-million-word deficit compared to students who do not live in poverty (Bergland, 2014). English learners often struggle with the academic vocabulary necessary to succeed in school. For these reasons, a schoolwide vocabulary focus would increase learning across subject areas.

Using the same methods for learning vocabulary schoolwide adds consistency and the cohesiveness necessary for students to understand expectations and at the same time learn strategies for approaching words that they do not know. Teachers determine the most important academic vocabulary (Marzano & Simms, 2013) to include at each grade level or in each course. These words are not domain specific like science or mathematics words, but words that are essential for students to know in any subject area. Teachers bring in domain-specific words, such as *mitosis* in the science unit, for example; students do not tend to struggle with these types of words. It is the other words in a paragraph or assessment item that students may need help to understand. Consider Sharon's experiences working with students as they were taking a science test: she noticed the students struggled to get through the questions. So at the end of the test, she asked them to circle the words they were unsure of on copies of the exam. The students did not circle *mitosis*. Instead, they circled words like *merely*. This was an eye-opening experience for Sharon, and an easy way for teachers to clearly understand the need for academic vocabulary instruction. The teachers with whom Sharon was working began to use word walls and vocabulary games to reinforce the meaning of specific academic vocabulary (power words) across the curriculum.

There is a great deal of power, and improvement is more likely to happen, when an entire school works together to improve a specific area of need. Another example of an impactful schoolwide initiative from our experiences is teachers adding an extended-response question to every formative assessment in each subject area and then using a universal rubric to score the question. This forces students to write in every class, a difficult skill and one they seldom practice enough through instruction. Teachers in any classroom can include an extended-response or essay question on each formative assessment, including those in subject areas that typically use performance assessments like art, music, and physical education. For instance, a basketball physical education unit usually includes a test on the rules of the game. The physical education teacher could use the same test as always, but add one extended-response item that asks students to read a scenario about the action in a game and be the referee by making the call and then giving the reasons why the call was warranted.

Sarah identified another opportunity for a schoolwide focus after walking through several elementary mathematics classrooms. She noticed that each classroom had an anchor chart describing how to solve word problems, but no two classrooms from a grade-level collaborative team, let alone across grade levels, had the same poster or steps. How confusing for a student to go from one teacher to the next only to relearn how to solve a mathematics word problem! When Sarah brought this issue to the attention of the teacher leaders, the leadership team took on the challenge of designing a common graphic organizer to use with students when problem solving in every grade level.

When using a rubric or graphic organizer schoolwide, teachers and students benefit because expectations are clear and consistent from one year to the next. Alternately, at the secondary level, subject areas might have some consistent strategies, content, or skills that they address from one course to the next so they are not teaching the strategy every year, but using it as a vehicle for students to learn the content in that grade level or course. For example, science teachers might construct a template for lab reports, social science teachers might consistently use a Venn diagram for initial compare-and-contrast activities, and all teachers might use the same rubric to evaluate student essays. Once students understand the consistent strategy, graphic organizer, or rubric, they can also give feedback to one another and self-evaluate as they use it during learning. Use figure 3.3 to determine a possible schoolwide focus to improve student learning.

---

Answer the following questions as a leadership team or as a collaborative grade-level or course team to determine consistent strategies and tools to use with all students that will improve student learning. Record your answers in the chart.

1. List those skills students must demonstrate proficiency with repeatedly throughout the year in your grade level or course (for example, problem-solving essay writing, informational text reading, and vocabulary development).

2. For the skills listed in item one, identify the strategies, tools, templates, rubrics, and so on that you use to teach and assess the student learning.

3. Determine which of the strategies, tools, templates, rubrics, and so on students should use schoolwide to enhance learning and list them. Then, for each one, create or identify a universal model for all teachers to implement and students to use.

---

**Figure 3.3: Schoolwide strategies and tools protocol.**

continued →

| Universal or Subject-Specific Skills Students Must Learn | Strategies, Tools, Templates, and Rubrics Used to Teach Each Skill | Schoolwide Use |
|---|---|---|
| | | |
| | | |
| | | |
| | | |
| | | |
| | | |
| | | |

*Visit **go.SolutionTree.com/PLCbooks** for a free reproducible version of this figure.*

There are many ways a school can harness the power within to improve student learning. Schools can determine and address the areas of greatest need by examining data from multiple sources including national, state or provincial, district, team, and teacher assessment data. After identifying the schoolwide focus, each team then works on the implementation plan at its grade level or content area. Improving schools are willing to do whatever it takes to increase student learning.

### Empower Students

It is impossible to increase student achievement without engaging the students—the actual people who learn—in the process. Experts reference student engagement often in articles, books, and presentations (Marzano, Pickering, & Heflebower, 2011; Sheninger, 2016; Stephens, 2015; Strong, Silver, & Robinson, 1995). Though it's a hot topic, student engagement is only a first step in a larger goal: to empower students to own their learning; students need to be equal partners in the learning process. Empowerment builds self-efficacy and promotes a growth mindset in students. Students must believe they can actually do difficult things. Teachers must stress that focused and intentional effort equals learning. If a student has not put forth effort to learn, he or she probably knew the concept before the teacher even introduced it. Teachers should encourage and celebrate productive struggle because it is learning in action—even if students fail along the way. Finally, nothing builds self-efficacy like actual success.

Students can measure success as they track their own progress—learning target by learning target (see chapter 5, page 79); they can celebrate it as they articulate what they have learned and what they have not learned *yet*. Regular formative feedback increases self-efficacy (Hattie, 2009). As students set incremental achievement goals, they build and reinforce efficacy. We discuss these strategies for student success in detail with examples and templates throughout this book.

In addition, honoring student learning with respectful tasks communicates that teachers value student work and accomplishments and consider them important. Honoring student learning means that students who have already demonstrated they are proficient or advanced in their learning receive extension of the learning, not more of the same. Honoring the learning for students who need more time and support to learn begins by finding the misconception and intervening accordingly, not starting instruction all over again. When teachers begin by teaching the concepts the students already learned, it sends the wrong message; students feel like the work that they did was entirely wrong or that the teacher thinks that they were not paying attention. They also may not realize that they actually have learned part of the lesson and lose hope at ever being able to learn at all. Honor each student's learning by providing respectful tasks that promote self-efficacy and empowerment.

Students will own their learning only if classroom roles shift from teacher-directed to student-directed learning. Often, teachers control and direct all the learning. These teachers present the content and then have students practice what they just introduced. They also tend to assume the responsibility of higher-order thinking to analyze and summarize the information, rather than sharing this with students to do so. This method is entirely dependent on the teacher with little to no involvement by students except to complete practice exercises. In *teacher-directed learning*, the focus is on the content, not on the learning. It is generally the teacher's job to present the material and the students' job to learn it.

In contrast, *student-directed learning* focuses on learning or mastery of knowledge and skills. Students play a greater role in the learning process from the beginning by clearly understanding the learning targets, setting goals, tracking their learning, and articulating their progress. Students work in partnership with their teachers to examine their assessment results and determine next steps. They are actively demonstrating the four Cs (communication, collaboration, critical thinking, and creativity) in their learning.

A simple way to determine whether learning is teacher directed or student directed is to walk through a school and listen to who is doing the talking—the students or the teachers? The ones doing the talking are the ones who are doing the learning. How much teacher talk is present and how many opportunities are there for students to talk about their thinking? Is it a fifty-fifty split, more, or less? In student-directed learning there is more student dialogue with peers and the teacher. This increases engagement and makes reasoning and thinking apparent in every aspect of the learning. Educators often expect student thinking and reasoning in teacher-directed learning but do not often teach them. In student-directed classrooms, it is easy to hear students' thinking as teachers ask them questions that require more than one-word answers.

Figure 3.4 features a tool to use during classroom observation to gather data about student-directed and teacher-directed classrooms. Use the tool to determine if the students can articulate the learning target for the lesson. Notice what the teacher and students are doing during each activity or task. Who is doing the talking or the work? Finally, document the percentage of time (or actual minutes) that the teacher spends doing the work and the talking versus the time the students get.

| Class: _____ Time: _____ Date: _____ | | |
|---|---|---|
| **Lesson Standard and Objective** | **Student Learning Target or Targets** | |
| **What Is the Activity or Task?** | **What Is the Teacher Doing?** | **What Are Students Doing?** |
| | | |
| | | |
| | | |
| **Percentage of Time Teacher Is Talking, Modeling, or Doing the Work** | **Percentage of Time Students Are Talking, Practicing, or Doing the Work** | |

**Figure 3.4: Classroom walkthrough tool.**

*Visit **go.SolutionTree.com/PLCbooks** for a free reproducible version of this figure.*

The following list shows strategies that focus on student-directed learning and ensure that students will own their learning. This is not an exhaustive list; however, each item on the list engages students in their learning from the beginning of the unit, not just when it is time to take a test. Student and teachers become partners in the learning process.

- Students name their learning targets.
- Students manage their materials and data and track their progress.
- Students set goals and learning plans or activities for themselves.
- Students self-assess their work.
- Students reflect on what they have learned and make connections to new learning.
- Students generate possible test items at appropriate rigor levels.
- Students participate in rubric development.
- Students engage in meaningful dialogue about their learning.
- Students support each other in addressing learning gaps.

Today's students are inundated with technology and media on a continual basis. They play interactive games that give them continual feedback as they problem solve ways to move to the next level. This one-more-level, one-more-level, one-more-level mentality is exactly what learning is all about. It is a great example of a growth mindset in which effort and preparation pay off. It is also an example of student-directed learning. As students work to get to the next level, they are problem solving and monitoring themselves along the way, often using each of the four Cs. Our 21st century learners are ready to take on the rigorous challenge of meeting the standards, but they need teachers to partner with them on the journey.

## Reflect and Take Action

The rubric in figure 3.5 shows collaborative team progressions in working with 21st century learners. Look at the rubric to determine team strengths and next steps related to the teaching and learning of all students.

| | Level 1<br>Beginning | Level 2<br>Attempting | Level 3<br>Practicing | Level 4<br>Embracing |
|---|---|---|---|---|
| **Using Classroom Intervention and Remediation** | Teachers respond to interventions as they occur in first-best instruction (may not be planned).<br><br>Teachers acknowledge interventions that they identify with common assessment data but move on to the next lesson regardless.<br><br>Teachers design remediation for students that pulls them from other learning during the day. | Teachers plan for intervention in first-best instruction.<br><br>Teachers make an individual plan to address interventions as necessary based on classroom data from a common assessment.<br><br>Teachers design individual remediation plans for specific skills. | The collaborative team plans for intervention in first-best instruction.<br><br>The collaborative team creates interventions based on data from common formative and summative assessments.<br><br>The collaborative team develops individual learning plans to remediate specific skills for students. | The collaborative team plans and reflects on the interventions it uses in first-best instruction.<br><br>The collaborative team creates and determines the effectiveness of team interventions designed from analyzing data from common assessments.<br><br>The collaborative team develops individual remediation plans for specific skills for students to learn during a scheduled time in the school day that does not interfere with grade-level learning. |

| Having a Schoolwide Focus on Student Learning | Teachers choose from schoolwide or collaborative team–determined strategies, tools, templates, rubrics, and so on to be used for student learning. Teachers choose from schoolwide interventions based on data. | The team determines strategies, tools, templates, rubrics, and so on to use in the collaborative team for student learning. The team determines collaborative interventions based on data. | The team determines strategies, tools, templates, rubrics, and so on to use schoolwide for student learning. The team determines universal schoolwide interventions based on data. | The team analyzes the success of schoolwide strategies, tools, templates, rubrics, and so on to use schoolwide for student learning and modifies them as necessary. The team analyzes the effectiveness of schoolwide interventions based on data. |
|---|---|---|---|---|
| Empowering Students | Teachers seldom ask students to self-reflect. Teachers create extra activities for students who finish early and those who need intervention. The classroom is most often teacher centered. | Teachers ask students to self-reflect occasionally. Teachers honor the learning of most students. Teachers create a student-centered classroom some of the time. | Teachers use student-reflection sheets with students consistently. Teachers honor the learning of students. Teachers create a student-centered classroom. | Students consistently reflect on their learning. Students can explain how what teachers ask them to do shows their learning. Students own their learning within a student-centered classroom. |

**Figure 3.5: 21st century learners rubric.**

*Visit **go.SolutionTree.com/PLCbooks** for a free reproducible version of this figure.*

Once teachers have agreement about their current status, they should use figure 3.6 to determine the next steps to meet the needs of 21st century learners.

| Action | Team-Level Rating | Next Steps |
|---|---|---|
| Plan for classroom intervention and remediation. | | |
| Plan for schoolwide student learning and interventions using common strategies and tools. | | |
| Empower students to own their learning. | | |

**Figure 3.6: Focus on 21st century learners reflection and action plan.**

*Visit **go.SolutionTree.com/PLCbooks** for a free reproducible version of this figure.*

**Collaborative Team Questions to Consider**

- What are the requirements of 21st century learning?
- Are your curriculum, instruction, and assessments aligned with the standards and learning targets, rigor, and content students need to learn?
- How will you establish a recurring cycle of interventions and extensions with respectful tasks that moves learning forward?
- Are teams providing additional time and support for students to learn based on common assessment data?
- How will you provide interventions while also remediating prerequisite skills?
- What are you currently doing to close the gap for students who have skill deficits?
- Are you currently doing whatever it takes to improve student achievement in your school? How?
- What are the areas you can address schoolwide to provide consistency in expectations while students are learning content?
- How can you design lessons that are more student centered than teacher centered?

CHAPTER 4

# Establishing a Common Guaranteed and Viable Curriculum

It is not unusual for educators in a district or school to assert that the core mission of their organization is to ensure that all students will learn. But until they collectively address the fundamental question, "Learn what?" such an assertion will remain empty rhetoric rather than a commitment to student success.

*—Richard DuFour*

When Sarah first became a teacher at a high school in Oregon, she had to ask her geometry students which teacher they had the previous year so she could understand what material they had an opportunity to learn. Some algebra teachers taught through chapter 6 on systems of linear equations, while others got through chapter 12, covering topics that included quadratics, exponential functions, and statistics. Despite their diverse understandings of algebra, the school expected all students to learn geometry well. She wrestled with the questions, Where do I begin? How do I re-engage all learners in the necessary prerequisites to be successful learners of geometry? Without ensuring a common commitment to what students would learn each year, the school was setting up students and teachers to fail their mission of all students learning at high levels. Being clear about a common curriculum changes this paradigm.

Robert J. Marzano (2003) concludes in *What Works in Schools: Translating Research Into Action* that the factor with the most impact on student achievement is a guaranteed and viable curriculum. A *guaranteed curriculum* is one that promises the community, staff, and students that a student at a school will learn specific content and processes regardless of the teacher to whom he or she is assigned. A *viable curriculum* refers to ensuring there is adequate time for all students to learn the guaranteed curriculum during the school year (DuFour & Marzano, 2011).

A common curriculum does not mean that all teachers teach from the same lesson or use the same worksheets each day; it is the guaranteed and viable curriculum that teachers deliver within each subject at each grade level. It addresses the first critical question of a PLC: what do we expect students to know and be able to do? (DuFour et al., 2016). It refers to agreements within a district and collaborative teams on the sequencing and pacing of grade-level standards as well as the intended rigor for each. It defines what students will know and be able to do at discrete moments of the year and informs what teachers should or should not commonly assess and collectively respond to when diagnosing the needs of students as they learn. The resources teachers use in the classroom are secondary to clarity about the consistent sequencing and rigor of standards with realistic pacing to ensure student learning.

The research identifies three types of curriculum in modern schools when addressing learning: (1) the *intended curriculum*, the standards the state, district, or school identify for each course by grade level or subject, (2) the *implemented curriculum*, the standards actually taught, and (3) the *attained curriculum*, the standards students actually learn (Marzano, 2003). The intended curriculum is usually a lofty goal and not altogether practical. It is why too many teachers self-determine what students should learn, knowing that learning all of it is not possible. Instead, collaborative teams need to build a shared understanding of what *all* students will learn. The implemented curriculum becomes the guaranteed and viable curriculum. Their goal is to match the implemented curriculum to the attained curriculum so students actually learn what they teach.

When a school is caught in a cycle of failure and needs to improve, often teachers focus on the lack of prerequisite skills instead of current grade-level standards students must learn. For example, a second-grade team we worked with had planned to spend the first two-and-a-half months of school reviewing first-grade content. This only left seven-and-a-half months to teach the second-grade standards designed for students to learn in ten months! It is critical to focus on grade-level content and process standards first, and then work in collaborative teams to address any remediation that needs to occur concurrently with learning grade-level material. A guaranteed and viable curriculum does not start with the premise that all students will learn it only if they come with the necessary skills at the start of the year. Rather, the collaborative team will work to ensure *all* students learn the grade-level standards at high levels. Clarity about the grade-level content to learn throughout the year is imperative to successfully addressing student deficiencies along the way through remediation (of prior grade-level content) and intervention (for current grade-level content).

If teachers do not follow the determined sequencing, rigor, and pacing of the common curriculum, students will not experience a guaranteed and viable curriculum. Instead, as DuFour et al. (2016) have noted, they get a lottery system for classroom assignment. Which students get the teacher who briefly skims all of the standards students must learn? Which students get the teacher who covers concepts in depth and so thoroughly that he or she never reaches the last few units' worth of standards? Is one of these classrooms better than the other for students? There must be another option. How can schools achieve a guaranteed and viable curriculum so all students receive the opportunity to learn essential standards? This chapter examines the work collaborative teams must engage in to create such a curriculum that provides rich learning opportunities for *all* students.

## Determine Vision Versus Reality

There are many roads between San Diego and New York City. When driving from California to New York, travelers must decide which route to take. Are there parts of the country they must see? Sites they want to experience? What is their time frame? Are they planning around a goal for minimal miles traveled or minimal time spent driving? If traveling with others, how do they meet the needs and desires of each person? Even with care and forethought, car trouble, bad weather, or unexpected construction can disrupt the best plans. How do they respond? Will they still make it to New York as expected? If not, what are the consequences for their journey along the way?

Much like the many roads between New York and California, there are many standards students must learn each year, and teachers must similarly plan a route that will get students to the destination. What is the plan to identify and ensure the learning of essential standards? How will teachers include all standards in the road map as they plan from the start to the end of the year? What are the consequences to the yearlong plan if additional days are necessary to re-engage students when the plan is disrupted? Answering these questions as a collaborative team helps the vision of academic success begin to form at your school for all students.

A school or district using a guaranteed and viable curriculum with common pacing establishes what is most critical for all students to learn. Collaborative teams build shared knowledge around what students must know and be able to do, which informs common formative assessment opportunities and deliberate practice with feedback and student action for greater learning (Hattie, 2012). Students receive focused opportunities for learning prerequisite skills tied to standards and interventions as they need them. Teams and support staff can rally around the learning of all students in a grade level or course.

Establishing a guaranteed and viable curriculum as a school or district provides a critical framework for collaborative teams as they work to do what is tight (team actions and commitments everyone will do) and use that information to move student learning forward in a way that is loose (teacher actions that can differ). In the context of a guaranteed and viable curriculum, teams reach this vision when they do the following.

- Determine *priority standards*—those standards that are more essential for students to learn than others.

- Ascertain when students will be proficient with standards throughout the year.

- Create a sequence of units with pacing criteria.

- Establish what students will have to know and be able to do as a result of learning the standards in each unit.

- Document unit plans and identify district or school resources teachers can use for their instruction of the identified standards.

With a guaranteed and viable curriculum, teams can work intentionally and focus their efforts on clearly defined student outcomes. Common grade-level classrooms or subject-specific classrooms learn similar content at the same time so students can work together, regardless of which teacher's room they are in. Teachers can make a collective plan for students who are learning and for those who have not learned yet.

Unfortunately, teachers in a building or across a district who have been working without a guaranteed and viable curriculum will not automatically agree on priority learning or general pacing and order of standards—even if everyone agrees on the value of doing so. Two excellent educators may strongly disagree on whether the year should start or end with poetry. Whether a teacher has taught for one year or twenty-five years, each has worked hard to ensure the learning of students and used his or her previous successes and failures to frame the current implementation of scope, sequence, and rigor. The team will have challenges to overcome when defining a common sequence and pacing and, to do so, it is critical to involve stakeholders in decisions and allow teachers a voice in the process.

Once teams overcome the difficulties of determining priority standards and common pacing, the challenges are not over. Students may lack prerequisite knowledge or exhibit behaviors that slow the pacing. What is a teacher or team to do? Is it more important to make sure students learn the standards the teacher is currently teaching or that they gain exposure to all of the standards? Teams will have to work to turn this question from *or* to *and*. How can we continue to teach standards the students have not yet learned *and* continue student learning? In other words, how do we accelerate learning to minimize gaps? Answers will often flow from the determined priority standards. Teams will work to ensure each student learns the priority standards at high levels and provide additional time and support for both remediation of prerequisite skills needed to access the grade-level standards and intervention related to the grade-level priority standards themselves.

Sometimes, schools within a district have different realities related to learning; keeping one building similarly paced with another can be a challenge. Likewise, within a school, one classroom of students may seem to struggle more than another. To mitigate this issue, we advocate eliminating tracking outside of honors or other accelerated courses at the secondary level and creating heterogeneous classes as a means to promote team collaboration and increase the learning of *all* students (Boaler, 2015). When planning for student learning, time can be built into units as flex days, so teachers can share students and best meet their learning needs and can plan for additional interventions as needed. Communication and collective responses to student learning are critical.

While the challenges to creating a guaranteed and viable curriculum can be daunting, it is important to stay the course so students can reap the benefits of a focused and intentional learning program. The culture shift from individual classroom learning expectations to grade-level learning expectations brings greater supports and resources to the students we serve and ensures equity.

## Start Now

There are many ways for a school or district to begin creating a common guaranteed and viable curriculum. Teams need not wait to do the work in the summer for the following year. They should start immediately, with a sense of urgency that the students in classrooms *this year* should experience equitable learning opportunities and guaranteed learning outcomes.

First, collaborative teams must identify the priority standards all students will learn and then create an overview for the year using a proficiency map to define how to sequence standards, pacing, and units. Next, teams create more details with a unit map and, finally, share a daily plan. Similarly, when planning a trip from San Diego to New York City, travelers first decide what is most critical to experience on the trip (priority standards) and then plan the route and how far they will travel each day (units within a year). Next, they determine the general structure of each day, such as the start and end times for driving and specific sites they want to visit that day (unit plan). Finally, each day, working within those parameters, they determine what they will eat and how long they will spend at various locations along the way and where they will stop to rest (daily plans). For educators, this work is the academic journey they have promised to all students in a grade level or course at their school.

### Identify Priority Standards

There are too many standards to teach each one to rigorous depth without rushing or denying students the time to actually learn them. When building shared knowledge about the standards in a grade level or course, teams must determine which standards are more essential than others for students to learn. These become the priority standards. It is important to note that these are not the only standards students will learn and that identifying them as a team is critical to creating equitable learning experiences for students. In the absence of teams identifying the priority standards, individual teachers will create their own, whether intentionally or not. The team-identified priority standards receive more instructional time in class and are the primary focus of common assessments, interventions, and extensions.

It is best to unpack standards to fully understand the intent and rigor of each before identifying any as priority standards. This means teams analyze each standard to break it into smaller learning targets that describe what a student must know and be able to do in order to be proficient with the standard (see page 63 for more about unpacking standards). However, in our experience, too many schools begin the process of unpacking standards, never finish, and then are unable to collectively determine which standards are most important for students to learn. Therefore, to start the work now, if teams are unable to unpack the standards first due to urgency, we recommend identifying the priority standards and then unpacking these and the remaining standards on a unit-by-unit basis.

If the school or district has never done this work before, consider starting with an activity designed to generate a vertical conversation around the standards students must learn, without yet identifying specific priority standards. Have each grade-level or course-alike collaborative team identify about ten essential skills or the knowledge students must learn in their grade level or course and the essential knowledge or skills students must learn in the previous grade level or course to be successful the next year. Once teams have articulated the knowledge and skills students in the current year and previous year must learn, have the teams share their answers vertically with one another to see how similar or different their answers may be. Ask them to create definitive lists, which will help inform which standards to name priority standards. See figure 4.1 to help with this protocol.

Subject: _____ Grade level: _____

1. What essential knowledge and skills should students in this subject and grade learn?

2. What essential knowledge and skills should students in this subject in the previous grade learn to be successful in this grade?

**Figure 4.1: Essential knowledge and skills.**

*Visit **go.SolutionTree.com/PLCbooks** for a free reproducible version of this figure.*

Douglas B. Reeves (2002) provides three criteria to use when determining priority standards.

1. **Does the standard have endurance?** A standard with endurance is one that requires students to learn knowledge and skills that will serve them for a lengthy period of time, not just until the next test.

2. **Does the standard have leverage?** A standard with leverage is one that requires students to learn knowledge and skills that they can apply to other curricular areas.

3. **Does the standard develop student readiness for the next level of learning?** A standard that meets the criteria of readiness will prepare students for a future unit, course, or grade level.

Larry Ainsworth (2003) identifies these priority standards as power standards and calls them the "safety net" of standards that all students *must* learn. He adds another criterion that teams should consider when determining the essential standards: the demands of district benchmark assessments and state assessments. Use the assessment blueprints or test specifications to determine those standards that receive more focus than others on assessments.

There are different protocols for having teams identify their priority standards. We often use the following three-step protocol.

1. Individual teachers, looking at a copy of the standards document, place the letters *E* (endurance), *L* (leverage), *R* (readiness), and *A* (assessment connected) next to each standard as appropriate. This is known as the R.E.A.L. criteria (Many, 2016).

2. Teachers determine individually eight to twelve priority standards from their classifications.

3. Teachers share their priority standard selections and come to consensus around the eight to twelve collaborative team priority standards.

Keep in mind that consensus does not mean everyone agrees; consensus is achieved when (1) all points of view have not only been heard but also solicited, and (2) the will of the group is evident even to those who most oppose it (DuFour et al., 2016).

We have found success using a slightly different version of this more common three-step protocol, especially in schools working to build shared knowledge of the standards due to emergency credentialed teachers or newer teachers on a team.

1. Copy each strand of standards on a different colored piece of paper. For example, from the Common Core State Standards, print Reading Informational Text on green paper and Writing on pink paper, or so on.

2. Cut the standards into strips and together write *E* (endurance), *L* (leverage), *R* (readiness), and *A* (assessment connected) on each strip of paper.

3. Once every standard is tagged, teams begin to collectively determine which eight to twelve should be the priority standards and document them as shown in in figure 4.2. (The standards are for seventh-grade Common Core English language arts.) Use the DuFour et al. (2016) definition of consensus: everyone has had a chance to speak and the will of the group is clear.

| Subject: _____ Grade level: _____ | | | | |
| Identify the priority standards and the reasons each is essential. | | | | |
| **Priority Standard** | **Endurance** | **Leverage** | **Readiness** | **Assessment Connected** |
|---|---|---|---|---|
| **RL.7.3:** Analyze how particular elements of a story or drama interact (e.g., how setting shapes the characters or plot). | X | | X | X |
| **RL.7.4:** Determine the meaning of words and phrases as they are used in a text, including figurative and connotative meanings; analyze the impact of rhymes and other repetitions of sounds (e.g., alliteration) on a specific verse or stanza of a poem or section of a story or drama. | X | X | X | X |
| **RL.7.6:** Analyze how an author develops and contrasts the points of view of different characters or narrators in a text. | X | | X | X |
| **RI.7.1:** Cite several pieces of textual evidence to support analysis of what the text says explicitly as well as inferences drawn from the text. | X | X | X | X |

| | | | | |
|---|---|---|---|---|
| **RI.7.2:** Determine two or more central ideas in a text and analyze their development over the course of the text; provide an objective summary of the text. | X | X | X | X |
| **RI.7.8:** Trace and evaluate the argument and specific claims in a text, assessing whether the reasoning is sound and the evidence is relevant and sufficient to support the claims. | X | X | X | X |
| **RI.7.9:** Analyze how two or more authors writing about the same topic shape their presentations of key information by emphasizing different evidence or advancing different interpretations of facts. | X | X | X | X |
| **W.7.1:** Write arguments to support claims with clear reasons and relevant evidence. | X | X | X | X |
| **W.7.2:** Write informative/explanatory texts to examine a topic and convey ideas, concepts, and information through the selection, organization, and analysis of relevant content. | X | X | X | X |
| **W.7.3:** Write narratives to develop real or imagined experiences or events using effective technique, relevant descriptive details, and well-structured event sequences. | X | | X | X |

*Source for standards: National Governors Association Center for Best Practices and Council of Chief State School Officers (NGA & CCSSO), 2010a.*

**Figure 4.2: Identify priority standards.**

*Visit **go.SolutionTree.com/PLCbooks** for a free reproducible version of this figure.*

It is important to remind teams that standards not identified as priority are supporting standards. Teams can think of a fence with posts and rails to visualize the relationship between priority and supporting standards. Posts are carefully placed and solidly constructed using deep holes and cement so they stand the test of time. The posts are the priority standards, those that all students must learn, which may require interventions and additional support and time to learn. The rails connecting the posts are the supporting standards, still critical to the structure of the fence and linking the posts together but not necessarily deeply learned at high levels for all students to be successful the following year.

Once teams have identified their priority standards, it is important to check two things.

1. Even though teams checked assessment blueprints, check them again to ensure that the chosen priority standards are valid in regard to the state assessment (if applicable). Not only must the content match, but the level of rigor should also be a consideration. If, for example, a team selects all standards at a DOK 1–2 level and the assessment is 60 percent at a DOK 3 level, the team may need to alter the priority standards or clearly define the rigor of each (for more information on DOK levels, see chapter 5, page 79).

2. Carefully review the priority standards, looking vertically through grade levels in a subject. Ideally, teams will not choose the same priority standard year after year; rather, teams will make decisions about when to prioritize each standard and provide focused additional time and support as well as when to devote that time and support to other standards based on the priorities of the previous or following years. Some priority standards for a grade level or course may change in this process.

Teams will have to further unpack the priority and supporting standards to define the knowledge and skills all students must learn to be proficient with each standard. However, first, it is important to determine when the team expects students to be proficient with all standards, priority and supporting, by sequencing and organizing them into units.

## Create a Proficiency Map

An overview of the year should be quick to read, reference, and use—ideally a single page. A proficiency map is one such document. It shows teams the units they will teach throughout the year and the length of time to spend on each unit, and it identifies the standards students will be proficient with by the end of each unit. An example of a fifth-grade mathematics proficiency map appears in figure 4.3 (page 64) and one for third-grade English language arts appears in figure 4.4 (page 66). We have emphasized the team priority standards with bold type within each unit. Note that each standard includes its number and a short phrase to give the reader an overview of the content students will learn.

In the examples, each unit has a name, a number of days in which to teach and assess the standards in each unit, and the end date according to a school calendar so a team can monitor its progress and adjust throughout the year while working together to ensure students learn the standards. Ideally, the sum of the instructional days on the proficiency map is less than the number of contact days with students. In fact, consider using about 155 days in a 180-contact-day calendar. This allows teams to add more time, if necessary, to a unit to account for interruptions like field trips, snow days, and state assessments that impact instructional time with students.

Note that the standards that appear in the proficiency map are those that teachers expect students to be proficient with by the end of the unit—not necessarily every standard teachers will teach or review in the unit. In spite of expectations, students can still demonstrate proficiency with a standard in a later unit; however, teachers should proactively devote all resources and supports to having students learn each unit's identified standards during that unit. If, according to the plan, students will be proficient with only part of a standard in one unit and another part in a later unit, place an asterisk next to the standard in both units and write a brief description distinguishing one part from the other in each unit.

In the proficiency map, each standard has a number and a short phrase to give the reader an overview of the content students will learn. The unit plan, however, should list the entire standard and unpack each standard for clarity (we describe this process later in this chapter). Try to list each standard only once and minimize the use of asterisks showing a standard has been separated over units. Later, when planning units, teams can plan to teach any prerequisite knowledge students need within each unit, rather than trying to teach all review material at the beginning of the year.

Some subjects are better suited to using a unit format. When working with teams to create proficiency maps, we have found that mathematics, science, and social science tend to work best by chunking learning as units. English language arts teams, however, usually are most efficient in creating a proficiency map when looking at unit names last. These teams can instead start by calling each unit a month of the year (August, September, October, and so on). Next, place standards the team expects students to be proficient in within each column next to the appropriate strand. Finally, look at the reading, writing, language, and speaking and listening skills in each unit to create a name for the unit based on the standards students will learn. In the unit plan, teams can address texts to use as vehicles for learning the standards.

If teams use colored strips of paper to identify priority standards, they can use them again by grouping the strips into units. Teachers can move the standard strips around, placing them according to when they expect proficiency. Some teams, especially in elementary school, may start by grouping standards by quarter or trimester. From there, they can chunk the standards further into roughly three-week units so they are not assessing several standards at one time. Next, teams create the proficiency map, finish organizing, and add unit names and time frames to the top of the map.

A checklist and template for a proficiency map appear in figures 4.5 and 4.6 (pages 68 and 69).

Even if the district or school has created a curriculum map with common sequencing and pacing, collaborative teams must translate the information into a one-page document (such as the one in figure 4.6) for teachers in a collaborative team to reference and use, much like a cover page to the curriculum map. If teams decide to extend a unit by a couple of days, they must note the new end dates for each future unit to ensure that all students have the opportunity to learn the remaining standards. When time becomes critical, they will use the proficiency map to determine which standards are more important by identifying the priority standards, teach those, and continue moving ahead to address all units. This keeps teams from suddenly realizing in April that they have four more units to teach and only five weeks for students to learn the standards in each one. There must be an accurate plan to ensure the curriculum is guaranteed and viable.

## Unpack Standards Into Learning Progressions and Student Learning Targets

Five different teachers can read a standard and interpret it five different ways. To have a guaranteed and viable curriculum that is equitable for all students, teachers on a collaborative team must share an understanding as to the content and skills students must demonstrate to be proficient with the standard.

Just as important is students' ability to articulate what they are learning and reflect on their progress toward mastering the standards within units and throughout the year. A teacher can tell a student what he or she has learned and not learned yet, as well as make a plan for continued learning, but the challenge is this: Can the student articulate what he or she has learned and not learned? If not, teachers may be working very hard to close a gap the student doesn't even know exists. Student learning targets bring students into the learning process.

There are many ways to unpack standards to develop a deeper understanding of student proficiency and create student-friendly learning targets. We offer the following five-step protocol, which we adapted from the work of Ainsworth (2003), for unpacking a standard with the examples in figures 4.7 and 4.8 (pages 70–71).

1. Circle the verbs and underline the nouns or noun phrases. Put a bracket around the context of the standard.

2. Write a list of the nouns or noun phrases to identify the content students must learn. This is what they must know to be proficient with the standard.

3. Write a list of the verbs with each noun or noun phrase to identify the skills students must demonstrate. This is what they must be able to do to be proficient with the standard.

4. Determine the rigor level intended in each target. (We use Norman L. Webb's [1999] DOK levels since they are most frequently aligned with the requirements of assessments; see chapter 5, page 79, for more information.)

5. Write student-friendly learning targets.

During this unpacking process, when a team becomes clear about the scope and depth of each standard students must learn, it is possible that they might determine that a standard they thought was a priority no longer makes the list. In that case, the team can revise their list of priority standards. The general template for unpacking a standard appears in figure 4.9 (page 71).

| | Multiplication and Division (Twenty-Five Days) Ends October 11 | Volume of Rectangular Prisms (Fifteen Days) Ends November 2 | Decimals and Conversion (Thirty-Five Days) Ends January 5 | Fractions: Addition and Subtraction (Twenty-Five Days) Ends February 10 | Fractions: Division and Multiplication (Thirty-Five Days) Ends April 10 | Graphing and Geometry (Fifteen Days) Ends May 1 |
|---|---|---|---|---|---|---|
| Operations and Algebraic Thinking (OA) | **\*5.OA.1: Evaluate expressions with parenthesis (whole numbers).** \*5.OA.2: Write and interpret expressions (whole numbers). | | **\*5.OA.1: Evaluate expressions with parenthesis (with powers of 10).** | | **\*5.OA.1: Evaluate expressions with parenthesis (with fractions).** | 5.OA.3: Understand number patterns. |
| Number and Operations in Base Ten (NBT) | 5.NBT.5: Multiply using the standard algorithm. 5.NBT.6: Divide up to 4 digits by 2 digits and show thinking. | | 5.NBT.1: Place value with 10s. **5.NBT.2: Multiply and divide by 10.** **5.NBT.3a: Read and write decimals.** **5.NBT.3b: Compare decimals.** 5.NBT.4: Round decimals. **5.NBT.7: Add, subtract, multiply, and divide decimals.** | | | |
| Number and Operations—Fractions (NF) | | | | 5.NF.1: Add and subtract fractions. **5.NF.2: Add and subtract fraction word problems using models.** | 5.NF.3: Interpret fractions as division. 5.NF.4a: Interpret fraction products. 5.NF.4b: Find area of rectangle. 5.NF.5ab: Explain and compare factors and products. **5.NF.6: Solve real-world fraction multiplication problems.** **5.NF.7abc: Divide whole numbers and unit fractions.** | |

| | | | | |
|---|---|---|---|---|
| Measurement and Data (MD) | 5.MD.3a: Recognize a cubic unit.<br><br>5.MD.3b: Identify volume as number of cubes.<br><br>5.MD.4: Find volume by counting cubes.<br><br>5.MD.5a: Discover the volume formula.<br><br>**5.MD.5b: Apply the volume formula.**<br><br>5.MD.5c: Add volumes to find the total volume. | *5.MD.1: Convert measurements to solve problems (decimals). | | *5.MD.1: Convert measurements to solve problems (fractions).<br><br>5.MD.2: Create a line plot with fractions and use it to solve problems. |
| Geometry (G) | | | | 5.G.1: Understand a coordinate plane.<br><br>5.G.2: Represent problems in first quadrant.<br><br>5.G.3: Know attributes of 2-D shapes.<br><br>**5.G.4: Classify 2-D shapes.** |

**Standard in bold = priority standard**

**\* = the standard is split over units**

**Figure 4.3: Proficiency map example—Grade 5 mathematics.**

*Source for standards: NGA & CCSSO, 2010b.*

| | Unit 1 Answer Text Questions (Thirty Days) Ends October 7 | Unit 2 Theme and Word Meaning (Thirty Days) Ends November 23 | Unit 3 Character Actions, Main Idea, and Produce Writing (Thirty Days) Ends January 20 | Unit 4 View Points, Main Idea, Narrative Writing (Thirty Days) Ends February 24 | Unit 5 Folklore Theme, Author Point of View, and Explanatory Writing (Thirty Days) Ends April 14 | Unit 6 Argument Writing Reading Grade-Level Texts (Thirty Days) Ends May 19 |
|---|---|---|---|---|---|---|
| Reading: Literature | 3.1: Answer text questions using evidence. **\*3.3: Describe characters.** | **\*3.2 Determine theme from stories using key details.** | **\*3.3: Describe character actions applied to sequence of events.** 3.4: Distinguish literal and nonliteral word meaning. 3.5: Refer to chapter, scene, and stanza. 3.7: Explain how text illustration contribute to the text. | 3.5: Refer to chapter, scene, and stanza. **\*3.6: Distinguish own view from character point of view.** | **\*3.2: Determine theme from folklore.** 3.9: Compare and contrast themes, settings, and plots (same author). | 3.10: Read grade-level text. |
| Reading: Informational Text | 3.1: Answer text questions using evidence. | | **\*3.2: Determine main idea with key details.** | 3.4: Determine meaning of academic and grade-specific words. 3.5: Use text features (headings) to locate information. **3.8: Describe text structure.** **3.9: Compare and contrast main idea and key details.** | **\*3.6: Distinguish own view from author point of view.** 3.7: Use information gained from illustrations. | 3.10: Read grade-level informational text in different subject areas. **\*3.3: Describe historical events, scientific ideas, steps and sequence, and so on.** |
| Writing | | | 3.6: With guidance, use technology to publish writing and collaborate. 3.4: With guidance, produce writing with organization to task and purpose. 3.5: With guidance, revise editing. | **3.3abcd: Write narratives.** 3.8: Recall and gather information from digital sources. | **3.2abcd: Write informative and explanatory texts.** 3.7: Conduct short research project | **3.1abcd: Write arguments with valid reasoning and evidence.** 3.10: Write routinely over short and extended time frames. |

| | | | | |
|---|---|---|---|---|
| **Speaking and Listening** | | 3.1abcd: Discussions—Prepare, use rules, ask questions, and explain ideas.<br><br>3.3: Ask and answer questions about information from a speaker, with details. | 3.2: Determine main idea and details of text read aloud.<br><br>3.4: Report on text, tell a story, or recount an experience.<br><br>3.5: Create audio of stories or poems—add visual displays.<br><br>3.6: Speak in complete sentences. | | |
| **Language** | 3.4d: Determine meaning using glossary or dictionary. | 3.4a: Use context clues in a sentence to determine word meaning.<br><br>3.4b: Determine meaning of words with affixes. | 3.1abcdef: Explain and form nouns and verbs.<br><br>3.2abcdefgh: Use conventions when writing—capitalization, punctuation, and spelling.<br><br>3.4c: Develop meaning of word using same roots (such as company and companion). | 3.1ghi: Form and use adjectives, adverbs, subordinating conjunctions, and sentence types.<br><br>3.6: Use grade-level conversational and academic words and phrases. | 3.3ab: Choose words and phrases for effect and compare differences between spoken and written English.<br><br>3.5abc: Find word relationships and nuances in word meanings (literal, nonliteral, real-life connections, shades of meaning). |
| **Foundational Skills** | | 3.3a: Identify and know common prefixes and suffixes.<br><br>3.3c: Decode multisyllable words. | 3.3d: Read irregularly spelled words. | | 3.3b: Decode words with Latin suffixes.<br><br>3.4abc: Read with fluency to support comprehension. |

**Standard in bold = priority standard**

**\* = the standard is split over units**

**Figure 4.4: Proficiency map example—Grade 3 English language arts.**

*Source for standards: NGA & CCSSO, 2010a.*

A proficiency map identifies which standards students should be proficient with by the end of the identified unit during the school year. The units appear in the top row of the chart, allocating a number of days for teaching the unit and including the title of the unit. The standards' domains or strands appear along the left column. Teachers complete the chart by writing in the standards students will demonstrate proficiency with by the end of each unit. Sometimes a standard may need to appear in more than one unit. If so, teachers should clearly identify the parts of the standard in which students are to demonstrate proficiency with an asterisk.

**Example:**

| | Multiplication and Division (Twenty-Five Days) Ends October 11 | Volume of Rectangular Prisms (Fifteen Days) Ends November 2 | Decimals and Conversion (Thirty-Five Days) Ends January 5 | Fractions: Addition and Subtraction (Twenty-Five Days) Ends February 10 | Fractions: Division and Multiplication (Thirty-Five Days) Ends April 10 | Graphing and Geometry (Fifteen Days) Ends May 1 |
|---|---|---|---|---|---|---|
| Operations and Algebraic Thinking (OA) | **\*5.OA.1: Evaluate expressions with parenthesis (whole numbers).** \*5.OA.2: Write and interpret expressions (whole numbers). | | **\*5.OA.1: Evaluate expressions with parenthesis (with powers of 10).** | | **\*5.OA.1: Evaluate expressions with parenthesis (with fractions).** | 5.OA.3: Understand number patterns. |
| Number and Operations in Base Ten (NBT) | 5.NBT.5: Multiply using the standard algorithm. 5.NBT.6: Divide up to 4 digits by 2 digits and show thinking. | | 5.NBT.1: Place value with 10s. **5.NBT.2: Multiply and divide by 10.** **5.NBT.3a: Read and write decimals.** **5.NBT.3b: Compare decimals.** 5.NBT.4: Round decimals. **5.NBT.7: Add, subtract, multiply, and divide decimals.** | | | |

**Proficiency Map Checklist**

☐ Does every standard appear one time when you expect proficiency? If part of a standard appears in one unit, have you accounted for the rest of the standard and do both parts have an asterisk?

☐ Have you identified the priority standards for each unit?

☐ Does every unit have a name and a number of days? Does the proficiency map account for a total of about 155 days? (These days include assessments.)

☐ How have you built horizontal coherence into the proficiency map? For example, have you woven in previous concepts from the year or used them to support learning in a later unit?

☐ How have you built vertical coherence into the proficiency map? For example, what did students learn last year and when? When will they use this learning during the next year? (Look at the proficiency maps for the grade level above and below, if possible.)

**Figure 4.5: Proficiency map checklist.**

*Visit go.SolutionTree.com/PLCbooks for a free reproducible version of this figure.*

| Grade: | Unit 1 Name: | Unit 2 Name: | Unit 3 Name: | Unit 4 Name: | Unit 5 Name: | Unit 6 Name: | Unit 7 Name: |
|---|---|---|---|---|---|---|---|
| School Year: | Total Days: End Date: | Total Days: End Date: | Total Days: End Date: | Total Days: End Date: | Total Days: End Date: | Total Days: End Date: | Total Days: End Date: |
| | | | | | | | |
| | | | | | | | |
| | | | | | | | |
| | | | | | | | |
| | | | | | | | |
| | | | | | | | |
| | | | | | | | |

**Figure 4.6: Proficiency map template.**

*Visit go.SolutionTree.com/PLCbooks for a free reproducible version of this figure.*

**Standard**

**3.MD.D.8.:** (Solve) [real-world] and [mathematical problems] involving perimeters of polygons, including (finding) the perimeter given the side lengths, (finding) an unknown side length, and (exhibiting) rectangles with the same perimeter and different areas or with the same area and different perimeters.

| Content (Nouns)<br><br>What Students Need to Know | Skills (Verbs)<br><br>What Students Need to Be Able to Do | DOK |
|---|---|---|
| • Real-world problems involving perimeters | • Solve real-world problems involving perimeters. | 2–4 |
| • Mathematical problems involving perimeters | • Solve mathematical problems. | 2–4 |
| | • Find perimeters of polygons. | 1–2 |
| • Perimeter | • Find perimeters given side lengths. | 1 |
| • Perimeter given side lengths | • Find perimeters with an unknown side length. | 1–2 |
| • Perimeter with an unknown side length | | 2–3 |
| • Rectangle | • Draw rectangles with the same perimeter and different areas. | |
| • Rectangles with the same perimeter and different areas | • Draw rectangles with the same area and different perimeters. | 2–3 |
| • Rectangles with the same area and different perimeters | | |

**Student Learning Targets**

1. I can find the perimeter of a polygon. . . .
   ➤ With known side lengths (DOK 1)
   ➤ With unknown side lengths (DOK 1–2)

2. I can draw different rectangles that have the same perimeter or the same area. (DOK 2–3)

*Source: Adapted from Ainsworth, 2003.*

**Figure 4.7: Example of unpacking standards in mathematics.**

Throughout the unpacking process, teams collectively determine what student proficiency means related to each standard. This will help teams more accurately align their common assessments (see chapter 5, page 79) and also determine the best lessons to use to teach students, keeping in mind the context of each standard. On the skills part of the unpacking chart, teams achieve clarity about the learning progressions students must undergo to thoroughly learn each standard (step 3 of the unpacking process). Of critical importance is the fact that teams develop student-friendly learning targets to share with students at the start of each unit (step 5 of the unpacking process). Students can then use their evidence of learning throughout the unit to articulate if they have learned each target or not learned it *yet*. (We discuss this further in chapter 5, page 79.)

Next in the process, teams need to determine how to collect and store their work so they can efficiently and effectively plan and learn from their units.

| Standard | | |
|---|---|---|
| L.RST.9–10.6: Analyze the author's purpose in providing an explanation, describing a procedure, or discussing an experiment [in a text], defining the question the author seeks to address. | | |
| **Content (Nouns)**<br>**What Students Need to Know** | **Skills (Verbs)**<br>**What Students Need to Be Able to Do** | **DOK** |
| • Author's purpose | • Analyze the author's purpose. | 2–3 |
| • Provided explanations | • Analyze the explanations provided. | 2 |
| • Described procedure | • Analyze the procedure described. | 2 |
| • Discussed experiment | • Analyze the experiment shown. | 2–3 |
| • Text | • Evaluate the text-argument relationship. | 2–3 |
| • Question the author seeks to address | • Define the central question of the text. | 2–3 |
| **Student Learning Targets**<br><br>1. In a text, I can analyze a given _____. (DOK 2–3)<br>   ➤ Explanation<br>   ➤ Procedure<br>   ➤ Experiment<br>2. I can define the central question of the text. (DOK 2–3) | | |

*Source: Adapted from Ainsworth, 2003.*

**Figure 4.8: Example of unpacking standards for science and technology subjects.**

| Standard | | |
|---|---|---|
| | | |
| **Content (Nouns)**<br>**What Students Need to Know** | **Skills (Verbs)**<br>**What Students Need to Be Able to Do** | **DOK** |
| | | |
| **Student Learning Targets** | | |
| | | |

**Figure 4.9: Tool for unpacking a standard into learning targets.**

*Visit go.SolutionTree.com/PLCbooks for a free reproducible version of this figure.*

### Create Unit Plans

A *unit plan* provides collaborative teams with more details related to the student learning they must address throughout each unit: big ideas, essential questions, learning targets, standards, resources, and reflection. The proficiency map determines the standards to list on the unit plan and the number of days allocated to the unit. The unpacking process defines the skills students need to learn and develops the student learning targets. As teams determine each of these elements, the unit plan becomes a place to record the work so the collaborative team can build from that shared understanding each year. This is the continuous-improvement cycle in action.

There are many ways to collect and store the work of collaborative teams as they address what they expect students to know and be able to do. The following template in figure 4.10 shows a way to organize the important parts of a unit that are tight—that is, required in the work of collaborative teams.

The time and unit name come from the proficiency map. Big ideas and essential questions usually come later in this work. Teams need to be clear about any common anchor texts they are using in a unit and any process standards students are also learning in addition to content. There is a place to list the student learning targets for a unit. (See chapter 5, page 79, for more on learning targets.) Try to limit these targets to about five so students do not get overwhelmed when reflecting on their progress throughout the unit.

Each standard that appears on the proficiency map appears in the standards column on the unit plan tool. If it is a priority standard, use bold text. If it is a standard identified with an asterisk on the proficiency map because students will only be proficient with part of the standard, write the full standard in the unit plan and strike through the part of the standard that the team does not expect students to be proficient with *yet*. Identify any academic vocabulary words students will need to know and be able to use to be proficient with the standard, and list the skills, or targeted learning progressions, from the skills section of the unpacking a standard document (step 3 of the unpacking process). Finally, identify from which resources students can learn the standards or whether other resources are necessary, and begin to discuss ways to assess student learning (see chapter 5, page 79, for more on assessment).

The last part of the template provides space for the collaborative team to reflect on the unit once it is complete, including notes for the following year. Identify which strategies worked to improve student learning and which might need changes. Are there any projects or graphic organizers to use next year? Should the team modify anchor texts? Should the team adjust the common assessments? All of this will make planning the unit in the following year more efficient and enhance opportunities for students to learn from the very beginning of the unit.

| *Course: Unit Plan* | |
|---|---|
| Time (Month or Days): | Unit: |
| Big ideas: | Essential questions: |
| **Common texts, process standards, or both:** | **Student learning targets:**<br>1. I can |

| Standards | Vocabulary | Skills | Activities (Resources) | Assessment |
|---|---|---|---|---|
|  |  |  |  |  |
|  |  |  |  |  |
|  |  |  |  |  |
|  |  |  |  |  |
|  |  |  |  |  |
| Reflection: |  |  |  |  |

**Figure 4.10: General unit plan template.**

*Visit* **go.SolutionTree.com/PLCbooks** *for a free reproducible version of this figure.*

### Create Daily Plans

Once the team has established unit plans and written the common assessments (see chapter 5, page 79), teachers can make their day-to-day plans (see chapter 6, page 113). Teams may want to account for assessment and review days and even plan ahead for flex days to leave open to re-engage students in learning as necessary. For example, if a unit is twenty days and teams take two days for common assessments, one day to review for the summative assessment, and two days for flex days, the team now has fifteen days for quality core instruction. Within those parameters is the loose aspect of collaborative teams; teachers may create their own daily lesson plans, all with a focus on students learning the identified standards, especially the priority standards.

## Reflect and Take Action

The rubrics in figures 4.11, 4.12, and 4.13 (pages 74–76) show collaborative team progressions in designing a common curriculum that is guaranteed and viable. Look at each rubric related to common proficiency maps (fig. 4.11), unpacking standards to targets (fig. 4.12), and unit plans (fig. 4.13) and determine team strengths and next steps related to each topic.

|  | Level 1<br>Beginning | Level 2<br>Attempting | Level 3<br>Practicing | Level 4<br>Embracing |
|---|---|---|---|---|
| **Structure** | Teams number units without using names. The time line is absent, has too many days listed, or only lists instructional days.<br><br>Teacher teams do not reference the document when planning. | Teams number and name units and indicate the number of days for each unit. The corresponding end dates may or may not be absent.<br><br>Teacher teams glance at the document when planning, but do not make modifications.<br><br>Teachers may be in different places in their pacing. | Teams name units so that the scope is clear. They list the total number of days including instruction, assessment, and intervention with end dates. There are fewer days than the school calendar to account for additional interventions, weather, field trips, and so on.<br><br>Teams reference the map and teachers pace themselves similarly. | Teams reference the document at the start of each new unit and make any necessary adjustments to pacing. Teams also make adjustments in pacing and end dates any time additional days are necessary for student learning. They make choices to be sure they teach all standards by the end of the year. |
| **Standards** | Teams list only the number of the standard. They list when they teach standards rather than when they expect proficiency and more than once without clarifying why. They copy standards from the curriculum materials without discussing them.<br><br>Teams skim the map and do not use the full standard when planning. | Teams list the standard number and a brief phrase. They list the same phrase if they list a standard more than once, so it is unclear which part students will be proficient with. They list standards when they teach them instead of when they expect proficiency. Too many standards are in one unit. They give equal importance to all standards.<br><br>Teams make the map but seldom reference it. | Teams list the standard number and a brief phrase. They place standards according to when they expect proficiency. If they list a standard more than once, it has an asterisk and clearly identifies which part students will be proficient with in each unit. They place the standards with secondary emphasis on the curriculum materials.<br><br>Teams reference the standards when planning units and discuss how to emphasize the priority standards identified. | Teams consistently reference the map and make adjustments to pacing and standard learning as necessary. They use the standards to make decisions related to assessment. Some standards may receive less emphasis in order to make sure students have the opportunity to learn all of the priority standards before the end of the year. |

**Figure 4.11: Proficiency map rubric.**

*Visit **go.SolutionTree.com/PLCbooks** for a free reproducible version of this figure.*

|  | Level 1<br>Beginning | Level 2<br>Attempting | Level 3<br>Practicing | Level 4<br>Embracing |
|---|---|---|---|---|
| **Content and Skills** | Teams only read the standards or discuss the content and skills. Teams do not document the work. Teams might simply copy the work of other teams that they find online or that of curriculum publishers. | Teams write a list of nouns for content and verbs for skills without making connections between the two. Teams omit the context of the standard. | Teams connect the verbs of the standard with each of its nouns, noun phrases, or context, as necessary. Teams record the work on a unit plan or curriculum map for reference. Teams identify the cognitive rigor of the standard. | Teams use the unpacked standards to build an understanding of what students must know and be able to do in a unit, to plan lessons and high-level tasks, and to inform assessments. Teams identify the cognitive rigor of the standard. |
| **Learning Targets** | Teams write student learning targets that use a less-rigorous verb than the intent of the standard. | Teams write too many student learning targets. | Teams write about five student learning targets for the unit that match the intent and rigor of the standards in the unit. | Teams align and reference all instruction and assessment to the rigor of the student learning targets. |
| **Teacher Use** | Teachers create student targets but do not use them for assessment design or as a way to frame instruction and classroom work or homework. | Teachers post student learning targets on the board or the wall but do not use them as part of instruction or student learning. At most, teachers read them at the start or close of a lesson. | Teachers post learning targets on the wall, on an assignment sheet, or on a reflection sheet for students to reference and use them to make learning connections with instruction.<br><br>Teachers teach to the rigor level of the standard. | Teachers flexibly integrate the student learning targets throughout the lesson—students and teachers use the language and identify content and skills learning.<br><br>Teachers identify with students the rigor of the target. |
| **Student Use** | Students are unaware there are learning targets for each unit or know they are posted but never reference them during instruction or assessment. | Students choral read, silently read, or listen to the teacher say the learning target at the start or end of a lesson. | Students reflect on their progress using the learning targets and evidence from classwork, homework, and assessments. They can articulate what they are learning. | Students identify goals for future learning based on their feedback from formative and summative assessments. They articulate what they have learned and what they have not learned yet. |

**Figure 4.12: Unpacking standards to student learning targets rubric.**

*Visit **go.SolutionTree.com/PLCbooks** for a free reproducible version of this figure.*

|  | Level 1 Beginning | Level 2 Attempting | Level 3 Practicing | Level 4 Embracing |
|---|---|---|---|---|
| Structure | The team creates only a day-to-day list of lessons to teach by unit, often omitting standards in the plan. | The team creates an overview by unit to include the time frame for the unit and the standards, the unpacked nouns and verbs (although not connected), and resources to use to teach during the unit. | The team creates an overview plan by unit to include a time frame; an essential question; practices and critical reasoning; standards and unpacked standards; resources, assessments, common assignments, and tasks; and a list of the student learning targets. | The team uses the curriculum map and unit plan to be clear about student learning in the unit and assessment items, and to make an instructional plan that aligns to the standards. |
| Reflection | Teams do not record reflections to use in the next school year. | Teams make notes about what assessment items they need to modify in the next school year. | Teams make notes relative to best instructional practices, interventions and extensions, and necessary modifications in assessment, as well as helpful hints to remember and connections to make between the unit and other units. | Teams proactively make notes to identify trends in student learning and how to improve learning for all students in the next year. Teams modify the map as needed based on student data they analyze during the unit. |

**Figure 4.13: Unit plan rubric.**

*Visit **go.SolutionTree.com/PLCbooks** for a free reproducible version of this figure.*

Once teams have reached agreement about their current status, they should use figure 4.14 to determine the next steps to strengthen their practice in working to ensure all students learn the guaranteed and viable curriculum.

| Action | Team-Level Rating | Next Steps |
|---|---|---|
| Identify priority standards. | | |
| Create a proficiency map. | | |
| Unpack standards into learning progressions and student learning targets. | | |
| Create a unit plan. | | |

**Figure 4.14: Guaranteed and viable curriculum reflection and action plan.**

*Visit **go.SolutionTree.com/PLCbooks** for a free reproducible version of this figure.*

**Collaborative Team Questions to Consider**

- What must all students learn and how will we ensure that they do?
- What are the priority standards all students will learn at high levels?
- How will you ensure students receive the opportunity to learn all of the standards?
- How will you articulate the learning outcomes you expect with students?
- How will you plan each unit once you know the number of days for the unit?
- How will you plan for unexpected bumps in learning along the way?
- How will you organize and keep the artifacts the collaborative team makes so you can use them one year to the next and modify them yearly as necessary?

## CHAPTER 5

# Creating and Using Common Assessments

Classroom assessment is central to every teacher's success and every learner's success. It is central to addressing the standards. It is central to guiding instruction. It is central to making individual and program improvements. It is more than just a measure of learning; it must *promote* learning.

—*Cassandra Erkens, Tom Schimmer, and Nicole Dimich Vagle*

"But, Sarah—you don't understand," exclaimed an elementary teacher with whom Sarah was working. "We can't create our own assessments," the teacher continued, "because we don't have time." Sarah naively assumed the teacher meant not enough time to create the tests as a team. However, as the teacher went on, Sarah realized it was much worse.

The teacher explained, "We already give the STAR assessment every month, and our district created English language arts and mathematics unit pre- and postassessments for us to administer at the beginning and end of every three weeks. Plus, we have to give a district benchmark test at the end of each trimester. And then there is the state test in the spring. We can't use more class time to test—we have to teach!"

Unfortunately, when a school is not getting the results it, the district, community, or state desires, one solution is to find more nationally normed or recognized assessments and create district assessments to measure the learning across sites in the same grade levels or courses. In addition, too often these assessments occur in rapid succession. As Richard DuFour (2015) makes clear:

> When students struggle on tests created by others—the textbook, the district, the state—it is not uncommon for educators to attribute their struggles to the poor quality of the test. That likelihood is diminished when the teachers themselves create an assessment that they agree is a valid way to gather evidence of student learning. (p. 176)

It is not that one type of test is good and another bad; rather, the lack of a balanced assessment vision in a school often leads to over-testing and under-instructing. What is the purpose of each assessment? Who is using the information and how? Where do collaboratively planned common assessments fit in? State or district assessments generally do not improve student learning. Improvement comes from real-time feedback from teacher-created common assessments. A balanced assessment system means the school places a larger emphasis on team-created common assessments with an occasional district benchmark assessment, progress-monitoring assessment, or state assessment as further evidence of student learning. These assessments are how a team addresses the second, third, and fourth critical questions of a PLC: (2) How will we know if each student has learned it? (3) How will we respond when some students do not learn it? and (4) How will we extend the learning for students who have demonstrated proficiency? (DuFour et al., 2016).

A *common assessment* is a grade-level or course-alike assessment that teams plan collectively that matches one or more identified standards in a unit. Every teacher on the collaborative team agrees on the questions or prompts that appear in the assessment, scores the items on the assessment using agreed-on points or a rubric, administers it the same way, and administers it at the same time. Common assessments take various forms from pencil-and-paper and computer-assisted assessments to essays and performance-based assessments, to name a few.

There are many reasons why common assessments are critical to the work of collaborative teams as they focus on improving student learning. For teams to create valid and reliable assessments, they must first determine what students will learn by identifying what students must know and be able to do for proficiency with each standard, as we discussed in chapter 4 (page 55). This helps teachers as they plan instruction and give feedback to students throughout a unit. Furthermore, Richard DuFour, Rebecca DuFour, Robert Eaker, and Thomas Many (2010) assert:

> Common formative assessments are frequently administered throughout the year to identify (1) individual students who need additional time and support for learning, (2) the teaching strategies most effective in helping students acquire the intended knowledge and skills, (3) program concerns—areas in which students generally are having difficulty achieving the intended standard—and (4) improvement goals for individual teachers and the team. (p. 214)

Nicole Dimich Vagle (2015) adds the following:

> Using assessment well means capitalizing on the information collected and using those insights to facilitate learning and foster hope for students. When students see their work in terms of their strengths and what they understand, and see deficits as opportunities to grow, assessment provides more information about how to get better. (p. 2)

Through the work of creating and responding to the results of common assessments, both teachers and students have opportunities to learn.

Some of the common assessments collaborative teams create will be formative in nature and others summative. Richard Stiggins, Judith Arter, Jan Chappuis, and Stephen Chappuis (2006) describe formative assessments as "assessments *for* learning" and summative assessments as "assessments *of* learning." John Hattie (2012) asks that educators think of formative assessments by considering "assessments as feedback" (p. 125). Kim Bailey and Chris Jakicic (2012) state that formative assessments occur "during the learning process" while summative assessments occur "after the learning is complete" (p. 14). Common formative and summative assessments do not differ in their construction or how they look; rather, they are distinguished by how teachers and students *use* them.

Common formative assessments are only part of the formative assessment process, which we explore in more detail in chapter 6 (page 113). Educators first began focusing on formative assessments with the meta-analysis research of Paul Black and Dylan Wiliam (1998) in their article "Inside the Black Box." In it, they conclude that formative assessment does improve student learning and argue it does so with an effect size between 0.4 and 0.7, a significant range in education research. Marzano (2003), Hattie (2009), and W. James Popham (2003), among others, confirm this research to show the power that quality formative practices and assessments have in improving student learning. Again, this includes ongoing daily instructional practices in core instruction (as we explore in more detail in chapter 6) as well as common formative assessments that teachers create, analyze, respond to, and involve students within a course or grade-level classroom.

Some resources label every assessment a collaborative team gives as formative if students and teachers reflect on and respond to the data. While this is an important feature of formative assessments, we stipulate that it is not unique to formative assessments and that the data from summative assessments, those assessments designed to measure expected student proficiency, also require students and teachers to reflect and respond to the data. Common summative assessments are those that teachers use as evidence of learning and to determine a student's final grade or level of proficiency with standards in a course. Common formative assessments are those assessments that teachers give within a unit for one or two standards and use to proactively encourage students and teachers to respond to the data before the unit concludes. Students can retake both common formative and summative assessments because they learn at different rates and may demonstrate proficiency at a later date. To determine the type of assessment, ask what the purpose of the assessment is. To assign a grade as a measure of learning at a moment in time? Or to inform students and teachers about the progress students have made toward standard proficiency within a unit and alter instruction accordingly? Both summative and formative assessment serve useful instructional purposes and both are essential for teacher and student learning.

## Determine Vision Versus Reality

Assessment has become a very charged topic. Diane Ravitch (2016) as well as parent and student objectors to standardized assessments have created a minefield for educators to navigate. However, as the story at the start of the chapter suggests, it is possible that some states and districts do, in fact, use too many assessments, and many use them for the purposes of evaluating students and educators rather than as a valuable instrument to analyze instructional practices and student learning.

State assessments in certain grade levels and subjects measure the successes of one school over another. While it is important to know about these successes, such assessments are seldom useful as guides for future instruction or for students to articulate their strengths and needs related to their learning. There are simply too few assessment items per standard, and it takes too much time from implementation of the assessment until teachers and students see the results.

Robert Eaker and Janel Keating (2012) note:

> Students are more apt to perform well on high-stakes summative assessments if the quality of their learning has been regularly monitored along the way—especially if the results of the assessments were used to provide students with additional time, support, or enrichment. (p. 121)

This means that although state assessments are important in their design to measure student learning, they should not be the sole focus of collaborative teams. Rather, through a balanced approach of common formative and summative assessments that continually monitor student learning and indicate the need for interventions and extensions, student learning will improve and a culture of learning will emerge. State assessments, then, become just another indicator that students are learning.

Teachers should consider their team's or school's vision for assessment. What does assessment look like and sound like when teachers do it well? How can teachers best use assessment to *improve* student learning and not just measure student learning? Rarely does the vision include the urgent need to grade more papers or the desire to sacrifice more class time and the promise of stressed students. Instead, the vision should include meaningful and purposeful assessments designed to promote learning, and it should provide clarity to all stakeholders about what students should learn as well as the rigor of that learning and how teachers expect students to demonstrate it. These high-quality assessments provide teachers and students with information that strengthens instruction and furnishes hope for students to continue persevering in their learning. In a nutshell, when schools do it right, assessment is meaningful, insightful, and necessary for teachers and students to advance learning.

When thinking about how instruction and assessment merge to improve student learning, it is critical to clarify for collaborative teams the compelling vision for instruction and assessment and the actions teams must take to realize that vision. Consider using the instruction and assessment vision protocol in figure 5.1 (page 82) with collaborative teams and the leadership team. Teams clearly define the expectations for each subgroup and then focus on what teachers must do to make the vision a reality.

| Imagine what your school looks like and sounds like when you reach your vision for quality instruction and assessment. Write your ideas below. | | | |
|---|---|---|---|
| Brainstorm what different people within the school are doing to make that education vision for instruction and assessment a reality by answering the questions below. | | | |
| **What are teachers doing?** | **What are administrators doing?** | **What are students doing?** | **What are other staff and community members doing?** |
| | | | |
| Write a statement using twenty words or fewer that explains what teachers must do to make the instruction and assessment vision a reality. | | | |
| | | | |

**Figure 5.1: Instruction and assessment vision protocol.**

*Visit **go.SolutionTree.com/PLCbooks** for a free reproducible version of this figure.*

## Start Now

Creating meaningful common formative and summative assessments requires intentional planning. To create assessments that are useful to both teachers and students, the team must determine what to assess, how to assess, and how to communicate and respond to the assessment results.

### Determine What to Assess Using Standards and Proficiency Scales

Before a team can write any common assessment, it is critical that it knows which standard or standards the assessment should address. We designed the proficiency map in chapter 4 (page 55) for this purpose. It identifies the standards that teams expect students to have learned by the end of each unit. Chapter 4 also describes a method to identify priority standards. Often, teams start by writing common formative assessments around each priority standard in a unit. These short assessments give feedback on essential learning for students that a team uses to design possible interventions and extensions both during and after a unit.

For each standard that it will assess, the team unpacks the standard (as we described in chapter 4) to understand what students will have to know and be able to do in order to be proficient with the standard. This work also informs the types of assessment questions necessary to adequately determine whether or not a student has learned a standard and to what level.

Marzano (2006, 2010) has contributed much work in the area of proficiency scales. A proficiency scale lays out what is adequate (level 3) for student proficiency related to a standard. Level 4 describes what a student must know and be able to do if he or she exceeds the expectations of the standard. Level 2 describes the partial understanding or application of a standard a student has when close to proficiency, and level 1 describes the minimal knowledge or application of a standard a student might have when still far from proficiency. (It does not describe what a student cannot do, but rather the minimum he or she can do). While Marzano also shows how to define a 1.5, 2.5, and 3.5 on the scale, Thomas R. Guskey (2015) states that fewer categories allow for greater scoring reliability among teachers, so we encourage using only levels 1, 2, 3, and 4.

Consider the two examples in figures 5.2 and 5.3 (pages 85–86) that show how to move from a standard to a proficiency scale.

---

**Standard 3.D.1.1 from the Oklahoma State Standards, Grade 3:**

3.D.1 Summarize and construct a data set with multiple categories using a frequency table, line plot, pictograph, and/or bar graph with scaled intervals.

| Content (Nouns) | Skills (Verbs) | Depth of Knowledge (DOK) Level |
| What Students Need to Know | What Students Need to Be Able to Do | |
| --- | --- | --- |
| • Data set with multiple categories<br>• Frequency table<br>• Line plot<br>• Pictograph<br>• Bar graph with scaled intervals | • Summarize data in a frequency table with multiple categories. | 1–3 |
| | • Summarize data in a line plot with multiple categories. | 1–3 |
| | • Summarize data in a pictograph with multiple categories. | 1–3 |
| | • Summarize data in a bar graph with scaled intervals that has multiple categories. | 1–3 |
| | • Construct a frequency table from a data set with multiple categories. | 1–4 |
| | • Construct a line plot from a data set with multiple categories. | 1–4 |
| | • Construct a pictograph from a data set with multiple categories. | 1–4 |
| | • Construct a bar graph with scaled intervals from a data set with multiple categories. | 1–4 |

**Figure 5.2: Standard to proficiency scale mathematics example.**

continued →

| Student Learning Targets | 1–3 |
|---|---|
| 1. I can answer questions about data shown in a:<br>  ➤ Frequency table<br>  ➤ Line plot<br>  ➤ Pictograph<br>  ➤ Bar graph with scaled intervals | |
| 2. I can construct a:<br>  ➤ Frequency table<br>  ➤ Line plot<br>  ➤ Pictograph<br>  ➤ Bar graph with scaled intervals | 1–4 |

**How Might a Student Demonstrate Advanced or Extended Mastery of the Standard?**

A student might compare and contrast two data sets as shown in two different representations (for example, shown a bar graph and a pictograph of students who like chocolate, vanilla, and strawberry ice cream from two different classrooms, the student can find the total number of students who like each flavor or can determine how many more students like one flavor over another). This is more advanced if the scale of the bar graph does not match the number of students represented by each cone in the pictograph. Students might also gather data themselves on a topic and then create an appropriate graphical representation of the data.

**Standard** (Learning progression ends here with mastery of this standard.)

Summarize and construct frequency tables, line plots, pictographs, and bar graphs with scaled intervals.

| 4 | Compare the information from two different data sets shown in two different ways.<br><br>or<br><br>Ask a question, gather data, and construct a frequency table, line plot, pictograph, or bar graph with scaled intervals to show the data. |
|---|---|
| 3 | Construct and answer questions about the data shown in frequency tables, line plots, pictographs, and bar graphs with scaled intervals. |
| 2 | Construct frequency tables, line plots, pictographs, or bar graphs with scaled intervals. |
| 1 | Identify the total number of data in each category shown in a frequency table, line plot, pictograph, and bar graph with scaled intervals. |

*Source for standard: Oklahoma State Department of Education, 2016.*

*Visit **go.SolutionTree.com/PLCbooks** for a free reproducible version of this figure.*

Note that in figure 5.3 (page 85–86), the verb *analyze* is possibly a DOK 1 level for rigor. That happens when a student is restating learning he or she gathered from analyzing in class. In this case, the student might only be remembering the learning, having not truly analyzed for meaning him- or herself.

**Standard 3 for U.S. History from the Texas Essential Knowledge and Skills for Social Studies**

The student understands the political, economic, and social changes in the United States from 1877 to 1898. The student is expected to:

(A) Analyze political issues such as Indian policies, the growth of political machines, civil service reform, and the beginnings of Populism;

(B) Analyze economic issues such as industrialization, the growth of railroads, the growth of labor unions, farm issues, the cattle industry boom, the rise of entrepreneurship, free enterprise, and the pros and cons of big business;

(C) Analyze social issues affecting women, minorities, children, immigrants, urbanization, the Social Gospel, and philanthropy of industrialists; and

(D) Describe the optimism of the many immigrants who sought a better life in America.

| Content (Nouns) What Students Need to Know | Skills (Verbs) What Students Need to Be Able to Do | DOK Level |
|---|---|---|
| • Political changes in the United States from 1877 to 1898 | • Understand political changes in the United States from 1877 to 1898. | 1–2 |
| • Economic changes in the United States from 1877 to 1898 | • Understand economic changes in the United States from 1877 to 1898. | 1–2 |
| • Social changes in the United States from 1877 to 1898 | • Understand social changes in the United States from 1877 to 1898. | 1–2 |
| • Political issues such as: <br> ➢ Indian policies <br> ➢ Growth of political machines <br> ➢ Civil service reform <br> ➢ Beginnings of Populism | • Analyze political issues such as: <br> ➢ Indian policies <br> ➢ Growth of political machines <br> ➢ Civil service reform <br> ➢ Beginnings of Populism | 1–3 |
| • Economic issues such as: <br> ➢ Industrialization <br> ➢ Growth of railroads <br> ➢ Growth of labor unions <br> ➢ Farm issues <br> ➢ Cattle industry boom <br> ➢ Rise of entrepreneurship <br> ➢ Free enterprise <br> ➢ Pros and cons of big business | • Analyze economic issues such as: <br> ➢ Industrialization <br> ➢ Growth of railroads <br> ➢ Growth of labor unions <br> ➢ Farm issues <br> ➢ Cattle industry boom <br> ➢ Rise of entrepreneurship <br> ➢ Free enterprise <br> ➢ Pros and cons of big business | 1–3 |
| • Social issues such as those affecting: <br> ➢ Women <br> ➢ Minorities <br> ➢ Children <br> ➢ Immigrants <br> ➢ Urbanization <br> ➢ Social Gospel <br> ➢ Philanthropy of industrialists | • Analyze social issues such as those affecting: <br> ➢ Women <br> ➢ Minorities <br> ➢ Children <br> ➢ Immigrants <br> ➢ Urbanization <br> ➢ Social Gospel <br> ➢ Philanthropy of industrialists | 1–3 |
| • Optimism of many immigrants seeking a better life in America | • Describe the optimism of immigrants seeking a better life in America. | 1–2 |

**Figure 5.3: Standard to proficiency scale social studies example.**

continued →

| Student Learning Targets | 1–3 |
|---|---|
| 1. I can analyze and explain changes between 1877 and 1898 related to:<br>➤ Political issues<br>➤ Economic issues<br>➤ Social issues | |
| 2. I can describe the optimism of immigrants seeking a better life in America. | 1–2 |

**How Might a Student Demonstrate Advanced or Extended Mastery of the Standard?**

A student might compare and contrast the political, economic, or social issues between 1877 and 1898 to those of today. The student might also explain how one set of issues (political, economic, or social) affected another set of issues.

**Standard** (Learning progression ends here with mastery of this standard.)

Analyze political, economic, and social issues in the era between 1877 and 1898.

| 4 | Compare and contrast the political, economic, or social issues that occurred between 1877 and 1898 to those of today.<br>or<br>Explain how the political, economic, or social issues that occurred between 1877 and 1898 were intertwined. |
|---|---|
| 3 | Analyze and explain changes in political issues, economic issues, and social issues between 1877 and 1898, including the optimism of immigrants seeking America. |
| 2 | Explain changes in political issues, economic issues, or social issues between 1877 and 1898. |
| 1 | Identify key aspects of some political issues, economic issues, and social issues between 1877 and 1898. |

*Source for standard: Texas Essential Knowledge and Skills, 2011.*

*Visit **go.SolutionTree.com/PLCbooks** for a free reproducible version of this figure.*

Teams can use the blank template in figure 5.4 to create proficiency scales.

| Standard: | | |
|---|---|---|
| **Content (Nouns)**<br>**What Students Need to Know** | **Skills (Verbs)**<br>**What Students Need to Be Able to Do** | **DOK Level** |
| | | |

| | |
|---|---|
| **What Are the Student Learning Targets?** | |
| **How Might a Student Demonstrate Advanced or Extended Mastery of the Standard?** | |
| **Standard** (Learning progression ends here with mastery of this standard.) | |
| 4 | |
| 3 | |
| 2 | |
| 1 | |

**Figure 5.4: Standards to proficiency scales tool.**

*Visit **go.SolutionTree.com/PLCbooks** for a free reproducible version of this figure.*

As teams use the template to determine the proficiency scale, they should first consider what an advanced-level student who is exceeding the standard would demonstrate. Exceeding the standard does not mean that a student must move forward to another grade-level standard, but rather that the student might deepen or extend the intent of the current grade-level standard. Sometimes it is helpful to consider the proficiency scale descriptions in table 5.1 when creating scales.

Table 5.1: Proficiency Scale Descriptions

| Level | Adjective | Meaning |
|---|---|---|
| 4 | Exceed | **Beyond proficiency:** Student understanding and application extends beyond the intent of the standard. |
| 3 | Adequate | **Proficient:** If there is a mistake in student work, the student requires no additional instruction to correct his or her thinking. |
| 2 | Partial | **Close to proficiency:** The student requires intervention for part of the standard, but he or she clearly understands another part of the standard. |
| 1 | Minimal | **Far from proficiency:** The student needs remediation or intervention. |

The work of determining what to assess allows teachers to design effective instructional practices and intentionally differentiate to improve student learning. It also forces teams to deeply discuss what students will have to know and be able to do to be proficient on a standard and address the common misconceptions students have when learning the standard. All of this improves core instruction leading to the eventual common formative and summative assessments and defines what students must learn and what, consequently, teachers will assess.

### Determine How to Assess Using Assessment Design

There are many factors to consider when designing an effective assessment. Teams cannot assume that a publisher's test is a quality assessment. Though many of the items on an assessment might strongly match with the standards students must learn, the content and rigor of others may not, and some of the standards teachers need to assess might be missing altogether. In either case, the team must modify the assessment to best parallel the learning it expects students to demonstrate to ensure the resulting data are meaningful.

Consider the following questions when planning for a common assessment.

- How well do the assessment items match the standard's intended rigor?
- How well does the assessment method match the assessed standard?
- How well has the team represented each essential learning target on the assessment?
- How clear are the directions?
- How will the team commonly score the assessment?

Teams must also consider how students and teachers will respond to the assessment results.

#### Rigor of Assessment Items

Teachers are often familiar with Bloom's taxonomy as a tool for determining the reasoning complexity and difficulty of tasks that they use instructionally or place on an assessment (Bloom, Anderson, & Krathwohl, 2001). There are also other schemata teams can use to determine the amount of reasoning and skill required to demonstrate proficiency on a standard.  In this book, we use Norman L. Webb's Depth of Knowledge levels, which teachers commonly use to identify the cognitive complexity required to meet proficiency of a standard. Webb originally created the four DOK levels in the late 1990s at the Wisconsin Center for Education Research in the areas of mathematics and science, and they have since been applied to other subject areas by both Webb and others (Hess, 2004, 2005a, 2005b, 2010; Webb, 1999).

Webb's four DOK levels appear in table 5.2.

When using DOK levels to describe the cognitive demand of a task or assessment item, it is important to separate the difficulty of the task from the amount of reasoning required to address it. A kindergarten student solving $3 + 4 = ?$ and a fourth grader solving $1,245 + 3,917 = ?$ are both using reasoning at the recall and reproduction level (DOK 1), even though the second problem may be more difficult for students to solve. For both, a student quickly recognizes the need to add so the reasoning to access the task has the same cognitive demand. If every student succeeds, the problem is easy, if not, the problem is hard or of medium difficulty, but the reasoning is at DOK 1. Similarly, an assignment comparing and contrasting the themes in two novels using evidence at the secondary level would be at a higher level (DOK 3) as long as the student is not simply regurgitating the class discussion and the task is novel and new for the student (without these criteria it would be DOK 1). Again, when most students successfully accomplish the task, they signal that it is easy, and if not, that it is hard.

Table 5.2: DOK Levels and Descriptions

| DOK Level | Name | Description |
|---|---|---|
| 1 | **Recall and Reproduction** | Recite facts or use simple skills, procedures, or algorithms.<br>For example:<br>• Read a passage and answer a question found directly in the text.<br>• Use punctuation marks correctly.<br>• Add or subtract with an algorithm.<br>• Place words on a science diagram.<br>• Recite the preamble to the Constitution. |
| 2 | **Skills and Concepts** | This requires mental processing beyond recall or a habitual response. Students must make decisions about how to approach the task and may have to put ideas together.<br>For example:<br>• Predict the conclusion to a story.<br>• Write a summary that includes the important details in a piece of informational text.<br>• Solve a two-step word problem.<br>• Organize data from a science experiment.<br>• Explain Abraham Lincoln's influence on the Civil War. |
| 3 | **Strategic Thinking** | Reason and plan at higher levels than DOK 1 and 2. Students must analyze text, data, or student work and use evidence to support a conclusion or explain their thinking when reasoning deeply.<br>For example:<br>• Determine how the author's purpose affects the interpretation of a text.<br>• Edit an essay.<br>• Solve a nonroutine problem and show the solution pathway chosen to reach the answer.<br>• Use data from an experiment to form a conclusion as it relates to the original hypothesis.<br>• Describe how the geographic features of a region influence its economy. |
| 4 | **Extended Thinking** | Use complex reasoning with high cognitive demand. Students will often be applying knowledge to a new situation by analyzing, synthesizing, or planning. This often requires extended time.<br>For example:<br>• Read texts from throughout a time period and compare and contrast the themes using evidence from the texts and historical texts.<br>• Create an argument paper citing multiple sources as evidence.<br>• Create a design for a park within given parameters and prove the design meets the given criteria.<br>• Design and conduct an experiment with analysis of results.<br>• Read informational text about a current event and explain how it compares historically to different events in U.S. history, citing evidence. |

*Source: Adapted from Hess, 2004, 2005a, 2005b, 2010.*

Apart from separating difficulty from the reasoning required, it is also important not to just look at a verb to determine the DOK level of a task or assessment item. For example, a teacher might use the word *explain* in the following ways related to weather in a science unit (see table 5.3). It is important to read the entire stem of an assessment item or task to determine the complexity of reasoning it asks of students.

Table 5.3: DOK Level Examples in Science

| DOK Level | Task | Explanation |
|---|---|---|
| 1 | *Explain* what causes the noise of thunder in a storm. | This task requires an explanation that simply recalls factual information. |
| 2 | *Explain* how hurricanes and tornadoes are alike. | This task requires an explanation that asks students to determine the similarities and differences between knowledge they have learned related to these two types of storms. |
| 3 | *Explain* whether hurricanes are getting worse in recent years with evidence to support your argument. | This requires students to form an argument and then provide evidence to support that decision. |
| 4 | *Explain* how to design an experiment that tests the effects of wind in urban areas. | This task requires extended time to formulate a quality experiment design and then explain how it tests wind in urban areas. |

When the collaborative team has determined the DOK level or levels associated with a standard, that is the level it expects for *all* students, not just those performing at high levels. As a team it becomes important to write assessment items to that level and then design instruction that prepares each student for that level of rigor (see more on instruction in chapter 6, page 113).

When writing a common summative assessment that covers multiple standards, consider working toward half of the assessment being written at the DOK 2 level with the remaining half split between DOK levels 1 and 3. DOK 4 is usually its own assessment because extended thinking also requires extended time and planning. An essay, speech, or lab report might fall into this category.

### Assessment Types

There are different ways to design a quality common assessment. Assessments fall into the categories of selected response, constructed response, performance assessment, or personal communication (Stiggins et al., 2006; Vagle, 2015).

*Selected response* refers to multiple-choice, fill-in-the-blank, matching, true-or-false, or few-word answers to questions. These elicite right and wrong answers, which make these types of assessment items easier to grade and less subjective. However, it is difficult to assess DOK 3 or 4 with these types of items and, if written well, multiple-choice items are some of the most difficult to write. For more information about how to write such selected-response items you might reference *Raising the Rigor* by Eileen Depka (2017). Ideally each distractor (incorrect answer) gives the teacher as much information as the correct answer because each distractor represents a common student misconception; teachers can respond to these indicators of student learning with quality instructional re-engagement.

When writing selected-response items, consider the following.

- Multiple choice:

  ‣ Do not give away the answer in the stem (question part). This can happen when a question uses similar words in the stem and answer or the stem ends with a word like *an*, which might give away the need for the answer that begins with a vowel.

- Limit the number of words in the answer and distractors. Put as much of the reading as possible in the stem.

- Use parallel construction in the answer and distractors so they have roughly the same length and structure (for numeric answers this means if the answer is a decimal, there will be at least two decimals to choose from if the other distractors are integers).

- Seldom use "all of the above" or "none of the above."

- When there is more than one answer, let the students know that in the stem (for example, write "Select all that apply" or "Choose the two reasons why.")

- Refrain from clever distractors such as "Because I said so." Some students will choose this to be clever in return, which means teachers will not ascertain their understanding, and others are choosing from one less distractor.

- True or false:

  - Avoid double negatives in the statement.

  - Keep the reading level simple.

- Matching:

  - Keep the lists students must match to and from short.

  - Make the list students match to longer than the one they match from so they must continually choose the correct answer and not just connect the last two items on each list.

  - Keep the lists homogeneous (for example, don't mix dates, names, and places).

  - Consider allowing students to match to an answer more than once.

- Fill in the blank:

  - Provide one blank per answer.

  - Don't give away the response with the length of the line.

  - Put the line at the end of the sentence, rather than the beginning, for more valid results.

*Constructed response* refers to writing short answers or essays using sentences, completing a graphic organizer, showing work toward a mathematics solution, or other original written work from a student. These questions are typically easier for a teacher or collaborative team to write, yet more difficult to score consistently and more time intensive to grade. They do, however, provide an opportunity for students to demonstrate their reasoning and for teachers to look at student work and see the misconceptions students have in learning. They work well for DOK levels 2–4.

When writing constructed-response items, consider the following.

- Be clear in the stem what students should convey (for example, tell students if their responses must include complete sentences or if they must show their work for a solution).

- Determine as a collaborative team how to score each constructed-response item.

- Determine as a collaborative team what students must include in their responses for proficiency.

- Write the stem at the lowest reading level possible.

- Provide ample space for each student to answer the item.

*Performance assessment* refers to a performance a student gives or a product a student creates. Collaborative teams must determine in advance the rubric to use when scoring these types of assessments and later calibrate themselves to ensure their responses to learning are accurate. It is important that a team discusses whether a performance assessment is enough to determine proficiency. For example, when taking a driver's exam, there are two parts:

(1) the performance aspect of driving the car and (2) a written exam testing a person's knowledge of traffic signs, car design, and safety that the instructor cannot necessarily assess while the student drives the car. Similarly, a team may need a performance assessment and an additional assessment to determine student proficiency, especially if the performance assessment includes a group of students (such as a group project or choir performance). These assessments can often be time intensive in the classroom, so teams need to account for that loss of instructional time.

When writing a performance assessment, consider the following.

- Make sure the assessment matches the intent of the standard.

- Be clear what learning students should demonstrate (for example, not "Give a speech about the book," but rather, "Give a speech about a character and his or her development related to the theme of the book.").

- Create a rubric that describes the quality of the work the team expects rather than a scoring guide for points that students can earn.

- Clearly define team expectations for the performance.

*Personal-communication* assessments are the most difficult type of assessment to use as a common assessment because conversations meander in different ways between a teacher and a student. However, these are critical for interviews, demonstration of conversational world language acquisition, and for students who are unable to read or write responses (such as kindergartners). As such, we include it as an assessment type, though we encourage its use sparingly. When using this type of assessment, it is important that teachers all use the same script throughout the assessment and limit follow-up questions until after the teachers ask all scripted questions so as not to prompt a future answer inadvertently. Teams will also have to decide in advance what to look for in each response for proficiency and determine how to score responses.

When writing a personal-communication assessment, consider the following.

- Create a script that details word for word what each teacher will say and ask.

- Determine how each teacher will record and score student responses.

- Keep questions simple.

- Limit the number of personal-communication assessments due to the amount of instructional time it takes from class to administer one to every student.

Once a collaborative team has determined the standards to put on the common formative or summative assessment, it must determine which assessment method to use to score each one. Using a template like the one in figure 5.5 to determine an assessment plan can helps teams make this choice. If the assessment is pencil and paper, teams will generally want at least three to four questions per standard to determine student proficiency, unless the questions require a longer written response, in which case a rubric or scoring guide provides an explanation of proficiency. Ultimately, the collaborative team will need to determine if there are enough items to feel confident about a student's demonstration of learning as well as enough items for the team to design quality intervention and enrichment if necessary. Teams can use the planning template in figure 5.5 for smaller common formative assessments covering one standard or a larger common summative assessment.

The assessment design tool provides an overview of the type of assessment to use, but good practice requires further analysis of the questions teams choose.

| Standard or Learning Target | Selected Response | Constructed Response | Performance Assessment | Personal Communication |
|---|---|---|---|---|
| Quote accurately from a text when drawing inferences. | Read an original passage and answer two items.<br><br>DOK 1: Identify a quote to support a given inference. | Read an original passage and answer two items.<br><br>DOK 2: Make an inference and support it with a quote. | | |
| Compare and contrast two or more characters using details in a text. | Read an original passage and answer two items.<br><br>DOK 1–2: Identify two characters with similar or different impacts on the main idea of the story. | Read an original passage and answer one item.<br><br>DOK 3: Choose two characters and use details in the text to explain how they interact with one another and contribute to the main idea of the text. | | |

**Figure 5.5: Assessment design tool—Grade 5 English language arts example.**

Visit **go.SolutionTree.com/PLCbooks** for a free reproducible version of this figure.

### Target-Test Analysis

If teams start with an assessment they have used previously or that of a publisher, look at each item and determine which standard it measures. One way to do this is to use the template in figure 5.6. Start by identifying the standards students must demonstrate they have learned on the assessment. Next, identify which items match each standard and note the DOK level of the item and the points that the scoring guide or rubric allocates to the question on the assessment. When finished, determine if any standards are missing assessment items or if the assessment has items that do not correspond to any standards. In either case, adjustments may be necessary in the assessment or instruction for the unit.

| Learning Target or Standard | Assessment Items | DOK Level | Points or Rubric Score | Percentage of Test |
|---|---|---|---|---|
| I can write linear equations given: | 1 | 1 | 24 | 52% |
| • A slope and *y*-intercept | 7 | 2 | | |
| • A slope and a point | 12a | 2 | | |
| • Two points | 2 | 1 | | |
| • A graph (includes lines of best fit) | 8 | 1 | | |
| | 9 | 2 | | |
| | 3 | 1 | | |
| | 10 | 2 | | |
| | 4 | 1 | | |
| | *6 | 1 | | |
| | *16 | 2 | | |

**Figure 5.6: Target-test analysis.**

continued ➡

| Learning Target or Standard | Assessment Items | DOK Level | Points or Rubric Score | Percentage of Test |
|---|---|---|---|---|
| I can write an equation for a line parallel to a given line. | 5 | 1 | 4 | 9% |
| | 11 | 2 | | |
| I can use a linear equation or line of best fit to answer real-world questions. | 12 b | 2 | | 26% |
| | 13 abc | 2–3 | 12 | |
| | *14 abc | 2–3 | | |
| I can interpret the meaning of a graph. | 15 | 2 | 6 | 13% |
| | 14 d | 3 | | |
| **Team Analysis** | | | | |

1. Should the test be revised for this year and if so, how?

   We feel like we met the intent of the DOK levels for standards in this unit. However, the test is a little too heavy on computations with the first target and we need to add another word problem as well as an item related to parallel lines.

2. Should the instruction be revised and if so, how?

   We feel the instruction is a match to the changes we want to make to the assessment.

*Visit **go.SolutionTree.com/PLCbooks** for a free reproducible version of this figure.*

We worked with one seventh-grade prealgebra team in Minnesota who shared that students notoriously under-performed on their first unit common assessment. We decided to match the items to the standards the team expected students to learn. Upon doing so, we were surprised to learn that sixteen of the thirty-two questions did not adequately match any standard students were supposed to learn in that unit. "But, these are good questions!" the team lamented. We agreed. However, they did not belong on this assessment unless the team changed the standards it assessed in the unit. The team decided to save the questions and use them on upcoming assessments in which they made more sense.

While working with a U.S. history team in Oregon, Sarah aligned assessment items to targets and the team noticed that its multiple-choice assessment did not include any questions related to a target that asked students to write about an immigrant's experience coming to America. This team determined it needed to add an essay or short-response item to its assessment to meet the intent of the target.

Another team of algebra teachers conducted this analysis after giving their common unit assessment because the students did poorly. Results on the common formative assessments had predicted better results. After analyzing the linear-equations assessment, the teachers found that 50 percent of the points came from problem solving related to linear equations given a word problem or context. While this was their intent, they had actually taught the entire unit focused more on skills and taught only one day of problem solving before the unit assessment. They realized that the assessment was correct, but they needed to change their instruction to include problem solving daily to better match the key idea of the unit and the assessment.

This analysis allows the collaborative team to organize the assessment by standard or target which, in turn, enables it to review the results by standard as well as work with students to examine their work from each section and determine if they learned that standard or did not learn it *yet* based on the evidence they demonstrated. An example of this appears in the common summative assessment in figure 5.7.

The writers of this assessment organized it into three different learning targets identified by standard, gave it a balance of DOK 1–3 level questions, and specified how many points every question is worth (we discuss this further on page 99).

---

### Grade 3, Unit 4: Multiplication and Division

Name: _____     Date: _____

**3.OA.1–2:** I can interpret multiplication and division equations.

1.  Destiny found a mathematics picture on the floor after class. Here it is.

   a. What are different equations that this picture could represent? Circle all that apply.

   | | | | |
   |---|---|---|---|
   | $4 \times 5 = 20$ | $20 \div 4 = 5$ | $5 \times 2 = 10$ | 2 points _____ |
   | $10 \div 5 = 2$ | $5 \times 4 = 20$ | $20 \div 2 = 10$ | |

   b. Write a story problem that matches this picture.          1 point _____

---

**Figure 5.7: Grade 3 mathematics test example.**

continued →

2. Show how you can find the product of 5 × 6 on a hundreds chart.  2 points _____

| 1 | 2 | 3 | 4 | 5 | 6 | 7 | 8 | 9 | 10 |
|---|---|---|---|---|---|---|---|---|----|
| 11 | 12 | 13 | 14 | 15 | 16 | 17 | 18 | 19 | 20 |
| 21 | 22 | 23 | 24 | 25 | 26 | 27 | 28 | 29 | 30 |
| 31 | 32 | 33 | 34 | 35 | 36 | 37 | 38 | 39 | 40 |
| 41 | 42 | 43 | 44 | 45 | 46 | 47 | 48 | 49 | 50 |
| 51 | 52 | 53 | 54 | 55 | 56 | 57 | 58 | 59 | 60 |
| 61 | 62 | 63 | 64 | 65 | 66 | 67 | 68 | 69 | 70 |
| 71 | 72 | 73 | 74 | 75 | 76 | 77 | 78 | 79 | 80 |
| 81 | 82 | 83 | 84 | 85 | 86 | 87 | 88 | 89 | 90 |
| 91 | 92 | 93 | 94 | 95 | 96 | 97 | 98 | 99 | 100 |

Answer: 5 × 6 = _____

3. Brian's teacher gave him this mathematics problem: 3 × ☐ = 21  2 points _____

   a. Brian starts solving the problem by sketching an array. Finish his work to show how he solved the problem.

   b. Now, solve the equation 3 × ☐ = 21  ☐ = _____

4. The model below shows a division problem.

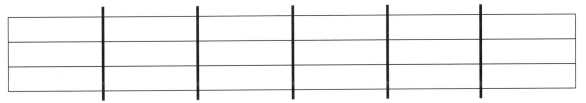

    a. Write a division equation that matches the picture.    2 points _____

    b. Write a story problem that matches your equation.    1 point _____

**3.OA.3:** I can solve word problems.

5. Kendra had 8 times as many pencils as Tracy. Kendra has 56 pencils. How many pencils does Tracy have? Use a picture, words, and/or an equation to show how you know your answer is correct.

    2 points _____

6. Peggy has 6 pieces of string. Each piece has a length of 8 inches. Peggy placed all 6 pieces of string in a long line with the end of one string touching the end of another string. What was the total length of the line she created? Use a picture, words, and/or an equation to show how you know your answer is correct.

    2 points _____

7. Martin had 4 goldfish bowls. This is what he did with the fish. He put:

| 10 fish in<br>the first bowl | 10 fish in<br>the second bowl | 7 fish in<br>the third bowl | and 13 fish in<br>the fourth bowl |
|---|---|---|---|

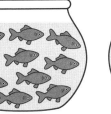
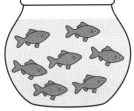
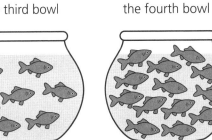

Martin says that he showed 4 × 10 using the bowls and the goldfish. Is he correct? Explain why or why not.

    2 points _____

continued →

**3.OA.4:** I can determine the unknown in an equation.

Determine the unknown number for each problem.

6 points _____

8. $6 \times ? = 42$      ? = _____

9. $\triangle \times 10 = 70$      $\triangle$ = _____

10. $7 \times 2 = \square$      $\square$ = _____

11. $* \times 9 = 0$      * = _____

12. $36 \div 9 = ?$      ? = _____

13. $24 \div \square = 8$      $\square$ = _____

*Source for standards: NGA & CCSSO, 2010b.*

### Clarity of Directions

Directions on an assessment are critical so students know how to write their answers or demonstrate their learning. We recommend that each teacher on the collaborative team take the assessment independently and then come together as a team to look at the desired responses. If directions are unclear, it will be evident from the teachers' varied responses. However, even still, directions may be unclear for students. A team might not learn about this lack of clarity until after giving or evaluating the test. In this case, the team can make adjustments to scoring or the assessment for the next year. If, however, the team needs the information to determine the current students' proficiency, teachers may need to give an additional assessment item to students to measure their level of understanding.

### Common Scoring

After working with teams to develop common assessments at an elementary school in Oregon, Sarah met with them to analyze the student results from the assessment. The teams hoped that as a result of the meeting, teachers could identify (1) which students had learned or not learned each standard on the assessment, (2) targeted interventions and extensions to use with students as a result of the data, and (3) effective instructional strategies they had used throughout the unit to grow the instructional toolkit of all teachers on the team.

All teachers on the third-grade team came armed with their data—they had even color-coded it red (far below proficiency), yellow (close to proficiency), and green (proficient) for each student by standard. Together, they looked at the percentage of students who were proficient with each standard and then identified how many students fell into each category. Next, Sarah and the team began to look at the student work on the assessment to identify what they should target to have more students learn. At that moment, an interesting problem developed.

Suddenly, it became very clear that not all four teachers had scored the assessment the same way. Two used a rubric to score answers on a scale of one to four and the other two assigned point values to each item on the test, though they were not in agreement about how many points each of the questions should be worth. No longer could the teachers talk about student proficiency, interventions, or instructional strategies because they had not agreed on what level of work students needed to demonstrate to show they understood the content. Though they had administered the same assessment to every third-grade student, it was not truly a common assessment because they had not agreed on scoring or considered calibration.

The team should have considered the following questions.

- What are the agreed-on scoring guides or rubrics your team uses to score each common assessment?

- If using points, how do you allocate them for a student response? In other words, how does a student earn each point?

- If using rubrics, what are the criteria and how do students know in advance your expectations for proficiency in each criterion?

Calibrating scoring using common scoring agreements is critical. Teachers should ask themselves how comfortable they are with a colleague grading their student assessments. If that answer gives them pause or concern, their team needs to address that area.

Before giving an assessment, a collaborative team must determine how it will score the assessment. It does not matter exactly whether a team uses points, scales, or a rubric. What matters is that the members all use the same tool in the same way. An assessment score becomes the communication tool teachers use with students and parents. These scores must be consistent for a collective response to student learning. Perhaps even more important, once the team has determined common scoring, each teacher can better give feedback to students during the instructional part of the unit because everyone is clear about what each student must do to demonstrate proficiency. Teachers can create the best lessons and activities to develop student understanding and application.

When using points, be clear about how students are earning each point based on the evidence they are demonstrating in their work. When using scales, be clear about the group of questions associated with a standard that will collectively earn a score. When using a rubric that shows categories and quality of student work, be clear about the interpretation of each category by value.

Answer the questions in the team assessment scoring protocol in figure 5.8 to determine how the collaborative team will score student work and provide meaningful feedback to students.

| 1. Determine independently how you would score each item on the assessment. |
| --- |
| > If you use points, be able to explain the student work required to earn each point. |
| > If you use a scale or rubric, be able to explain the work required for each value. |
| 2. Discuss as a team how you will score each item on the assessment and record your agreements. Be clear about how students will earn points or the scale or rubric values. |

| Assessment Item | Total Points or Rubric Values | Student Work Required to Earn Points or Rubric Values |
| --- | --- | --- |
| Learning Target 1 #1–5 (all multiple choice from reading a literary passage) | Scale score 1–4 for the entire section of the test | 1 = Student answers 0–1 of items correctly. <br> 2 = Student answers 2–3 of the items correctly. <br> 3 = Student answers 4 of the items correctly. <br> 4 = Student answers 5 of the items correctly. |

**Figure 5.8: Team assessment scoring protocol.**

continued →

| Assessment Item | Total Points or Rubric Values | Student Work Required to Earn Points or Rubric Values |
|---|---|---|
| Learning Target 2 #6 (compare and contrast by completing a Venn diagram) | Scale score 1–4 | 1 = Student identifies at least one similarity or difference in character development or sequencing. |
| | | 2 = Student identifies one similarity or if he or she lists several, they are not the two listed to earn a 3. |
| | | 3 = Student identifies at a minimum that both characters learned a lesson and each needed a pet to help on their journeys. Students note at least three differences between the characters (for example, Charlie wanted to run away, Mike wanted to spend time on vacation with his family, Mike wanted to go home). |
| | | 4 = Student lists many similarities and differences, including those listed for a 3. |
| Learning Target 3 #7 (short answer) | Scale score 1–4 | 1 = Student identifies a theme without evidence or cites a theme and provides evidence, but the theme is incorrect. |
| | | 2 = Student identifies a theme and supports it with one quote for evidence. |
| | | 3 = Student identifies theme and cites at least two quotes as evidence to support the theme. |
| | | 4 = Student identifies theme and cites at least two quotes as evidence to support the theme. Student extends the answer by including a personal example to illustrate the theme (this is part of an extension prompt). |

3.  After giving the assessment, bring in three student assessments and independently grade each by standard or learning target. Share your scores and calibrate your results through discussion so that the team grades all students consistently and equitably.

**Standard or Learning Target 1 on Assessment**

| | Student 1 Score | Student 2 Score | Student 3 Score |
|---|---|---|---|
| Teacher 1 | 4 | 1 | 2 |
| Teacher 2 | 4 | 1 | 2 |
| Teacher 3 | 4 | 1 | 2 |
| Teacher 4 | 4 | 1 | 2 |

**Standard or Learning Target 2 on Assessment**

| | Student 1 Score | Student 2 Score | Student 3 Score |
|---|---|---|---|
| Teacher 1 | 3 | 2 | 3 |
| Teacher 2 | 3 | 1 | 3 |
| Teacher 3 | 2 | 2 | 4 |
| Teacher 4 | 3 | 2 | 4 |

| Standard or Learning Target 3 on Assessment | | | |
|---|---|---|---|
| | Student 1 Score | Student 2 Score | Student 3 Score |
| Teacher 1 | 1 | 3 | 4 |
| Teacher 2 | 2 | 2 | 3 |
| Teacher 3 | 1 | 3 | 4 |
| Teacher 4 | 1 | 2 | 4 |

*Visit **go.SolutionTree.com/PLCbooks** for a free reproducible version of this figure.*

Figure 5.9 shows the common scoring agreements of the grade 3 team whose assessment appears in figure 5.7 (pages 95–98).

---

***Grade 3, Unit 4: Multiplication and Division***

**Scoring Agreements**

**3.OA.1–2:** I can interpret multiplication and division equations.

| | |
|---|---|
| Test question 1a: | 2 points if all three correct equations are circled<br>1 point if 1 or 2 correct equations are circled |
| Test question 1b: | 1 point for a correct word problem |
| Test question 2: | 1 point for correct model<br>1 point for correct answer |
| Test question 3: | 1 point for correct model in part a<br>1 point for correct answer in part b |
| Test question 4a: | 2 points for correct equation<br>1 point if dividend and divisor correct but wrong quotient |
| Test question 4b: | 1 point for a correct word problem |

Proficiency = 7 out of 10 points

**3.OA.3:** I can solve word problems.

| | |
|---|---|
| Test question 5: | 1 point for the picture or equation<br>1 point for the correct answer |
| Test question 6: | 1 point for the picture or equation<br>1 point for the correct answer |
| Test question 7: | 1 point for answering "No"<br>1 point for correct explanation |

Proficiency = 4 out of 6 points

**3.OA.4:** I can determine the unknown in an equation.

| | |
|---|---|
| Test questions 8–13: | 1 point each |

Proficiency = 4 out of 6 points

---

*Source for standards: NGA & CCSSO, 2010b.*

**Figure 5.9: Grade 3 mathematics test-scoring agreements example.**

There is much to think about when designing quality common assessments. The main things teams should remember are, again, to be clear about the standards assessed, determine the proficiency and rigor of each, design the assessment, and determine how to evaluate the assessment. Consider any released state assessment items while designing assessments to make sure all tests are in alignment.

When the collaborative team has done all of this before the unit of instruction begins, it helps every member better design lessons and give daily formative feedback to students. This intentional and purposeful planning improves student learning.

## Determine How to Communicate Results and Respond to Student Learning

Too often, teams give assessments and then simply move on to the next unit or concept. When this happens, the time they spent administering the assessment is no longer a part of the valuable instructional minutes schools receive each year. How can assessments be instructional and how can teachers use them for learning? Continual learning happens when teacher teams and individual students analyze and respond to the assessment results.

### Team Response to Assessment Results

Teachers need to grade common assessments in an agreed-on time frame and then collectively gather their results to see what specifically *all* students in a grade level or course learned. Analyzing the results numerically as well as through student work samples deepens the instructional response to learning for each student. The following is a four-step process for organizing and responding to results (Schuhl, 2016).

1. **Look at an overview of the data:** Teachers determine the percentage of students who are proficient by standard and learning target and gather their data onto one document for all members of the collaborative team to view while discussing them. (Google Docs is one possible tool to use.) Looking at this initial picture of the data allows teachers to address areas of strength and areas to grow related to student learning across the team and within each classroom. Teachers should also use this data to determine the instructional practices most effective in student learning by answering the following questions.

   ‣ Which teachers had the best results?

   ‣ In which area was each teacher's lowest result, and how can the result be improved?

   ‣ What strategies or resources did teachers on the team use that differed from one another?

   ‣ Is there a target on the assessment in which no teacher had great results? If so, what is the team plan?

They also can discuss any surprises in the data and make sense of the student learning in each classroom compared to the whole grade level or course. Additionally, teams can keep the data in a folder to look at in the following year and proactively address some of the common misconceptions students have had previously in the unit. The chart might look like the one in figure 5.10.

| | Target 1 | Target 2 | Target 3 | Target 4 |
|---|---|---|---|---|
| **Teacher A** | 62% | 70% | 81% | 92% |
| **Teacher B** | 71% | 65% | 68% | 64% |
| **Teacher C** | 82% | 78% | 83% | 81% |
| **Team Total** | 69% | 72% | 76% | 78% |

Figure 5.10: Team data chart showing student proficiency by target.

2. **Identify students by standard proficiency:** Once the team has achieved common understanding of student learning, it is then critical to acknowledge and discuss which students are proficient and not proficient—or proficient, close to proficient, and far from proficient—by target. Elementary

teachers often do this by listing the names of students in each category by target. Secondary teachers often highlight class rosters in green, yellow, and red to see the name and number of students in each classification because they have so many more students.

3. **Identify trends and patterns in student work from the highest to the lowest performers:** First, teams identify the trends in student thinking and work that demonstrated that a student was proficient. What did these students do in their evidence of learning to set their work apart from the others? Next, they address the evidence in the work shown by students close to proficiency and compare and contrast that student work to the work of proficient students. Is there something to target that might be a catalyst to move students who are close to proficiency into the proficient category? Last, the team looks at the work of those students far from demonstrating proficiency and continues the process, looking at what the teachers might target in future learning (see figure 5.11).

1. Determine the percentage of students proficient on the assessment for each standard or target by teacher and then for all students within the team. Write the information in the following chart.

|  | Target 1 | Target 2 | Target 3 | Target 4 |
|---|---|---|---|---|
| **Teacher A** |  |  |  |  |
| **Teacher B** |  |  |  |  |
| **Teacher C** |  |  |  |  |
| **Teacher D** |  |  |  |  |
| **Total Team** |  |  |  |  |

2. For each standard or target, determine the number of students who are proficient, close to proficient, and far from proficient by teacher and as a team (write the number or the names of the students).

| Target 1 | | | |
|---|---|---|---|
|  | **Proficient** | **Close to Proficient** | **Far From Proficient** | **Total** |
| **Teacher A** |  |  |  |  |
| **Teacher B** |  |  |  |  |
| **Teacher C** |  |  |  |  |
| **Teacher D** |  |  |  |  |
| **Total Team** |  |  |  |  |

| Target 2 | | | |
|---|---|---|---|
|  | **Proficient** | **Close to Proficient** | **Far From Proficient** | **Total** |
| **Teacher A** |  |  |  |  |
| **Teacher B** |  |  |  |  |
| **Teacher C** |  |  |  |  |
| **Teacher D** |  |  |  |  |
| **Total Team** |  |  |  |  |

**Figure 5.11: Data-analysis protocol.**

continued →

| Target 3 | | | | |
|---|---|---|---|---|
| | **Proficient** | **Close to Proficient** | **Far From Proficient** | **Total** |
| **Teacher A** | | | | |
| **Teacher B** | | | | |
| **Teacher C** | | | | |
| **Teacher D** | | | | |
| **Total Team** | | | | |

| Target 4 | | | | |
|---|---|---|---|---|
| | **Proficient** | **Close to Proficient** | **Far From Proficient** | **Total** |
| **Teacher A** | | | | |
| **Teacher B** | | | | |
| **Teacher C** | | | | |
| **Teacher D** | | | | |
| **Total Team** | | | | |

3. What skills did the proficient students demonstrate in their work that set their work apart? Which instructional strategies did teachers use that effectively produced those results?

4. In which area or areas did my students struggle? In which areas did our team's students struggle? What is the cause? How will we respond? Which strategies will we try next?

5. Which students need additional time and support to learn the standards or targets? What is our plan?

6. Which students need extension and enrichment? What is our plan?

7. Do these data show we are on track to meet our SMART goal? Why or why not?

4. **Make re-engagement and extension plans:** From these discussions, teachers can make a collaborative plan to re-engage students in learning. Does the team need to stop, shuffle students, and plan a full lesson for each group of students? Does the team need to address learning by spending ten to fifteen minutes three days a week during core instruction with specific activities all students can learn from? Does the team need to plan for more focused and targeted intervention? (See chapter 6, page 113.) Also, how are students part of the plan by identifying what they learned and what they still need to learn in this process?

By analyzing data as a team and collectively responding, collaborative teams learn and students learn—a win for both. Looking at numbers first is helpful to see the overall picture, and it is in analyzing student work that targeted instructional responses become apparent to best improve the learning of each student.

### Student Response to Assessment Results

It is not enough for teachers to respond to the common assessment data. Assessment evidence is meaningful to students when they see that it informs what they have learned and what they have not learned *yet*. Teams should consider how they will work to have students actually look at their assessment results, fix their errors in thinking, and find out from the assessment what they have learned and what they still need to work on learning. Ask students to identify their learning plan or, if they are part of a team-designed intervention or extension, to acknowledge why they are engaged in that learning experience. Ultimately, how can *students* articulate what they have learned and not learned and become part of the solution?

Collaborative teams may have other examples as well. Making reflection routine and a part of regular practice helps students identify what they have learned and in which areas they still need to focus. Students can set their own goals for learning or performance on progress-monitoring assessments, benchmarks, or state assessments. With guidance, they can learn to participate in student-led parent conferences and talk about their level of proficiency with the standards addressed.

Figure 5.12 shows a half-sheet self-reflection for the grade 3 mathematics assessment in figure 5.7 (pages 95–98). Students determine their score for each target, find out the total points they need in each target in order to circle "I got it!" or "Still learning it . . . " and then rewrite the targets they learned and those they still need to learn. Students take the reflection home for a parent signature and then bring it back to school.

| Learning Target | Test Questions | Score | How Did I Do? (Circle one.) |
|---|---|---|---|
| **3.OA.1–2:** I can interpret multiplication and division equations. | 1–4 | _____ out of 10 | I got it! <br> Still learning it . . . |
| **3.OA.3:** I can solve word problems. | 5–7 | _____ out of 6 | I got it! <br> Still learning it . . . |
| **3.OA.4:** I can determine the unknown in an equation. | 8–13 | _____ out of 6 | I got it! <br> Still learning it . . . |
| **Learning Targets I Know and Can Do:** | | **Learning Targets I Am Still Learning:** | |
| | | | |

**Figure 5.12: Grade 3 mathematics test student self-reflection example.**

Figure 5.13 shows a generic tracker that students can use to identify at what level of proficiency they have learned a standard.

**Standard:** _____

| | Assignment or Assessment | Score | Percentage |
|---|---|---|---|
| 1 | | _____ out of _____ | _____ % |
| 2 | | _____ out of _____ | _____ % |
| 3 | | _____ out of _____ | _____ % |
| 4 | | _____ out of _____ | _____ % |
| 5 | | _____ out of _____ | _____ % |
| 6 | | _____ out of _____ | _____ % |

**Assignment and Assessment Tracker**

| | | | | | | |
|---|---|---|---|---|---|---|
| 100% | | | | | | |
| 90% | | | | | | |
| 80% | | | | | | |
| 70% | | | | | | |
| 60% | | | | | | |
| 50% | | | | | | |
| 40% | | | | | | |
| 30% | | | | | | |
| 20% | | | | | | |
| 10% | | | | | | |
| | 1 | 2 | 3 | 4 | 5 | 6 |

**Figure 5.13: Student tracker example.**

*Visit **go.SolutionTree.com/PLCbooks** for a free reproducible version of this figure.*

Figure 5.14 shows an error-analysis sheet students can complete after teachers have scored their assessments. It is adapted from work by Stiggins et al. (2006). This example is from a writing assignment related to *To Kill a Mockingbird* in which teachers scored the writing using a rubric.

*Freshman English*

Reading test: *To Kill a Mockingbird*

Name: _____

**What did I learn? What do I still need to learn?**

**Analyzing Your Results**

After your test has been corrected:

- Identify on which problems you earned a 1–2 or a 3–4.

- For each score of 1–2, determine the edits you need to make to earn a score of 3 or 4.

**Evaluate your strengths and areas you still need to study for by answering the following questions.**

**What I Have Learned**

Learning targets I can do:

**What I Have Almost Learned**

Learning targets I got wrong but know how to edit to make the answers stronger:

What I can do to keep this from happening again:

**What I Still Need to Learn**

Learning targets I got wrong and I'm not sure what to do to correct them:

What I can do to get better at them:

*Source: Adapted from Stiggins et al., 2006.*

**Figure 5.14: Error-analysis sheet example.**

When thinking about a common formative assessment over one or two learning targets or standards, consider putting the information together using the template in figure 5.15. Identify the standards, create the assessment items, determine proficiency, and then preplan for possible interventions and extensions that teams can later refine once they have analyzed data and student work. These should happen on a routine basis so teams can consistently respond to the student learning of an entire grade level or course effectively and efficiently.

| Learning Target or Targets |
| --- |
| Assessment Items |
| Proficiency Level (How many items need to be correct for a student to be proficient?) |
| Possible Interventions |
| Possible Extensions |

**Figure 5.15: Common formative assessment plan.**

*Visit **go.SolutionTree.com/PLCbooks** for a free reproducible version of this figure.*

Schools in need of improvement often have many district, state, and national assessments they administer to students. Unfortunately, these are not the ones that most influence or impact student learning and teacher instructional practices. In this chapter we explained how collaborative teams can create quality common formative and summative assessments to focus instructional practices and grow student learning.

## Reflect and Take Action

The rubrics in figures 5.16 and 5.17 (page 110) show collaborative team progressions in designing a common assessment and analyzing the data from the common assessment. Look at each rubric to determine team strengths and next steps related to each topic.

| | Level 1<br>Beginning | Level 2<br>Attempting | Level 3<br>Practicing | Level 4<br>Embracing |
|---|---|---|---|---|
| **Common Formative Assessment (During Unit)** | Assessment is too long—uses too many instructional minutes to get data for students and teachers.<br><br>The assessment is at a lower level of rigor than the intent of the standard or the items on the unit assessment.<br><br>Each teacher on a team makes his or her own assessment. | Assessment is appropriately short in length.<br><br>Assessment is common; however, teachers may not score it together or may not determine proficiency in advance.<br><br>Teams write the assessment without considering the final expectations as determined on the summative assessment. | Teams determine proficiency before giving the assessment, and scoring agreements are clear.<br><br>The rigor matches the intent of the standards and matches the summative assessment.<br><br>Teachers reflect on the data to make instructional decisions. | Teams analyze trends in student work to determine what students who exceed, meet, nearly meet, and do not meet expectations demonstrate in terms of their understanding and application.<br><br>Teams take differentiated instructional actions.<br><br>Students analyze their results and set goals. |
| **Common Summative Assessment (End of Unit)** | Teams create the assessment at the end of the unit just before the assessment day.<br><br>Teams use a publisher test or other assessment as is without making sure every test item aligns to a standard in the unit.<br><br>Directions or questions are unclear.<br><br>Scoring details are unclear or not specified.<br><br>Assessment includes only multiple choice or only constructed response.<br><br>Teachers may give assessment at the same time.<br><br>Teachers may modify the assessment. | Teams create the assessment before the unit begins.<br><br>The assessment contains clear directions and questions.<br><br>Teams make scoring agreements in advance of giving the assessment.<br><br>Assessment may only be one format (multiple choice or constructed response).<br><br>All the teachers on a team give the assessment at roughly the same time.<br><br>Teachers may modify the assessment or administer it differently from the rest of the team.<br><br>Teams look at data and then move on. | Teams create the assessment before the unit begins. Items are clearly aligned to the learning targets and standards.<br><br>Teams determine proficiency by learning target or standard in advance of giving the assessment.<br><br>Scoring agreements are clear to teachers and students and teams calibrate their scoring.<br><br>The assessment has a variety of formats.<br><br>The assessment matches the rigor of the standards.<br><br>Teams analyze data and teachers determine next instructional steps. | Teams create the assessment before the unit, align items, and emphasize priority standards.<br><br>There are enough items to determine proficiency on the standards assessed.<br><br>There is a balance of rigor on the assessment.<br><br>Teachers analyze the data by standard and by student to determine what students learned and have not learned yet and which students learned and have not learned yet. The team makes a targeted plan.<br><br>Students analyze and reflect on their assessment data and make learning goals. |

**Figure 5.16: Common assessment rubric.**

*Visit go.SolutionTree.com/PLCbooks for a free reproducible version of this figure.*

|  | Level 1<br>Beginning | Level 2<br>Attempting | Level 3<br>Practicing | Level 4<br>Embracing |
|---|---|---|---|---|
| **Gathering Data to Analyze** | Teams compare team data from different assessments, assessments that they administer in different ways, or assessments that they grade with no scoring agreements.<br><br>Teams analyze the data too long after giving the assessment.<br><br>Teams analyze data for a few teachers who gave the assessment each unit.<br><br>Teams collect class or student averages instead of proficiency data. Or each team member brings different data to analyze (by test item, standard, or class average, or the overall test). | Teams wait until all teachers have given the assessment and then analyze the data. This means some students have the data immediately and others wait a long time.<br><br>All teachers give the common assessment within a five-day window.<br><br>Teams gather their own data and determine the percentage of students who are proficient, but do not collect it in one location to visually show others on the team and discuss as a team. | Teams analyze data quickly after giving the assessment. Team members immediately grade the common assessment using common scoring agreements.<br><br>All teachers give the common assessment on the same day so they can include all student data in the analysis.<br><br>Teams collect all data in a central spreadsheet or Google Doc so the data are available to all team members. | Teams analyze data quickly and teachers calibrate their scoring using samples of student work.<br><br>Teams gather all data and collect them effectively for future use. |
| **Analyzing Data** | Teachers verbally relate their data or only give descriptions (such as, "My students did well") without visually looking at team numbers and do not have teachers' data in a central location.<br><br>After they share data, teams have limited to no conversation and instead move on to planning the next unit. | Teams only look at individual students and miss the teacher and team data or only analyze the teacher and team data without looking at individual students.<br><br>Teams respond by trying to reteach everything or ignoring enrichment for students who are already proficient. Teams might also insist on taking extra days for intervention after every unit instead of using a schoolwide intervention or weaving the content into the next unit. | Teams look first at the percentage of students who are proficient on each standard or learning target by teacher and as a whole team and then look at each student and each standard.<br><br>Teams use a protocol to identify the strengths and weaknesses of learning in each classroom and by student to plan for effective interventions and enrichments, as necessary. Teams analyze and modify instructional practices. | Teams efficiently gather and analyze data and record their results for future use within the school year and the following year.<br><br>Not only do teachers look at the trends in student work to make targeted intervention and enrichment decisions, but students also analyze their data and self-reflect on their progress. Teams use the data to promote a growth mindset in students. |

**Figure 5.17: Data-analysis rubric.**

*Visit **go.SolutionTree.com/PLCbooks** for a free reproducible version of this figure.*

Once teams have reached agreement about their current status, they should use figure 5.18 to determine the next steps to strengthen their practice in working to ensure all students learn through common assessments and data analysis.

| Action | Team-Level Rating | Next Steps |
|---|---|---|
| Using common formative assessments | | |
| Using common summative assessments | | |
| Gathering and organizing data from common assessments to analyze | | |
| Analyzing trends in student work and collectively responding | | |

**Figure 5.18: Common assessment reflection and action plan.**

*Visit **go.SolutionTree.com/PLCbooks** for a free reproducible version of this figure.*

## Collaborative Team Questions to Consider

- Which standards are you assessing to make sure all students learn?
- How does your team define the rigor necessary for a student to demonstrate proficiency with each standard on an assessment?
- How does your team create scales to define proficiency on a standard or standards?
- What is the best way to assess each standard?
- How will you make sure each target is represented on the common assessment?
- How will your team create scoring agreements and calibrate grading?
- How will your team organize and analyze data from common assessments?
- How will your team respond to student learning on the assessments in future instruction and prepare a tiered intervention system?
- How will students routinely respond to their assessment data and learn from the results?

# Planning Meaningful and Effective Instruction

> Regardless of the research basis, it is clear that effective teachers have a profound influence on student achievement and ineffective teachers do not.
>
> *—Robert J. Marzano*

Designing meaningful and effective instruction is one of the most critical tasks that teaching requires—and one that greatly influences student learning. How does a teacher and his or her collaborative team best plan for the learning of every student? Which routines and tasks will most effectively move learning forward? How will each student learn from feedback and engage during the lesson? These are just a few of the questions to address every day with each lesson plan.

As part of her work in schools, Sarah does walkthroughs to observe student learning. In one elementary school, she observed a fourth-grade classroom in which students stood to recite a poem in front of their peers. As the lesson progressed, Sarah realized every student had memorized the same poem, reciting it one after the other. Sarah asked one of the students what he was learning during the lesson. He answered, "We just have to say this poem. I don't even know what it means."

In another fourth-grade classroom in the same school, Sarah observed students as they worked in pairs to write poems after reading and discussing five poems the previous day. Once they wrote their poems, they shared them with the class. When Sarah asked a student in that class what she was learning, the student replied, "We are learning how to write a poem and listen to each other."

Both of these fourth-grade teachers teach poetry using the same number of instructional minutes; however, their results are very different. In the first fourth-grade classroom, students listened passively (if they listened at all). In the second classroom, students talked about how to write a poem and used feedback from one another to make their poems better. Later, when sharing their poetry, students listened because their peers crafted each original poem and students wanted to hear the results.

It is important for students to know what they are learning and believe they can learn it. In *Classroom Instruction That Works: Research-Based Strategies for Increasing Student Achievement*, Ceri B. Dean, Elizabeth Ross Hubbell, Howard Pitler, and Bj Stone (2012) note:

> If students do not see the relevance of the learning objectives or believe they can successfully achieve them, it is unlikely they will fully engage in the learning activities their teachers identify. When teachers reinforce effort, provide recognition for accomplishments, and involve students in cooperative learning, they can positively influence how students think about their ability to succeed. (p. 155)

Each lesson must give each student an *a-ha* moment—when he or she makes a connection to previous learning. This builds meaning for students and also helps them see that they can learn. Teachers must consider the question, How are my students learning through reading, writing, and discourse? When students are reading to learn, writing about their learning, and talking about learning with one another, they own their learning. How are students involved in understanding what it is they are learning? Are they developing a belief they can learn with focused effort? Students can set goals and articulate what they are learning. A growth mindset builds a learner's disposition (Dweck, 2006). Addressing these questions is often challenging in schools in need of improvement; however, they are absolutely critical to changing the trajectory of student achievement.

At one time, convention held that teachers were successful when they had quiet classrooms in which students sat dutifully in rows, copying notes, politely listening to the teacher, and responding when called upon. That time has passed. Effective instruction does not happen in a teacher-focused classroom in which the teacher often works harder than the students. Instead, effective instruction focuses on what students are learning and doing throughout the lesson as the teacher facilitates and adapts the learning to meet a specific learning outcome.

Hattie (2012) identifies the following actions of expert teachers. These teachers:

- Can identify the most important ways in which to represent the subject that they teach
- Are proficient at creating an optimal classroom climate for learning
- Monitor learning and provide feedback
- Believe that all students can reach the success criteria
- Influence surface and deep student outcomes (pp. 25–27)

Further, Hattie (2012) notes that planning for student learning is not an isolated act. Rather, he states:

> Planning can be done in many ways, but the most powerful is when teachers work together to develop plans, develop common understandings of what is worth teaching, collaborate on understanding their beliefs of challenge and progress, and work together to evaluate the impact of their planning on student outcomes. (p. 37)

The world is a changing place, requiring knowledge and skills much different from those in years past. Similarly, process and content standards have evolved, which means instruction, too, is in second-order change and continuing to shift.

Teachers and teams must first ask themselves which standards students are learning each day and how they can best design instruction for students to achieve each standard. This requires some direct instruction, cooperative learning, discourse, higher-order reasoning, and productive routines, among other strategies, for all students. Teachers must emphasize analysis, summary, evidence for opinions and arguments, and problem solving rather than memorizing facts, which are all readily available with computers and electronic devices. How are students learning to discern and make sense of their world in each subject area and each grade level? Working together to determine the guaranteed and viable curriculum (addressed in chapter 4, page 55) and the common assessments (addressed in chapter 5, page 79) helps define the student learning that the lessons in each instructional unit require.

## Determine Vision Versus Reality

Teachers are always thinking about what they are teaching—whether they are designing formal lesson plans or just reflecting on activities to prepare when driving to school in the morning. However, Hattie (2012) notes that "attention needs to move from how to teach to how to learn—and only after teachers understand how each student learns can they then move on to make decisions about how to teach" (p. 92). In other words, it is not enough to think of fun activities and teacher actions. It becomes critical to determine with a collaborative team what students have to know and be able to do in order to demonstrate proficiency with a standard and then work to find the tasks and activities that will grow student learning of that standard.

A vision of quality instruction includes students learning from one another and from the teacher, as well as students knowing what they have learned, asking questions to learn more, and understanding content thoroughly. Additionally, it includes students learning through mistakes and productively struggling to meet the task demands. Seldom does the vision include silence and students sitting in rows; instead, it values discourse and cooperative groups working collectively. It also includes teachers learning from one another to improve the learning in each classroom. Teams should ask themselves how close this vision is to their current reality. This may be a good time to revisit the vision for instruction and assessment that teams established using figure 5.1 (page 82).

Too often we hear teachers complain that their instructional vision is not possible because of the students they serve—because of poverty or their behavior. Ruby Payne (2005), who has done much work in the field of understanding poverty, recognizes the challenges:

> One of the reasons it is getting more and more difficult to conduct school as we have in the past is that the students who bring the middle-class culture with them are decreasing in numbers, and the students who bring the poverty culture with them are increasing in numbers. (p. 61)

However, Payne does not think that poverty is an excuse. All students can still learn, regardless of their status as emotionally, physically, spiritually, mentally, or financially impoverished. The research from Marzano (2003), Marzano and Debra J. Pickering (2011), Hattie (2009, 2012), and Hattie and Gregory Yates (2014) confirms that students can learn and teachers can be effective, even when students face difficult circumstances. It becomes important for teachers to help students develop a growth mindset (Dweck, 2006) so students believe learning is possible through focused effort. This allows teachers to more effectively work together to design lessons so all students learn at high levels.

Achieving the team's vision of quality instruction involves team discussion and clarity around intentionally using quality higher-level and lower-level tasks. It also requires discussions about effective ways to involve students in their learning as well as reflection about how they are learning. Working together means teams have established common pacing and all students are learning the same standards within a grade level or subject area (see chapter 4, page 55). The PLC process does not dictate that members of a teacher team must teach a specific lesson the exact same way, but rather that they should use the collaborative process to learn together, identify, and implement more effective teaching practices.

Teams must ensure they have established their instructional vision. To test it, they should imagine their school is the very best place for students to learn and for them to teach, and then ask themselves what they see and hear in the classrooms, hallways, lunch area, playground, main office, and staff lounge. Think about what the teachers must do to accomplish that instructional vision. Write a statement that describes the work of teachers in accomplishing the vision. For example:

> We will work collaboratively to ensure the learning of each student by being clear about what students will learn, designing common assessments with proficiency agreements, discussing how to give quality formative feedback to students, determining research-affirmed practices to use in lessons, and having students reflect on their learning.

To reach this instructional vision, when planning a lesson, ask the following questions.

- What are students learning today? (Not, what am I teaching today?)
- Which standard is the focus?
- How will students get feedback on their learning and take action on the feedback?
- How will students learn from one another during the lesson?
- What is the teacher doing and what are the students doing during each part of the lesson?

- Which instructional strategies are most effective with students?
- How are students able to articulate what they learned by the end of the lesson?

When planning effective instruction as a collaborative team using the actions this chapter outlines, individual teachers' lessons become stronger and more focused, and teachers provide ample opportunities for students to learn from meaningful feedback.

## Start Now

There are many factors to consider when planning effective instruction. In addition to lesson design, rigor, task selection, and differentiation, the classroom environment and its culture play a role.

### Design Classroom Culture

*Classroom culture* refers to the many aspects of the classroom environment and behaviors of the teacher and students, from the arrangement of classroom furniture and artifacts on the walls, to routines and procedures, to a collective willingness to learn through mistakes, to developing a growth mindset that promotes learning through continual effort. All of these elements combine to form the classroom culture. One important characteristic of a classroom culture focused on learning is respect for students and teachers alike—even when they make mistakes.

While in one classroom in Minnesota, Sarah watched a teacher make a mistake at the board. After a student pointed it out and together they corrected the error in reasoning, he turned and said, "That's okay, class, because when we make mistakes . . ." The whole class happily shouted, "We learn!" Teachers and students must embrace mistakes as learning opportunities so students persevere and do the work necessary to learn without the pressure of doing it right the first time.

From the beginning of the year, consider how to show samples of student work, asking students, (1) "What is strong in the work?" and (2) "How can you make the work even stronger?" After going through one sample together, give students back their own work and have them use a colored pencil or pen to make their own work stronger (without erasing the original work). Not only will students learn how to improve their own work using this strategy, through evaluating and analyzing their own work they will learn how to evaluate the work of others and give meaningful feedback to others as well. From the beginning, develop student understanding that they can make all work even stronger.

Consider the arrangement of the classroom. How are the desks set up? Arranging desks into groups of three or four promotes pair-sharing opportunities and cooperative learning experiences during lessons. Consider using assigned seats so students feel safe to talk to one another and, especially in the secondary grades, do not feel the peer pressure of choosing who to sit next to or talk to. Number the seats or use pictures to facilitate giving directions quickly (for example, "Partners 1 and 2 will work together, and partners 3 and 4 will work together" or "In each group, student 2 will share the group's thinking").

What are the routines in the classroom? According to Gayle Gregory and Martha Kaufeldt (2012), the brain constantly seeks patterns and structure:

> Consistent familiar patterns and organizational systems within the classroom can improve behavior and encourage independence. When students don't know what is going to happen next and what behaviors are expected, they can experience anticipatory anxiety. (p. 37)

Gregory and Kaufeldt (2012) propose that well-designed classroom procedures should address the following:

- Who the students may work with
- Where the students may work

- What behaviors are acceptable (talking levels, standing/sitting, and so forth)
- What materials the students may use
- When activities take place (appropriate times or how long) (p. 38)

When teachers want students to engage in a pair-share, let them know which partner to talk with. When they are working in groups, teachers should outline their expectations regardless of the activity or task. What are the expectations for moving from the carpet to tables (in elementary classrooms)? How long should they spend on each part of the lesson? Consider using a timer to help establish the time frames. Establish these expectations and others from the start of school to minimize time lost to transitions and to maximize student learning.

With any classroom expectations, it is important to be clear with students about what they should be doing and avoid negative statements that focus on what students should not do. For example, if a teacher tells a student not to run when the student is skipping, the student will be quick to argue she is not running—and she is correct. However, if the teacher tells her to walk when she is skipping, she can't argue about the behavior and the teacher has quickly reminded the student of the appropriate behavior. So students feel safe in an environment with clear expectations and routines, it is also important to avoid escalating situations. Instead, defuse them to keep a continual focus on learning. Marzano and Pickering (2011) recognize that "if students sense that they are not welcome, accepted, or supported in the classroom, it is unlikely that they will engage in classroom activities" (p. 6). Classroom culture impacts student learning.

## Plan Units

As Hattie (2012) notes, there are many ways to plan; the most powerful way, however, is to work together. Planning a unit requires teams to determine the daily unit structure, integrate student goal setting and reflection, and make corrections to previous learning.

### Determine the Daily Unit Structure

When preparing to teach a new unit, look first at the proficiency map and unit plan (see the process in chapter 4, page 55). Suppose, for example, that a unit has a length of twenty days. Determine as a team when to give a common summative assessment and when to give common formative assessments. Identify whether or not to spend a day reviewing for the common summative assessment. If, for example, teams choose to review for one day, give the common summative assessment for one day and give two common formative assessments, each about twenty minutes in length and together accounting for one class period, there are then seventeen days left for instruction. However, teams might also decide to have two buffer days—flexible days to use if a lesson needs two days instead of one or if a teacher or the team decides to stop and re-engage students in learning around a priority standard in the unit. Now there are fifteen instructional days. As a team, look at the curriculum materials and determine the best lessons, tasks, and instructional practices to use in those fifteen days. Figure 6.1 (page 118) shows a diagram of this process.

It is important that teams design their own units and do not rely on textbooks. Marzano (2003) states, "Unfortunately, teachers frequently do not make the decisions about how to sequence and pace content within their lessons and units. Rather, they rely on the design of textbooks for guidance" (p. 107). While publishers produce their materials with the intent of improving student learning, they do not create them specifically for meeting the needs of *our* students. As chapters 4 and 5 show, teams must be clear about the standards and how to measure student proficiency for each, and then design common summative and formative assessments to create meaningful and effective instruction. Publisher materials are a resource when designing the best lessons for student learning; they shouldn't be the only source of input.

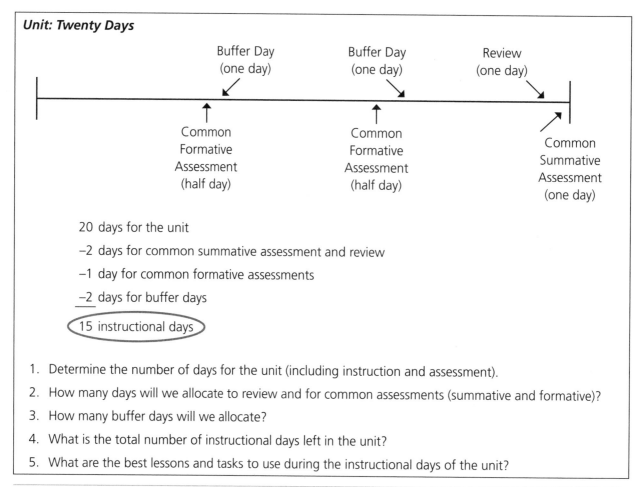

**Figure 6.1: Planning a unit protocol.**

*Visit **go.SolutionTree.com/PLCbooks** for a free reproducible version of this figure.*

### Integrate Student Goal Setting and Reflection

We expect students to learn a lot of information and skills in multiple subjects or classes each day. Teachers can help students make sense of the learning through their use of student learning targets (as we detailed in chapter 4, page 55). Consider as a collaborative team how to use student learning targets so students set goals and reflect throughout the unit about whether they have learned each target or not learned it yet. Some teachers write the learning targets on the board each day, others post them on chart paper for the unit once the unit begins, and still others may give students a tracker sheet featuring the learning targets for them to use throughout the unit as a reflection tool. Figure 6.2 shows a protocol for determining how students will set goals and reflect.

Figure 6.3 (page 120) shows a reflection sheet for seventh-grade mathematics students to use throughout a semester. The chart's thick black lines separate each unit. There are one or three student learning targets per unit. Students identify their initial learning of each target and their final learning of each target while also addressing the questions at the bottom of the page.

Sometimes student self-assessment and reflection sheets include check boxes or color-coded stickers students might use next to each target. One kindergarten team of teachers uses take-home folders for student self-assessment and reflection. Each folder contains four Velcro strips on the right inside of the folder. On the left side of the folder, teachers put a piece of paper with four printed learning targets on it, spaced to match the Velcro strips. Each Velcro strip has a Velcro dot. Students move the dot to the right as they learn. The added benefit of such a tool is that parents and guardians can see how their children are progressing to reach each target.

*How Will Students Set Goals and Reflect During the Unit?*

1. What are the student learning targets for the unit? (Write them using "I can . . ." statements.)

2. How will students know the learning target for each lesson (or know where to look to articulate the learning target for each lesson)?

3. Where and how will students write their reflections related to learning (such as using a tracker sheet, marking a number line to show learning of a target, or writing a goal in a journal)?

4. What will students use as evidence of learning in a unit (such as an exit ticket, a quiz, homework, classwork, or online resources)?

5. How will your team teach students to reflect on their learning during a unit?

**Figure 6.2: Student reflection expectations protocol.**

*Visit **go.SolutionTree.com/PLCbooks** for a free reproducible version of this figure.*

| | Preassessment | | | | Postassessment | | | |
|---|---|---|---|---|---|---|---|---|
| | I Don't Know Anything | I Know a Little | I Can Explain It | I Can Teach It | I Don't Know Anything | I Know a Little | I Can Explain It | I Can Teach It |
| 1.  I can simplify an expression. | | | | | | | | |
| 2.  I can solve an equation. | | | | | | | | |
| 3.  I can solve and graph an inequality. | | | | | | | | |
| 4.  I can explain the parts of a linear function. | | | | | | | | |
| 5.  I can represent a linear function with a graph, a table, or an equation. | | | | | | | | |
| 6.  I can analyze a function. | | | | | | | | |
| 7.  I can solve problems using ratios and proportions. | | | | | | | | |
| 8.  I can solve percent problems. | | | | | | | | |
| 9.  I can compare rational numbers and estimate square roots. | | | | | | | | |
| 10.  I can find the area and perimeter of triangles, quadrilaterals, and composite shapes (and circumference and area of circles). | | | | | | | | |
| 11.  I can determine the probability of an event. | | | | | | | | |

| Where Am I Now? | Where Am I Going? | How Do I Close the Gap? |
|---|---|---|
| What have I learned so far this semester? | What do I still need to learn? | How will I learn it? What is my plan? |
| | | |

**Figure 6.3: Student self-assessment and reflection sheet for grade 7 mathematics.**

*Visit **go.SolutionTree.com/PLCbooks** for a free reproducible version of this figure.*

*Make Connections to Previous Learning*

David A. Sousa and Carol Ann Tomlinson (2011) state that the reality for many students is that the learning experience in school is made up of memorizing data and practicing skills out of context:

> Students lose a great deal of what they memorize, often in a short period of time. Similarly, skills that are practiced without leading to student reasoning have a short shelf life. In both instances, the student's brain is unable to detect in the new learning the patterns or meaning necessary for long-term retention. (p. 52)

They argue that teachers spend too much time working to have students make sense of the new learning without providing meaning for the new learning by relating it to previous student learning or previous experiences to make it relevant. As such, students do not necessarily learn the concept taught and quickly forget the new learning because they cannot attach it to an understood idea or skill. Take time as a team to determine how to help students make connections from previous learning to the new learning so they can grow their understanding and avoid learning concepts fleetingly and in isolation.

## Use First-Best Instructional Practices

After establishing a framework for the unit, it is time to consider how best to spend the instructional minutes each day—how to engage students in learning content. Ideally, students will learn during core instruction and not need additional time and support with interventions to learn the grade-level content at high levels. Intentional differentiation for students during a lesson is part of first-best instructional practices.

*Focus on Lesson Design*

There are many things to consider when designing a lesson. First, and most important, it is vital to identify what students should learn by the end of the lesson. What content or skills will they know and be able to demonstrate as an outcome of the learning? Also, some students will get stuck in the lesson and others will finish early. What is the plan to continue to engage all learners throughout the lesson (Kanold & Larson, 2015)? Figure 6.4 shows the questions to answer when designing a quality and meaningful lesson.

| | Lesson-Planning Question | How to Plan |
|---|---|---|
| Lesson Frame | Which content standard or standards are students learning in the lesson? | Identify the actual content standard or standards the lesson addresses. |
| | Which process standards are students learning during the lesson? | Identify the process standards. This relates to the habits of mind students are developing in the lesson. For example, in science, does the lesson address an engineering practice? In mathematics, does the lesson address a mathematical process standard? In English, does the lesson address an English language arts capacity? |
| | What is the "I can . . ." statement students are learning? | Determine the "I can . . ." statement from the unit related to the lesson. |

**Figure 6.4: Lesson-design protocol.**

continued →

| | Lesson-Planning Question | How to Plan |
|---|---|---|
| **Differentiation and Formative Feedback** | How will you know if students learned throughout the lesson? How will students take action on feedback throughout the lesson? | Consider when you will check in with students to see if they are learning. How will student learning be visible or audible so you and other students can give feedback to students who will make immediate corrections in thinking during the lesson? |
| | How will students interact with one another during the lesson and learn from one another? | How will student pairings and groupings allow for students to learn from one another? What are the routines and expectations for student actions? |
| | What is your plan for students who struggle during the lesson? | Some students will get stuck during the lesson. Determine your plan to move them forward without giving away the answer or how to accomplish the task. What questions will you ask? What prerequisites might you need to address? What manipulatives or alternate activities might you need? |
| | What is your plan for students who finish early? | Some students will understand quickly and well. Determine how you can extend parts of the lesson so students continue learning the content in a meaningful way. |
| **Lesson Structure for Student Learning and Engagement** | How will the lesson begin? | Determine what students will be doing during the start of the lesson. Identify how the warm-up or initial activity connects previous learning to the day's lesson, reviews learning, or asks students to explore what they will learn during the lesson. Determine how to clarify the learning target for the day with students. |
| | What are the different parts of the lesson and what will students do during each? How long will you spend on each part of the lesson? | Determine the parts of the lesson (such as notes, group work, reading, writing, lab work, and so on) and how long students will spend on each part. Students can learn at most fifteen minutes of new information before doing something to apply that knowledge (Hattie & Yates, 2014). Consider how to have students learn through reading, writing, and discussion. Determine how you will actively engage students in learning throughout the unit. Focus not just on the teacher aspects of the lesson, but more on what students will do to learn during each part of the lesson. |
| | How will the lesson end? | Determine how to have students close the lesson by articulating what they learned (as a whole class, with journal writing, using pair-share, and so on). The conclusion might also include an exit ticket, but this alone does not provide an opportunity for students to reflect on what they learned unless you add a specific question. |
| | What materials will you need? | Make a list of necessary materials for the lesson and determine how to provide them to students in a way that minimizes transitions. |

*Visit **go.SolutionTree.com/PLCbooks** for a free reproducible version of this figure.*

When planning for learning, it is also important to recognize the types of learners in the classroom. Who are the auditory, visual, tactile, and kinesthetic learners? How will the lesson plan or a series of lesson plans in a unit address these multiple intelligences?

A strong and intentional lesson plan that addresses the questions in figure 6.4 provides students with focused and clear opportunities for learning. It also allows collaborative teams to reflect on their most effective instructional practices and strengthens future plans to grow student learning.

### Choose Effective Instructional Practices

There are many effective instructional practices to use at various grade levels and within different subject areas. Marzano, Pickering, and Jane E. Pollock (2001) identify nine categories of instructional strategies that affect student achievement through their research on the average effect sizes of strategies and by determining those that translate to student learning gains. Dean et al. (2012) study these further in the second edition of *Classroom Instruction That Works*. From greatest effect size (1.61, which is a percentile gain of 45 for a student) to least (0.59, which is a percentile gain of 22 for a student) these are:

- Identifying similarities and differences
- Summarizing and note taking
- Reinforcing effort and providing recognition
- Homework and practice
- Nonlinguistic representations
- Cooperative learning
- Setting objectives and providing feedback
- Generating and testing hypotheses
- Questions, cues, and advance organizers (Dean et al., 2012, as cited in Marzano, 2003, p. 80)

This, of course, does not mean that if a teacher has students take notes, for example, learning will improve. Rather, how the teacher implements these practices in the classroom affects the student learning that results. Each practice requires students to learn at high levels, a continual challenge if this experience is new to them. Selected tasks and activities require students to productively struggle so they can achieve learning.

### Identifying Similarities and Differences

Students must use their critical-thinking skills to adequately identify similarities and differences. In class, students develop this skill and demonstrate proficiency with such activities as completing a Venn diagram, comparing and contrasting the themes from two novels, or creating similes and metaphors. Students might also relate addition to subtraction or compare the lab results from two different trials in a science experiment. The key is that *students* are analyzing, evaluating, generalizing, comparing, and reasoning to make connections and deepen understanding. These are the higher-level thinking skills that 21st century learners need.

### Summarizing and Note Taking

Sharon observed one geography class during which the students dutifully took guided notes from a PowerPoint lecture. Every few minutes, the students filled in a blank line on a copied handout to create notes. Students, however, were not necessarily listening, making connections, or asking themselves questions as they learned. Instead, the majority were daydreaming, looking at cell phones under their desks, or just sitting passively. They did, however, write the correct word in the appropriate blank when it appeared during the lecture. During a conversation with Sharon, the teacher lamented the time he spends making and copying notes each day and the frustration he feels over students not using them. The teacher was working much harder than the students.

No single type of note taking is best for all subjects and all students, and there can be a benefit to guided notes. However, students learn through any note taking when they synthesize or summarize the information they received through reading, class discussions, or direct instruction. Too often guided notes mean teachers have used multiple sources and learned the content deeply before doing the high-level task of synthesizing the information into the parts they feel students need to know. This means teachers are doing the thinking and learning and then simplifying the higher-order reasoning to a list of facts for students to simply recall.

When using note taking, consider how students are making sense of the information. When the teacher needs to share new information, minimize the telling and think about how students can summarize, ask questions about, or apply the learning at least every ten to fifteen minutes through pair-share, an activity, or a written component in the margin of their notes. Ideally, taking notes is minimal in direct instruction and students will learn through higher-order questioning and activities that require productive struggle. The notes have value as evidence of the learning and reference material, and students correct their own notes after talking with other students in groups or as a class.

### Reinforcing Effort and Providing Recognition

As we mentioned previously in this chapter as well as in chapter 5 (page 79), there is much value in teachers and students assessing progress toward learning. Students can self-assess their understanding of learning targets using evidence of classwork, homework, and common formative and summative assessments.

Carol Dweck (2006) is the leading researcher on the importance of developing a growth mindset in both teachers and students—the disposition that all students can learn through focused effort. Praising a student for working hard can backfire if the teacher and student both know the effort is not producing the desired result. The student thinks, "Even if I work hard I can't do it." Make sure when reinforcing effort, teachers tie the effort to learning evidence the student is demonstrating. Help the student see that with effort, he or she can write a sentence with a period, write an equation to solve a word problem, draw the start of a life cycle, read the headings in a social studies text, or play a musical instrument. Have students reflect on their progress and the work they did to accomplish that growth. Too many students fear failure and never productively struggle to learn. Reinforcing effort applied to learning helps develop the growth mindset in both teachers and students.

### Using Homework and Practice

The value of homework is a much-debated topic in many schools, especially if the trend is that students are not doing it. It is true that teachers cannot control whether or not a student does homework; however, homework provides a valuable opportunity for formative feedback to students. How does one bridge the gap? First, careful lesson design needs to ensure students are maximizing their learning while at school, but students often need additional practice to deepen their learning. It is important to determine as a collaborative team the best homework problems or tasks to assign for additional student practice and learning, and avoid penalizing students by requiring them to use resources at home that are not available to them.

Keep any homework minimal and consider what will happen with it the next day so students see the relevance and value in trying it. For example, perhaps assign each student one word problem in mathematics and then begin class the next day with students sharing their solution strategies. Perhaps students can read a story and then share the main idea during carpet time the next day.

Additionally, use homework as an opportunity for students to show they have mastered a learning target. When an assignment requires explanations or work shown, consider providing answers to homework before students complete it so students can reflect on their learning as they are doing it and not practice in error. This allows students to receive immediate feedback on their thinking and adjust, if needed. Meaningful practice assigned to the learning target of the lesson provides another opportunity for formative feedback to students.

It can be helpful for students to have access to the learning targets and homework at the start of a unit in the intermediate grades and above. Figure 6.5 shows an English language arts homework sheet that students at Moriarty Middle School used, showing one week's worth of assignments related to each learning target.

| ELA: Unit 1, Fiction Versus Nonfiction |
| --- |

**Learning Targets**

1. I can identify the types of conflict in a story.
   - Main conflict
   - Internal conflict
   - External conflict

2. I can determine the meaning of a word by using context clues.

3. I can write explanatory text using compare and contrast.

4. I can publish my writing using APA style format.
   - Font: Times New Roman
   - Font Size: 12 point
   - Double spaced
   - Including headers and headings
   - Indenting paragraphs

**Vocabulary:** Create a student-friendly definition in five words or fewer.

| Main Conflict | |
| --- | --- |
| Internal Conflict | |
| External Conflict | |

**Schedule:** Week of 9/25–9/30

| Day | Learning Target, Classwork, Note, and Homework | Points Earned on Classwork and Homework |
| --- | --- | --- |
| Day 1 9/25 | Learning target: I can identify the types of conflict in a story. Classwork: Use a graphic organizer (three-column chart) to identify the conflicts—internal and external—in your reading selection. Note: See anchor chart. Homework: Finish draft of essay. | |
| Day 2 9/27 | Learning target: I can write explanatory text using compare and contrast. Classwork: Peer edit rough drafts. Homework: Read through edits and prepare for final draft. | |
| Day 3 9/28 | Learning target: I can publish my writing using APA format. Classwork: Type final draft. Homework: Read selection and explain the conflict. | |

**Figure 6.5: Homework tracker example.**

continued →

| Day | Learning Target, Classwork, Note, and Homework | Points Earned on Classwork and Homework |
|---|---|---|
| Day 4 9/29 | Learning target: I can identify a conflict in a story. Classwork: Brainstorm how to identify conflict in a story. | |
| Day 5 9/30 | Learning target: I can identify a conflict in a story. Common summative assessment | |

| Student Reflection | | | | | | |
|---|---|---|---|---|---|---|
| **Learning Target** | **Confidence Level (0–4)*** | | | | | |
| I can identify a conflict in a story. | 0 | 1 | 2 | 3 | 4 | |
| I can determine the meaning of a word using context clues. | 0 | 1 | 2 | 3 | 4 | |
| I can write explanatory text using compare and contrast. | 0 | 1 | 2 | 3 | 4 | |
| I can use APA style format. | 0 | 1 | 2 | 3 | 4 | |

*0 = No confidence; 1 = Little confidence; 2 = Somewhat confident; 3 = Mostly confident; 4 = Completely confident

*Source: Moriarty Middle School, Moriarty, New Mexico. Used with permission.*

Consider how to share with students the learning targets and the relationship of those targets to daily work and homework. Let them see that there is a plan, an expectation for learning, regardless of which teacher they may have in the grade level or subject area.

## Including Nonlinguistic Representations

In addition to requiring written work, consider how to make learning visible or audible. What picture can a student draw to summarize a process or make sense of a word problem? What is a mental image a student might see when thinking about a novel? Ask students to draw pictures, create graphic organizers, or make models to show their learning and demonstrate higher-level reasoning like clarifying, interpreting, and creating. When students make their thinking visible, they also invite feedback from peers and teachers, which furthers learning.

## Using Cooperative Learning

Cooperative learning is more than students talking with one another or sitting in close proximity to one another. While these are vital elements to quality cooperative learning, they do not in and of themselves promise learning, nor develop the collaboration and cooperation skills necessary in the world today.

Choosing the right task as the catalyst for learning is critical to students' ability to work together meaningfully and learn. According to Sousa and Tomlinson (2011):

> The most powerful tasks ask students to use essential knowledge and essential skills to explore or extend an essential understanding. Knowledge and skills are not sacrificed, as teachers sometimes fear they might be, to achieve understanding. Rather they are used in service of making meaning. Students who work consistently with such tasks are likely to learn more, retain more, apply their learning more naturally, and transfer what they learn more readily than students who simply attempt to master knowledge and skills out of context. (pp. 53–54)

Consider higher-level-cognitive-demand tasks (DOK 2–4, see chapter 5, page 79) that authentically promote student discourse because students *want* and *need* thoughtful discourse for understanding and sense making. As Hattie (2012) states, "Learning is collaborative and requires dialogue, and this requires teachers to be attentive to all aspects of peer-to-peer construction and mediation" (p. 39). The tasks teachers choose and the expectations they have for students working together are essential to productive, cooperative learning.

David W. Johnson and Roger T. Johnson (1999) name five elements for an effective cooperative learning model.

1. **Positive interdependence:** Students must work together and rely on one another because each student has a unique role or contribution to make in order to complete the task.

2. **Face-to-face promotive interaction:** Students engage in productive discussions as they attempt to work on the task. This includes students giving feedback to one another, brainstorming a solution pathway, trying multiple ideas or strategies, and refining each until all students in the group understand the team's thinking.

3. **Individual and group accountability:** Each student contributes and learns through working on the assigned task. Together, the students contribute to the success of the task.

4. **Interpersonal and small-group skills:** Students use effective group skills such as talking in turn, giving constructive feedback to one another, determining consensus, and trusting one another to build a community of learners.

5. **Group processing:** Students reflect on how they worked as a team on the task, and they receive feedback from the teacher related to their ability to work cooperatively.

Determine how students will share their learning with one another. One way is to use role cards with students so each student is clear on his or her role within the group (for example, facilitator, questioner, recorder, or resource manager). Will they feature their final thinking on chart paper so their peers can view their work during a gallery walk? Another way is a "three stay, one stray" activity in which the teacher chooses one student from each group to move to another group and explain his or her own group's thinking to the three remaining in the new group. The important thing to remember is to build accountability into lessons by including sharing with the class or another group of students.

Much learning happens through interaction with others, but ultimately students must master many concepts individually. Thus, it is important to balance students working in collaborative settings and independent settings with an emphasis on collaboration while learning. Using discourse and high-level tasks during the instructional minutes of a school day impacts student achievement and provides the time necessary for students and the teacher to give feedback and correct student thinking.

## Setting Objectives and Providing Feedback

Throughout this chapter and also in chapter 5, we have emphasized the importance of students self-assessing their progress through team-created student learning targets and clear targets for each instructional lesson. Students can set goals for themselves at the beginning of a unit and monitor their learning throughout when the team has determined a systematic process for those things to happen. Students can also assess their learning after each common formative and summative assessment.

Teachers can give feedback to students on common assessments, which in turn will help students self-assess their progress going forward. Part of this effective instructional practice is teachers giving formative feedback to students and students giving it to other students in the context of daily lessons and activities. This requires students to make their thinking visible or audible so students or a teacher can look at the thinking, acknowledge its strengths, and provide specific suggestions for improvement, if needed, that students can immediately take action on and learn from.

Dean et al. (2012) have four recommendations for classroom practice with regard to providing feedback:

- Provide feedback that addresses what is correct and elaborates on what students need to do next.
- Provide feedback appropriately in time to meet students' needs.
- Provide feedback that is criterion referenced.
- Engage students in the feedback process. (p. 11)

Through feedback, students and teachers learn. Collaborative teams can address the most common misconceptions that students demonstrate and work together to improve the learning of all students and strengthen future lessons.

## Generating and Testing Hypotheses

This effective instructional practice means choosing tasks for students to engage in that promote higher-level thinking and reasoning skills. Students problem solve, investigate, explore, experiment, invent, test, and make decisions during projects and tasks. Students may read a passage and make an inference using evidence to support it before continuing the reading. Afterward, students might write or discuss the accuracy or inaccuracy of the inference, again using evidence. Alternately, students might read a word problem or a scientific question and make a conjecture or hypothesis about the solution or findings before solving the problem or performing an experiment. Students might analyze the life cycle of a bird and use that to predict other life cycles or analyze major events in history to infer what happened in a time period they have not yet studied. All of these examples require students to make meaning of the task at hand using previous knowledge and understanding, which strengthens their learning.

## Using Questions, Cues, and Advance Organizers

For Marzano (2003), this instructional practice refers to activating students' prior knowledge while they are learning a new concept or skill. Consider a K-W-L chart where students list what they *know* (before the learning), what they *want to know* (before the learning), and what they *learned* (after learning has occurred). Teachers might also provide pictures of a time period or era or of a location that students will study, encouraging students to wonder about the photos prior to the new learning.

Additionally, consider the types of questions to use in each lesson. Do questions require one-word or simple-phrase answers each time? Who is answering each question? Ideally, questions should require thinking and all students should have the opportunity to answer by sharing their answers with a partner. Then, randomly select students to share their own thinking or the thinking of their partners. This holds all students accountable to think and reason when the teacher poses a question. Ask why after nearly every response, and have students elaborate on one another's answers. Develop a culture of questioning, thinking, reasoning, and learning from both incorrect and correct answers in class, and have students learn to listen deeply and critically to one another.

Each of these effective instructional practices, when done well, engages students in learning. When planning a lesson, consider having students learn through work and discourse at least 60 to 65 percent of each lesson (Kanold & Larson, 2015). The start and end of each lesson is also critical to students' understanding of the day's learning related to the learning target. Teams will discover additional effective instructional practices through their own work and experience; they can record these for future use in lessons.

### Use Lesson Study and Instructional Rounds

A collaborative team learns a lot about instruction when members have the opportunity to observe student learning in one another's classrooms and plan lessons together. Teams can accomplish this in several ways.

We have found success when teams participate in a lesson study in which the team collectively creates a lesson, one teacher teaches the lesson while the other members observe and note student behaviors and learning throughout the lesson, and then the team debriefs the strengths and weaknesses of the lesson related to student learning. A second teacher might then teach a modified lesson while the team members again observe students and then debrief, finishing with ideas for teachers to use in future lessons related to student engagement. When designing a lesson, the team determines a goal related to student engagement (such as quality student discourse, meaningful cooperative learning, or making thinking visible) and gathers student data related to that goal for the debrief to strengthen instructional practice. The focus of the lesson observation is on the students, not the teacher. We adapted this model from Mona Toncheff and Timothy D. Kanold's (2015) *Beyond the Common Core: A Handbook for Mathematics in a PLC at Work, High School*.

Sometimes, teams collaboratively plan a lesson with a student-engagement goal, and then each teacher delivers the lesson to students. Teachers may or may not record student actions during the lesson and then come back as a team to reflect on the strengths and weaknesses of the lesson that students experienced in each classroom. Again, the focus is on student engagement and learning. Team members look for commonalities and areas that require changes in practice that will continue to improve student learning.

Initially and throughout the year, teachers and administrators might conduct walkthroughs of one another's classes to observe student learning in action. These are typically shorter in duration (about ten minutes per class-room) with a meeting to reflect as a concluding activity. These are most effective when the team has established a goal prior to student observations that the observer can collect data on. However, observers can also effectively use their findings to establish a goal or give feedback to teachers related to student learning. We offer the following template in figure 6.6 for administrators or teachers to use as a general recording tool or feedback tool.

| **Observer:** _____ **Grade and subject:** _____ **Date:** _____ |
|---|
| **Activity observed:** What are students doing? (Engaging in dialogue, doing independent work, completing worksheets, doing project-based learning, using manipulatives, writing, reading, and so on) |
| **Cognitive demand:** Circle the thinking you observe or that the teacher facilitates.<br><br>Analyze, interpret          Apply                    Use cause and effect<br>Compare, classify, categorize   Create, develop          Draw conclusions<br>Generalize                 Infer                    Justify, evaluate<br>Make connections, summarize   Predict, estimate        Sequence, order<br>Synthesize |
| **Locus of control:** Who is responsible for most of the thinking and talking—the teacher or students? Note the evidence you observed. |
| **Learning targets:** What is the connection between what the students are doing and the posted learning targets? |
| **Evidence of differentiated instruction:** What scaffolding or support for differentiated learning did you observe? (Such as modeling, using graphic organizers, offering visual supports, implementing small-group instruction, using manipulatives, featuring project-based learning, giving extended time, and so on) |

**Figure 6.6: Instructional observation recording tool.**

continued →

| |
|---|
| **Classroom environment:** How is the classroom arranged? What is posted on the walls? What is the structure of the learning spaces? (Such as desk configuration, use of anchor charts, a literacy- and numeracy-rich classroom, and so on) |
| **Instructional strategies:** Which instructional strategies does the teacher use during the lesson? |
| **Final reflections:**<br><br>• I liked . . .<br><br><br>• I wonder . . . |

*Visit* **go.SolutionTree.com/PLCbooks** *to download a free reproducible version of this figure.*

This instructional observation recording tool focuses on the key ideas related to lesson design: rigor of thinking (cognitive demand), locus of control (teacher or student), meaningful activities, evidence of differentiation, classroom environment, and instructional strategies. Additionally, there is a place for feedback where an administrator or teacher can document those things he or she liked in the lesson because they are strong instructional practices that engaged students in learning and those things he or she wonders about because there may be other ways to get even more students productively learning. The tool helps teams develop a list of first-best instructional practices to use each year with students.

Teachers continue to build shared knowledge of quality instructional practices by identifying those practices used in class and then looking at data from common formative and summative assessments and anecdotal data from classwork to determine which strategies translate into student learning most effectively.

## Respond to Student Learning

Even with the best lesson designs that include classroom engagement and differentiation, some teachers will still have students who need additional time and support to learn at high levels. The teacher schedules this additional support systematically during the school day. Chapter 7 (page 137) explores this concept more as an accountability measure. Visit the Tools and Resources section on AllThingsPLC (www.allthingsplc.info/tools-resources), and select Make Time for Collaboration in the right margin under Building a Collaborative Culture to view examples of K–12 school schedules within PLCs that show ways to handle this challenge.

For the purposes of this chapter, we focus on instructional practices that are necessary to develop a collective response to student learning. Collaborative team discussions need to focus on the possible interventions (grade level), remediation (prior grade level), or enrichments and extensions to student learning that are necessary based on evidence from common formative and summative assessments. Some schools call this scheduled additional time in the day *WIN time*, which stands for *What I Need*; teachers regroup students as needed during that portion of the schedule.

After giving a common formative or summative assessment, identify those students by target who are advanced, proficient, close to proficient, or far from proficient (see chapter 5, page 79). Bring samples of student work to the collaborative team meeting in order to share with one another the work students have demonstrated in each category. Identify trends in student work to strategically target a skill in which to grow student learning. In *Simplifying Response to Intervention*, Austin Buffum, Mike Mattos, and Chris Weber (2012) state, "The more targeted the intervention, the more likely it will work. Most schools' interventions are ineffective because they are too broad in focus and rarely address a child's individual learning needs" (p. 136). Figure 6.7 shows a template teams can use to determine the instructional re-engagement needs of each student.

| 1. Identify the assessed standard and student learning target. | | | |
| --- | --- | --- | --- |
| | | | |

| 2. Identify the students who demonstrated learning at levels of advanced, proficient, close to proficient, or far from proficient. | | | |
| --- | --- | --- | --- |
| Advanced | Proficient | Close to Proficient | Far From Proficient |
| | | | |

| 3. Look at samples of student work. What did the advanced students show in their work that set them apart? Next, look at the proficient students and look at the trends in their work. Continue with each level and write down the trends in student work for each. | | | |
| --- | --- | --- | --- |
| Advanced | Proficient | Close to Proficient | Far From Proficient |
| | | | |

| 4. Determine a collective plan to target learning for each group of students. How will you re-engage each group in learning and who will be responsible for the learning? When will you re-evaluate groups to see if learning occurred? | | | |
| --- | --- | --- | --- |
| Advanced | Proficient | Close to Proficient | Far From Proficient |
| | | | |

**Figure 6.7:** Re-engagement protocol.

*Visit **go.SolutionTree.com/PLCbooks** for a free reproducible version of this figure.*

As a collaborative team, decide how to regroup students and re-engage them in learning during any allocated additional time and support for learning during the school day. Depending on a school's schedule, only those students who need intervention or remediation may have additional time and support to learn or the school may schedule an intervention time for all students (Buffum & Mattos, 2014). The team should decide how to differentiate instruction and use manipulatives and activities that re-engage students in learning, rather than simply reteach a concept. Be clear, too, about the target for that re-engagement so teams can design the best lessons for students. Consider how to assess student learning at the end of the time the schedule allocates for the continued learning. Groups for intervention and support should never be determined solely based on individualized education program (IEP), English learner status, or other education classifications. Rather, base groups on which students have learned the targets or not learned them yet, with the collaborative team analyzing the root cause to improve the learning of every student.

Planning for meaningful and effective instruction focuses primarily on the work teachers do during core instruction and includes necessary differentiation in lessons. However, teachers on a collaborative team will have to address the learning of students throughout the year and design effective instruction for intervention, remediation, and enrichment and extension as necessary during additional time in the school day. Consider again the vision for quality instruction and challenge teams to reach that vision through quality lesson planning and team reflection about best practices related to instruction.

## Reflect and Take Action

The rubric in figure 6.8 shows collaborative team progressions in planning meaningful and effective instruction. Teams should look at the rubric and determine where they rate related to each topic.

| | Level 1<br>Beginning | Level 2<br>Attempting | Level 3<br>Practicing | Level 4<br>Embracing |
|---|---|---|---|---|
| Classroom Culture | Teachers see mistakes as bad or challenges to overcome rather than a learning tool.<br><br>Students sit in rows and seldom, if ever, discuss learning with one another.<br><br>Teachers establish routines and procedures for movement in the classroom but not necessarily for expectations during learning. | Students begin to learn from mistakes, but may not feel safe making mistakes.<br><br>Students sit in groups but may not fully utilize one another as resources for learning.<br><br>Teachers establish routines and procedures, but neither they nor students always follow them. | Students and teachers authentically learn from mistakes and feel safe making mistakes while productively struggling to learn.<br><br>Students sit in groups for learning and utilize one another as resources.<br><br>Teachers and students practice routines and procedures to maximize the time they spend learning. | Teachers see mistakes as opportunities for learning and embrace them in a manner that encourages all students to try any task.<br><br>Students sit in groups and learn from and challenge one another.<br><br>Teachers and students establish and practice routines and procedures for learning. |

| | | | | |
|---|---|---|---|---|
| **First-Best Instruction: Lesson Design** | Instruction is lecture only (telling information) with optional note taking.<br><br>The lesson is the same for all students throughout the class period or block of time.<br><br>The lesson focuses on an activity rather than a standard, or students simply mimic what teachers model throughout the lesson.<br><br>There is no closure present beyond instructions for preparing to leave or put things away. | Teachers instruct using the guided release method with structured I do, you do, we do. We do is independent.<br><br>Teachers intervene for students struggling in a lesson.<br><br>Teachers tie the lesson to a standard but do not make that clear to students.<br><br>Students complete an exit slip for closure. | Teachers use flexible instruction with students doing the work and learning through reading, writing, and discussions that include inquiry.<br><br>Teachers plan for intervention and keep students who finish early busy with tasks.<br><br>Teachers tie the lesson to a standard and students understand the relationship to the learning target. Tasks include various levels of rigor for which critical thinking and reasoning are necessary. Teachers give time for productive struggle.<br><br>Students close the lesson by explaining what they learned related to the learning target. | Teachers act as facilitators, managing some direct instruction with more student-led involvement.<br><br>Teachers plan for intervention and enrichment so all students are engaged in learning throughout the lesson.<br><br>Teachers tie the lesson to a standard and students understand and can articulate the connections in the lesson to the unit and other units. Students experience different levels of rigor and productively struggle as necessary.<br><br>Students close the lesson and reflect on their understanding of the learning target. |
| **First-Best Instruction: Discourse** | Teachers are the primary person talking in class.<br><br>Teachers ask "right there" questions, which match the language in the text, and students call out answer or raise their hands to answer.<br><br>Students only learn from the teacher. | Teachers are the primary person talking in class and directing all conversations.<br><br>Teachers affirm or refute all answers from questions students pose.<br><br>Students primarily learn from the teacher, though sometimes from one another. | Teachers pose higher-level questions and students listen to the responses and justifications.<br><br>Students listen to one another and respond to one another.<br><br>Students work in groups and learn from one another as well as from the teacher. | Teachers and students pose questions in class and listen and respond fluidly to answers.<br><br>Students initiate conversations as necessary to learn and make sense of the standard. |

**Figure 6.8: Instructional practices rubric.**

continued →

| | Level 1 Beginning | Level 2 Attempting | Level 3 Practicing | Level 4 Embracing |
|---|---|---|---|---|
| **First-Best Instruction: Formative Process** | Teachers focus on finishing a lesson and do not check student work or think to provide quality feedback.<br><br>Lessons do not provide opportunities for visible or audible student thinking that teachers can give quality feedback to quickly and effectively. | Teachers check for understanding by having students show thumbs up or down, for example, and then continue teaching accordingly.<br><br>Lessons provide opportunities to see or hear student thinking, but teachers make no adjustments to instruction. | Teachers provide feedback to students or student groups who are able to connect their thinking as necessary.<br><br>The teacher sees or hears student thinking in the lesson and adjusts instruction as necessary. | Teachers provide feedback to students and students provide feedback to one another throughout the lesson.<br><br>Teachers and students see and hear one another's thinking and work together to learn. |
| **Response to Student Learning** | Collaborative teams discuss student learning (not always using data) and make individual plans after the discussion to address student learning. | Collaborative teams determine trends and misconceptions in student learning and each design in-class opportunities for remediation, intervention, or extension as necessary. | Collaborative teams determine trends and misconceptions in student learning to design quality intervention, remediation, and extension as necessary. | Collaborative teams analyze data to collectively design intervention, remediation, and extension as necessary and use data to monitor the effectiveness of each. |

*Visit **go.SolutionTree.com/PLCbooks** for a free reproducible version of this figure.*

Once teams have reached agreement about their current status, they should use figure 6.9 to determine next steps to strengthen their practice in working to ensure all students learn through meaningful and effective instruction.

| Action | Team-Level Rating | Next Steps |
|---|---|---|
| Designing classroom culture | | |
| Planning units | | |
| Using first-best instruction: daily unit design | | |
| Using first-best instruction: student reflection | | |
| Using first-best instruction: formative process | | |
| Responding to student learning | | |

**Figure 6.9: Effective instruction reflection and action plan.**

*Visit **go.SolutionTree.com/PLCbooks** for a free reproducible version of this figure.*

**Collaborative Team Questions to Consider**

- How will your team make sense of the standards students are learning and develop a plan for the lessons?
- How will your team determine the best homework to assign during the unit?
- How will your team have students self-assess their learning throughout the unit?
- How will students make connections to the new learning from previous learning or experiences?
- How will you design a quality lesson using the protocol in figure 6.4 (pages 121–122)?
- How will you work together to determine high levels of learning for all students?
- How might you learn from one another through lesson study, instructional rounds, or walkthroughs?
- How will you use trends in student work to determine targeted re-engagement for students?

## CHAPTER 7

# Embracing Accountability

We hold students accountable by analyzing their work, providing feedback, providing focused interventions and additional time and support, and insisting students redo their work when it is not to standard. So too must adults—specifically teacher teams, principals, and district office leaders—be held accountable for the work connected to improving student learning.

—Robert Eaker and Janel Keating

Why do teachers do the difficult, time-consuming, and at times spirit-draining work of designing lessons, creating and administering assessments, responding to student learning, and taking time to really know students? This entire book rests on the premise that the answer is this: because of a desire for all students to learn at high levels and to open the doors of opportunity to every student. Many educators can attest that their drive to improve the lives of students through education is relentless despite the toll it sometimes takes. So how does one know if all the effort is paying off? How do teams learn what actions they should replicate for future student learning? How do they know how to extend the learning for students who have demonstrated proficiency, the fourth critical question of a PLC (DuFour et al., 2016)? The answers to these questions come from a careful and continual look at data to evaluate learning and programs.

A second-grade team at an elementary school in Louisville, Kentucky, discovered while analyzing its district benchmark assessment data that students in two mathematics classrooms were outperforming those in the other two mathematics classrooms. This had happened on the three previous benchmark assessments as well. Though the teachers on the team planned lessons together and designed common assessments, there was not much change in student performance. After analyzing the most recent benchmark data and beginning a meeting to brainstorm solutions, one teacher asked a question: "What if we teach each other's classrooms and our own each week? We can teach our own class on Monday and Friday and rotate through the others on Tuesday through Thursday. What do you guys think?"

Teachers A and B, whose students had been performing well, were a little nervous about sharing their students with teachers C and D, who were not getting the desired results. However, they recognized that all the second graders were "their" second graders and decided to give it a try. The team spent the next six weeks closely planning lessons and being clear about standards and expectations of proficiency in short common formative assessments. They shared student progress and the aspects of the lesson implementation that worked for student learning. After an intense six weeks of constant planning and learning from one another, they found that the scores of nearly all second-grade students improved. The students from classrooms C and D improved dramatically and, to the surprise of teachers A and B, those in classrooms A and B also showed improvement. One teacher exclaimed, "Oh no! It worked." When asked why she didn't sound excited, she answered, "It was a lot of work. How can we go back to the old way knowing what we know now? We are going to have to keep doing this!"

This second-grade team has embraced accountability. These teachers do not see the data related to student learning as an evaluation or judgment; rather, they see it as an opportunity to learn from one another, to become better educators, and to better meet the needs of each student. The team members are accountable to students to grow their learning and accountable to one another to work as a team toward that commitment. They focused their efforts to improve the learning of all students and saw the results of these efforts in the data.

There are many types of data in two categories to collect and review: (1) numbers—quantitative data—which teachers generate from such things as common assessment results or student discipline records, and (2) narrative records—qualitative data—from such things as classroom observations or student work descriptions. Quantitative and qualitative data promote accountability and team learning through constant probing, analyzing, inferring from, and responding to student learning. Who benefits from these actions? Students, teachers, and administrators all benefit as teams determine those antecedents, including instructional practices, that most profoundly affect student achievement.

## Determine Vision Versus Reality

Too often administrators and teachers in schools in need of improvement use data as a means to judge or confirm the poor performance of teachers and students. The culture of fear around data and accountability that results from this misuse of information hinders the opportunity that data can represent to improve student learning in a focused and meaningful way.

When the mission and vision of a PLC include high levels of learning for all students, data become a learning tool. From the data, each stakeholder can identify and address what students have learned and what they have not learned yet. Teams routinely and continually collect data and have data conversations that cause them to shift and change their instructional practices to meet the needs of each student. This is not something one administrator, teacher, or student can do; rather, it takes a collective effort to achieve.

Schools that embrace accountability comprise adults who are willing to learn from the data so all students really do learn. Teams do not only look at data after a state assessment or benchmark assessment, nor do they give common assessments only once per month and analyze the data a week after giving the test. Instead, they seek opportunities to give short common formative assessments (as we discussed in chapter 5, page 79) and quickly analyze and respond to the data and the student work. They continually address learning in the classroom using anecdotal observations or data from exit slips and discuss how to best use schoolwide intervention and enrichment time to benefit learners.

When the school achieves this vision of accountability, not only are teachers embracing and modeling the power of accountability to each other and their students, but administrators and learning teams also focus on continual accountability to student learning. Leadership is always a collective endeavor and "no one person has all the expertise, skill, and energy to improve a school or meet the needs of every student in his or her classroom" (Kramer, 2015, p. 44). Administrators hold one another and teachers accountable. Teachers hold themselves accountable to student learning and hold students accountable to their learning when they routinely analyze and learn from data. Students hold themselves accountable when they monitor their learning against the targets in each unit.

Embracing accountability does not mean that the school ranks and penalizes teachers and students; it means identifying learning needs and realizing learning opportunities because everyone is accountable for the learning of each student. It means there is a healthy culture of adults and students learning from the data and the narrative that a school produces. It means learning comes first.

# Start Now

The mission of any school should include working toward grade-level or higher learning for all students. How will teachers and school leaders know if the hard work they have dedicated to this mission is achieving results? How will they know when they need to make corrections so more students learn? How will they know what and who to celebrate in the quest for more students learning?

When building the culture of embracing accountability, it is important to identify the actions adults in the school will hold one another accountable to and determine what stakeholders will continually monitor and respond to in the school to improve the learning of each student. We separate this work into three sections—the work of (1) collaborative teacher teams, (2) leaders, and (3) students—though there is some overlap among them.

## Hold Collaborative Teacher Teams Accountable

The school holds collaborative teacher teams accountable for the learning of the students they serve. Learning includes academics and behavior impacts it, which means teams must work together to determine how to eradicate gaps that prevent students from learning grade-level content. They must also work to determine the processes that can minimize behaviors that impede learning. At the same time, teams must also serve students who are ready to learn and in need of extensions. This is a large task and the stakes are high. By working together in a culture of accountability, however, teacher teams can meet these demands.

### Do the Right Work

Student learning improves when teachers work collaboratively to address the four critical questions of a PLC:

1. What do we expect students to know and be able to do?

2. How will we know if each student has learned it?

3. How will we respond when some students do not learn it?

4. How will we extend the learning for students who have demonstrated proficiency? (DuFour et al., 2016, p. 59)

To address these questions with maximum impact on student learning, teams must do the right work, as we outline in chapter 1 of this book (page 7). Teachers must hold each other accountable to addressing these questions during each collaborative team meeting as they set agendas. We have found, however, that sometimes teams believe they are addressing these questions when, in fact, they are not quite meeting their intent. Figure 7.1 (pages 140–141) shows some of the common actions collaborative teams take when addressing each of the critical questions, as well as common actions we have seen teams take during meetings that actually do not address each of the critical questions.

Team members should consider how they hold one another accountable to answering each of the four critical questions. What are their current strengths as a team and in which areas do they need to challenge themselves? Accountability starts by recognizing the work ahead and determining how to monitor progress related to student learning.

| 1. What is it we expect students to know and be able to do? | |
|---|---|
| **Collaborative Team Actions** | **Non-Collaborative Team Actions** |
| <ul><li>Prioritize standards.</li><li>Group standards into units. Determine when proficiency with each is expected.</li><li>Develop scope and sequence (pacing).</li><li>Unpack standards to understand the learning targets and write student-friendly learning targets.</li><li>Determine rigor needed for proficiency of learning.</li><li>Identify practices or processes students need to learn with the content standards.</li></ul> | <ul><li>Group standards arbitrarily or spontaneously and teach without a plan or with a minimal plan.</li><li>Agree on a few standards, and individuals choose the rest.</li><li>Use a book as a guide for what to teach and when to teach standards.</li><li>Agree to disagree on the level of rigor needed to demonstrate proficiency.</li><li>Teach standards in isolation.</li><li>Individually interpret the meaning of standards.</li></ul> |
| **2. How will we know when they have learned?** | |
| **Collaborative Team Actions** | **Non-Collaborative Team Actions** |
| <ul><li>Create and use common formative and summative assessments.</li><li>Use common scoring guides and rubrics to assess student learning on common assessments.</li><li>Calibrate scoring of common assessments.</li><li>Analyze data from common assessments and respond.</li><li>Identify trends in student work and respond.</li><li>Identify and plan for classroom formative assessment processes in daily lessons.</li></ul> | <ul><li>Give independently teacher-created assessments to one's own class.</li><li>Agree on only some common items and leave freedom for teachers to independently choose the remaining items.</li><li>Score assessments independently.</li><li>Analyze data without a response (move on).</li><li>Give tests on different days.</li><li>Only give students feedback on unit assessments, ignoring formative assessment in daily instruction or vice versa.</li></ul> |
| **3. How will we respond when they do not learn?** | |
| **Collaborative Team Actions** | **Non-Collaborative Team Actions** |
| <ul><li>Look at trends in student work and re-engage all learners.</li><li>Re-engage all learners without lowering the cognitive demand of the target or standard.</li><li>Accelerate learning so students can access grade-level standards.</li><li>Base decisions on data, not a student's education label.</li><li>Create a systematic pyramid of interventions to meet the needs of all learners.</li></ul> | <ul><li>Focus solely on basic skills.</li><li>Slow down and stretch content without accelerating learning and including grade-level content.</li><li>Group students based on education label rather than academic ability.</li><li>Change (lower) expectations for student proficiency.</li><li>Reteach the same concept in a similar way or with lower expectations.</li></ul> |

| 4. How will we respond when they already know it? | |
| --- | --- |
| **Collaborative Team Actions** | **Non-Collaborative Team Actions** |
| • Look at trends in student work and re-engage all learners.<br><br>• Re-engage learners and deepen their understanding of a target or standard rather than skim future grade-level content.<br><br>• Raise text complexity, if appropriate.<br><br>• Base decisions on data, not a student's education label.<br><br>• Honor and advance student learning. | • Give students more difficult problems or activities.<br><br>• Speed through content to cover more or future content.<br><br>• Group students based on education label (gifted and talented education, English language learner, and so on) rather than ability.<br><br>• Change (raise) expectations for student proficiency.<br><br>• Reteach the same concept after it is learned.<br><br>• Require students to always help or teach others. |

*Sources: DuFour et al., 2016; Kramer, 2015.*

**Figure 7.1: Examples and nonexamples of addressing the critical questions for student learning.**

*Visit go.SolutionTree.com/PLCbooks for a free reproducible version of this figure.*

### Set SMART Goals

Collaborative teams within PLCs know they are making a difference in student learning when they establish SMART goals (goals that are strategic and specific, measurable, attainable, results oriented, and time bound) and monitor their progress toward reaching those goals (see chapter 1, page 7, for more information on SMART goals). One type of SMART goal is a program SMART goal. These measure the learning of students in a grade level or course from year to year. For example, a third-grade team will look at third-grade results from a previous year and write a third-grade goal for learning in the current year to improve these results. Another type of goal is a cohort goal, one that measures growth of student learning within a year or the growth of student learning throughout the time the students spent at a school from year to year.

To begin with, SMART goals are often program goals related to state assessment results. However, they can also be program goals that relate to student learning of priority standards, large topics, district benchmark assessments, and common unit assessments. Figure 7.2 (page 142) shows examples of SMART goals teams can set related to student learning results. Readers can consider these examples templates for goals, and teams can substitute their own current reality into the underlined portion of any goal they choose to use.

There is no magic formula to determine what a team will use as its new goal—it must feel like a stretch to meet but still be attainable. This requires the team members to hold one another accountable to meeting the goal and provides opportunities for celebration when they do so with hard and focused work.

Suppose a team starts with a state assessment goal. If its goal is for 60 percent of students to pass the assessment, team members can monitor progress toward that goal each time they give a common unit assessment (more than one standard) or a district benchmark assessment. Have at least 60 percent of students passed or exceeded expectations on the exam? If so (and assuming the test is of high quality and a predictor of future success), the team is on track to meet its goal of student learning.

**State assessment SMART goal:**

By the end of the 2017–2018 school year, the percentage of seventh-grade students passing the reading state assessment will increase from 27 percent to at least 45 percent.

**Priority standard or topic SMART goal:**

The percentage of eighth-grade students who meet or exceed the standards for writing an argument paper will increase from 14 percent (pretest given September 18, 2017) to at least 70 percent as measured on a schoolwide argument writing exam administered on March 4, 2018.

*Note: This is a cohort goal. If this is a yearly administered exam, one can use the percentage from the eighth-grade exam given in March 2017 to March 2018 to make it a program goal.*

**District benchmark SMART goal:**

By the end of trimester 2 in 2017–2018, the percentage of fourth-grade students passing the mathematics trimester 2 benchmark assessment will increase from 46 percent (in 2016–2017) to at least 75 percent.

**Common unit assessment SMART goal:**

By the end of Unit 2 Photosynthesis in 2017–2018, the percentage of students meeting or exceeding each of the targets on the common unit assessment will increase from 61 percent (in 2016–2017) to at least 75 percent.

**Grading SMART goal:**

By the end of the second semester in the 2017–2018 school year, the percentage of students earning a D or F in U.S. history will decrease from 36 percent (second semester in 2016–2017) to at least 20 percent.

**Figure 7.2: SMART goal examples.**

*Visit **go.SolutionTree.com/PLCbooks** for a free reproducible version of this figure.*

Once teams have set SMART goals, they must identify the collective actions they will take to meet them. These are focused and targeted actions teachers on a team will commit to doing related to norms (chapter 1, page 7), culture (chapter 2, page 27), student learning needs (chapter 3, page 41), a guaranteed and viable curriculum (chapter 4, page 55), common assessments with a collective response (chapter 5, page 79), and common instructional practices (chapter 6, page 113). They will, for example, hold one another accountable to do each of the following.

- Establish effective collective commitments (norms) for working with one another.
- Teach the guaranteed curriculum using common pacing.
- Create and administer common assessments with clear success criteria.
- Analyze and respond to the data from common assessments.
- Work collaboratively to improve the learning of students using formative assessment processes.
- Create effective intervention and remediation plans, as needed.
- Create effective extension plans, as necessary.
- Monitor progress toward SMART goals.
- Celebrate short- and long-term wins.

When teams are discussing their plan to achieve their SMART goals, consider using the protocol in figure 7.3 to address the necessary adult and student actions for success.

Team: _____   Date: _____

**SMART goal:**

> By the end of the 2017–2018 school year, the percentage of students proficient on the fifth-grade state mathematics assessment will increase from 42 percent to at least 55 percent.

1.  **What will we look for in student work as evidence we have reached the goal?**

    - At least 55 percent of fifth-grade students will meet or exceed proficiency on the state mathematics test.
    - At least 55 percent of fifth-grade students will meet or exceed each target on the common summative assessments.
    - Students will show their thinking when solving problems.
    - Students will productively attempt problems in class and on assessments.
    - Students will apply the concepts they learned in fifth-grade mathematics.

2.  **Consider the initial data necessary, whether from a test teachers administered in a previous year or a pretest for the current year. What do the initial data show related to strengths and areas of improvement for student learning?**

    - Students need to focus on communicating their reasoning and problem solving.

3.  **What will your team commit to doing to reach the team SMART goal?**

    - Determine priority standards and common pacing.
    - Administer common assessments and collectively respond to the data.
    - Include higher-order reasoning in instruction and on assessments so students have to show their work and can learn to build stamina for problem solving. In each unit, we will agree to at least three high-level tasks to use with students.

4.  **When will we give common formative and summative assessments to measure progress toward the SMART goal? How will we analyze the data from the common assessments and determine a response to student learning?**

    - See the proficiency map for common unit assessments—one per unit. We will also give at least two common formative assessments on priority standards in each unit.
    - We will analyze the data from common assessments within two days of giving each test and use the data to determine how to re-engage students in learning during core instruction or during WIN time for targeted additional support.

5.  **Which instructional strategies will your team commit to using in order to accomplish this SMART goal?**

    - We will give students high-level tasks (at least three common tasks per unit).
    - We will agree on the strategies students should demonstrate during each unit.
    - We will have students exchange papers and give feedback to one another, which we will use to make every student's solution stronger.
    - We will use a commonly designed word problem template with students as a graphic organizer for solving multistep word problems.

**Figure 7.3: SMART goal plan example.**

*Visit **go.SolutionTree.com/PLCbooks** for a free reproducible version of this figure.*

It is important to hold one another accountable to the instructional strategies the team has chosen, common assessments it has committed to administering, and data analysis it will conduct from those assessments to determine the necessary evidence from student work to know the team has achieved the goal. Along the way, celebrate the short- and long-term wins to contribute to the desired culture (as we outlined in chapter 2, page 27).

### Conduct Data Analysis

There are many types of data to analyze related to student learning. When doing this work, it is important to start with data from common assessments, observations during lessons, and ongoing monitoring of student learning with targeted plans for students by skill as necessary.

### Using Common Assessment Data

The most crucial data for teams to continually monitor and collectively respond to is from team-created common assessments, which show the learning of each student by standard or target (see figure 5.11, pages 103–104). Using this data, teams can make a plan to address student remediation needs by differentiating core instruction, employing grade-level targeted interventions during a school system intervention time, or using building resources.

As we outlined in chapter 5 (page 79), when analyzing data, team actions include the following four steps.

1. Look at an overview of the data.
2. Identify students by standard proficiency.
3. Identify trends and patterns in student work from the highest to the lowest performers.
4. Make re-engagement and extension plans.

Consider, too, how to use data to determine the success of any intervention or remediation plan. If, for example, a team chooses to use the first fifteen minutes of each lesson addressing how to balance chemistry equations or edit writing because assessment data show students need it, what short common assessment will the team give and analyze to determine the effectiveness of that strategy and when will they give it? If they regroup students during the day for a schoolwide intervention time, how will the team know that the strategies they employed helped more students learn? They should collect and analyze data not just for each assessment, but also to determine the effectiveness of interventions related to student learning. Analyzing data is cyclical rather than something team members can check off a list. Teachers use data to learn to collectively determine the practices that most impact student learning and to brainstorm ideas to ensure each student learns when struggles persist.

### Using Observational Data

Teams can also collect data throughout a lesson using observation sheets and share this information as a team to address student learning. Consider a recording sheet for each priority standard (as we discussed in chapter 4, page 55) or for each teacher using a larger task that addresses a priority standard. During the lesson, note the type of thinking a student or group of students uses and the success of that thinking, using student work as evidence. Discuss as a team which strategies students use that succeed and how to engage more students in using that reasoning. An example of a recording sheet for observations in a lesson appears in figure 7.4.

If the team already has an idea of the common misconceptions students might demonstrate during learning, it can list those across the top of an observational data tool. Be sure to leave one column blank for possible unanticipated misconceptions. Teachers can use check marks to determine which students or groups of students erred using each type of reasoning during the lesson or document other errors in reasoning. The team can analyze the form later to determine best ways to target strategies to ensure each student learns the standard in future lessons or through purposeful interventions.

| Classroom Observations | | |
|---|---|---|
| Standard: _____ | Activity: _____ | |
| **Student or Group** | **Reasoning or Strategy** | **Evidence of Learning** |
| Group 1 | Use Unifix cubes to show addition. | Students accurately found the sum by skip counting by tens and counting ones. |
| Group 2 | Add tens and then ones. | Students accurately found the sum. |
| Group 3 | Add tens and then ones. | Students made a minor calculation error when summing tens, but still regrouped and added ones correctly. |
| Group 4 | Draw dots to represent each addend and then count the dots. | While students had the correct answer, they did not show evidence of addition, rather of counting as a conceptual piece of adding. |

**Figure 7.4: Observation sheet example.**

*Visit go.SolutionTree.com/PLCbooks for a free reproducible version of this figure.*

## Using Status-Check Data

When a person is in an accident and sent to the hospital, medical personnel quickly develop a triage plan to determine the importance and order of issues to address. Similarly, teams need to periodically stop and assess student learning to develop a triage plan for students who have not yet learned grade-level standards at high levels. They identify those students who are proficient, close to proficient, or far from proficient with the standards the class has addressed to that date. Once teachers have listed every student in a group, they can analyze trends and needs to develop a plan to improve the learning of the students in each category.

We have found that teachers estimate the students in each category best when they imagine that they will administer a state assessment to their students the following day covering only the standards they have taught so far and think about how students would perform. This question works for grade levels and subjects that the state does not generally assess (such first grade or physical education) as well as for those that it does. Teachers can look at common assessment data to place students and determine the number of students they have in each category for the entire team. See figure 7.5 (page 146) for a possible template to use for this activity.

Though teams can use this status-check protocol several times throughout the year, the greatest success comes from doing this activity at the start of the second semester or at the start of each trimester. This leaves time for teams to plan classroom interventions as well as targeted and intensive interventions that require additional time and support. Teams can work to move names to higher levels within two months of identifying the students in each category and measure their success accordingly.

Another way to check the status of student learning is to use grade data from report cards. However, be cautious using these data if the grades do not tie directly to student learning of standards (often called proficiency grading). If teachers on a collaborative team are not all grading using the same system and weights for activities or have not calibrated themselves on grading practices, other problems emerge. These are critical to address since grades reflect the learning of students and should be meaningful and consistent in a grade level or course, regardless of teacher. When calibrated, teams can also use grades as a status check every six weeks or between progress reports and report cards. Obviously, teams then need to identify the targeted and specific interventions to employ for students not yet proficient, so the check never ends with only identifying the number of students earning each letter grade. The team learns from the data when they make a plan for more student learning and then assesses the effectiveness of that plan.

Course: _____ Date: _____

Where are we now?

Suppose you will give a state assessment tomorrow in your grade level or course. Which students in your classes would earn scores of level 4 (exceeds proficiency), level 3 (meets proficiency), level 2 (nearly meets proficiency), and level 1 (does not meet proficiency) based on your common assessment data? List the names of your students in the appropriate columns.

| | Level 4 (Exceeds) | Level 3 (Meets) | Level 2 (Nearly Meets) | Level 1 (Does Not Meet) |
|---|---|---|---|---|
| Teacher: | | | | |
| Teacher: | | | | |
| Teacher: | | | | |
| Teacher: | | | | |
| Total Number: | | | | |

What is your specific plan to have students increase in proficiency before _____ [date]? Check on your goal often to see if students would move based on your common assessment data.

**Team Plan**

| Up From Level 3 Meets Proficiency | Up From Level 2 Close to Proficiency | Up From Level 1 Far From Proficient |
|---|---|---|
| | | |
| Goal: This plan will help move _____ students by _____ [date]. | Goal: This plan will help move _____ students by _____ [date]. | Goal: This plan will help move _____ students by _____ [date]. |

**Figure 7.5: Status-check protocol.**

*Visit go.SolutionTree.com/PLCbooks for a free reproducible version of this figure.*

As teams analyze data, it is critical to document those strategies and instructional practices that improve student learning. That way, when planning the unit the following year, the team can proactively include these in their core instruction throughout the unit to grow their success as a program in a grade level or course and have more students learn each year, as the program SMART goal charts their progress. Teachers hold one another accountable to the work by analyzing the success of student learning across that team. A relentless focus on collecting, analyzing, and responding to data as a collective team improves the learning of students.

## Model Leadership Accountability

Leadership accountability is critical to create a culture focused on student learning that celebrates the success of that learning with students and teachers alike. In order for team members to hold one another accountable to their work by looking at the evidence of learning from common assessments, leaders must also model how to work as collaborative teams and hold teams accountable to the work.

Leadership refers at times to the work of the principal and administrative team as well as the work of the leadership team (as we described in chapter 1, page 7) or other leaders on campus. Often, the role of leadership is to create the necessary systems for collaborative teams to address student learning as well as provide ongoing feedback to the work of those teams throughout the year.

### Establish Systems for Academics and Behavior

Effective schools have clarified systems that address the academic and behavior needs of students. As a leader or with a leadership team, consider the protocols in place for responding to student learning and the time the school allocates to accommodate that response. For example, if a student needs additional time and support to learn a standard, it does not make sense to pull the student out of core instruction and widen his or her learning gap. Instead, teams should ask themselves how the student can learn core instruction and receive additional time during the day to address learning grade-level or prior grade-level skills. How will each student learn during this time of the day? This requires a structural change to the schedule that only leaders can provide so collaborative teams can design the instruction necessary to improve student learning. Leaders still hold teams accountable for having students learn during the core instruction using effective instructional practices that include differentiation. But for those students who still need additional time and support, consider the structures of time required for that type of learning response. As DuFour and Marzano (2011) state:

> One of the most persistent brutal facts in education is the disconnect between the proclaimed commitment to ensure all students learn and the lack of a thoughtful, coordinated, and systematic response when some students do not learn in spite of the best efforts of their individual classroom teacher. (p. 173)

Leaders cannot hold teams accountable for improvement without holding themselves accountable to problem solve any structural and system changes necessary so teams can work effectively.

Similarly, consider the protocols for responding to student behaviors, which might impede their ability to learn. Are teachers or collaborative teams addressing behavior concerns on their own or following schoolwide guidelines? Too often one teacher will mark a student tardy who is not in his or her seat when a bell rings while another only marks a student tardy if he or she is later than two minutes after the bell. What message do students receive regardless of teacher, grade level, or course? When will teachers make phone calls to parents? How will teachers work to de-escalate situations and minimize any loss of class time for a student? When a team troubleshoots issues related to student behavior, how are they documenting their work with the student and the possible successes and failures that resulted? Who are the adults on campus who can and should contribute to the solution? These sorts of information, too, are data and leaders can hold teams accountable to them provided they have created protocols that allow them to do so.

The leadership team should consider periodic agenda items to look at this type of behavior data and determine which structure, if any, needs adjusting in terms of schoolwide practices, as well as to problem solve how to minimize those behaviors that occur most frequently on campus and disrupt student learning (such as bullying or disrespect). Are there classes or minilessons teachers or counselors can provide? Can they relay their expectations for students in a positive and consistent manner to proactively address any negative behaviors (for example, "Participate in class discussions" instead of "Don't text during class")? The focus of the conversations will always be to have students in class learning rather than in-school or out-of-school suspension, which removes students entirely from the learning environment.

The leadership team can also review common assessment data, grade data, and status-check plans from collaborative teacher teams to look at the academic learning of students on campus and develop the necessary structures to provide students with additional learning time and support. In this process, leadership team members can also give feedback to one another and to the collaborative teams. In addition, they can analyze data related to state assessments, district benchmark assessments, growth of student learning by subgroups, number of students in advanced or remedial courses, and results from student surveys to arrive at solutions to improve student learning. Finally, they must celebrate the successes of teams and discuss action steps for teams to take as they work to meet their SMART goals. They can accomplish this in team meetings as well as by having teams share their work with one another at staff meetings for continual learning.

Through this accordion-style leadership, teams come together to solve problems and then expand back out with the solutions. Collaborative teams bring their concerns related to student learning to the leadership team members who then collectively work to minimize any structural impediments while learning from one another to better meet the students' needs. This, in turn, carries back to each team, who shares solutions and learning. Together, the adults in the building work with a focus on students learning grade-level or course standards at high levels.

### Consider Team Evidence and Provide Feedback

As previously addressed, Hattie (2009, 2012) has documented the importance of feedback in improving learning. In *School Leadership That Works*, Robert J. Marzano, Timothy Waters, and Brian A. McNulty (2005) find in their meta-analysis that successful schools had the following specific behaviors and characteristics related to feedback from leaders. These schools are:

- Continually monitoring the effectiveness of the school's curricular, instructional, and assessment practices
- Continually aware of the impact of the school's practices on student achievement (p. 56)

Ultimately, collaborative teams must be clear about the right work and know what specifically their leaders are holding them accountable to in terms of actions. Leaders, in return, must look for evidence of those team actions and provide meaningful feedback to nurture the learning of teams. Throughout this text, at the end of each chapter, we have provided rubrics to describe required actions and give meaningful feedback to teachers and leaders in the building.

Administrators should consider how to look for evidence of team actions from team meetings or classroom walk-throughs. In meetings, do administrators see and hear teachers do things like unpack standards and plan units, create common assessments, analyze data from common assessments, and make plans to respond to student learning? What is the quality of these discussions or the products they create? When walking through the classrooms of a collaborative team, do administrators see the same student learning targets in use, and the teachers giving the same assessment or the same instructional strategy? These would all indicate teachers are working together to improve student learning. How will administrators give feedback to teams about their observations?

Often leaders hold teams accountable to the right work by making them turn in agendas and simply collecting them after every meeting without any type of immediate feedback. This makes teachers feel like the work is really just one more thing to do, rather than a critical part of improving the learning of students and themselves. In addition, if an agenda simply states a team is going to analyze data and a leader does give timely feedback, how can a leader make that feedback meaningful? Stating what a team will discuss is different from seeing a product or hearing a discussion related to the agenda item. Instead, what if the team explained or shared the data they analyzed and the resulting decisions they made? Now, feedback is more meaningful and direct. Taking this one step further, consider having teams email their analyzed data using the protocol in figure 5.11 (page 103–104). They use this protocol during their meeting to record their discussion comments and team agreements, but rather than turn in a separate document, they might email this to the administrator and receive feedback. Similarly, if a team creates a common assessment with scoring agreements or unpacks a standard, they can submit this for feedback. That feedback can come from the principal, another administrator, or even from the learning team to hone the common vision of the work. Schools might also create electronic folders for team and leadership access, which provide an opportunity for continual feedback on artifacts, providing the administrator or leadership are accessing the folders to provide it.

As a leader, also consider surveys in order to hear from teachers what is working well and what needs to change to better meet the needs of students. The leadership team can determine the merits of the responses and brainstorm any necessary actions. All of this contributes to a transparent culture focused on student learning. It is important that all team members see any leader as a support and model in this work, rather than an evaluator or dictator. Be clear about those things that are non-negotiable (such as common assessments and data analysis with learning responses) and those areas with latitude (such as lesson planning). Student learning requires both.

## Hold Students Accountable

Students are also accountable for their learning in a culture that embraces accountability. How are students reflecting on their learning and setting goals for themselves? Chapter 5 (page 79) includes some protocols of how to have students self-reflect on common assessments and standards. How are collaborative teams using these tools with students? How are students using the tools to articulate what they have learned and not learned yet to themselves or to parents or guardians?

In addition to tracker sheets and reflection sheets, at many elementary schools, students set a goal for reading a certain number of books or a given number of words in a year. They track their progress on a bulletin board and earn medals or prizes along the way. These students can tell the teacher where they are related to their goal and if they will make it before the end of the year. There is a culture of "I can and I will" rather than a defeatist attitude that reading is impossible.

Holding students accountable for learning does not translate into giving students a zero for work they do not turn in. Rather, consider systems teams can put in place to have students actually *do* the work during the school day without loss of instructional time. Now the school is emphasizing the importance of learning and students can reflect and set goals because they have evidence of their learning to date. Holding students accountable for learning means ensuring they learn during instruction and through learning activities and then allowing them to recognize their success or the steps they need to take to continue. Just as teacher teams continually monitor student learning data, students relentlessly monitor their own learning.

Embracing accountability is not about judging and ranking teachers, leaders, or students. Rather it is about creating a culture of learning—one focused on each student learning grade-level standards at high levels. Together, with all stakeholders continually collecting and monitoring data, learning will improve. With a constant focus on that student learning and holding one another accountable to ensure the success of each student, each teacher, and each leader, the process will improve student learning.

# Reflect and Take Action

The rubric in figure 7.6 shows levels of embracing accountability as collaborative teams, leaders, and students. Look at the rubric to determine where each group ranks related to accountability.

| | Level 1 Beginning | Level 2 Attempting | Level 3 Practicing | Level 4 Embracing |
|---|---|---|---|---|
| **Collaborative Teams** | Teams give a common assessment and talk about the results without recording the data or the decisions they make.<br><br>Teams talk about how students performed during an activity and move on.<br><br>Teams acknowledge some students are learning and others are not and make individual plans to improve learning. | Teams gather and record common assessment data and look at it before moving on.<br><br>Teams talk about how students performed during an activity (no written record) and adjust instruction.<br><br>Teams record students who are learning and who are not learning and then reassess later without making a team plan to better the results. | Teams gather common assessment data, record it, and make a collective plan to improve the learning of students.<br><br>Teams gather observational data from a lesson related to a standard and adjust instruction.<br><br>Teams record students who are learning and not learning and work collaboratively to improve the learning of students in each group. | Teams analyze trends in student work to determine student learning by target, and identify next steps by the team for each student.<br><br>Teams analyze common misconceptions from an observational tool and determine a team plan to ensure learning.<br><br>Teams work with stakeholders beyond the team to meet the needs they identify with a status check of students and improve their learning. |
| **Leaders** | Leaders rely on teams to create their own necessary systems and protocols to address academics and behavior.<br><br>Leaders monitor team actions only through submitted agendas.<br><br>Leaders provide evaluative feedback to teams related to their work. | Leaders create necessary schoolwide systems and protocols so they can address academics or behavior.<br><br>Leaders look for evidence of team actions only by attending team meetings.<br><br>Leaders recognize the work of collaborative teams without giving specific feedback that also suggests next steps. | Leaders create necessary schoolwide systems and protocols so teams can address academics and behavior.<br><br>Leaders determine how to collect evidence of team actions that improve student learning in meetings and classrooms.<br><br>Leaders provide meaningful feedback to teams on their progress toward improving student learning. | Leaders create and adjust as necessary schoolwide systems and protocols for teams to address academics and behavior.<br><br>Leaders clarify with teams how they will collect evidence of team actions that improve student learning.<br><br>Leaders provide meaningful and timely feedback to teams on their progress toward improving student learning. |
| **Students** | Students reflect on learning using the overall grade in a class or an overall test grade for a subject or course. | Students reflect on learning by target. | Students reflect on learning by target and set learning goals. | Students reflect on learning by target and set learning goals with a plan to achieve them. |

**Figure 7.6: Accountability rubric.**

*Visit go.SolutionTree.com/PLCbooks for a free reproducible version of this figure.*

Once teams have reached agreement about their current status, they should use figure 7.7 to determine the next steps to strengthen their practice in working to embrace accountability.

| Action | Team-Level Rating | Next Steps |
|---|---|---|
| Collaborative team accountability | | |
| Leadership accountability | | |
| Student accountability | | |

**Figure 7.7: Embrace accountability reflection and action plan.**

*Visit **go.SolutionTree.com/PLCbooks** for a free reproducible version of this figure.*

### Collaborative Team Questions to Consider

- How do teams address each of the four critical PLC questions?
- What is a possible SMART goal related to student learning for your team to work toward achieving?
- How will you work toward and monitor progress for meeting your team SMART goal?
- How will your team collect, analyze, and respond to common assessment data?
- How will your team collect, analyze, and respond to classroom observational learning data?
- How will your team check the status of student learning throughout the year and make strategic plans to improve student learning in each group?
- How will principals and administrators work to model the work of collaborative teams?
- How will leaders hold themselves and teacher teams accountable for student learning?
- How will students hold themselves accountable for their own learning?

# School Improvement for All—Start Now!

> Every superintendent, principal, and teacher is in a leadership position. Don't ask if you are leading. You are. Don't ask if you will make a difference. You will. The question is, "What kind of leader will you be, and what kind of difference will you make?"
>
> *—Richard DuFour and Robert J. Marzano*

Teaching is not for the faint of heart. The work is difficult, even perilous, because it affects students' lives—in the moment and into adulthood. There is an urgency to reach every student, and for all schools to improve in a continual quest for even more students to learn at high levels. Whether at the start, middle, or end of the school year, no time is better than now to begin the improvement journey.

Unfortunately, we cannot accomplish the work of improving schools with a magic bullet. Too often quick fixes entice educators to make easy structural changes. For example, a school might purchase an online intervention program or give every student an extra thirty minutes of independent reading during the school day. However, these are only first-order changes. The work we describe in this book requires second-order change, meaning that the school makes structural changes with purpose and as part of a mission and vision to improve student learning. There are no magic bullets; the work is demanding and requires a collaborative journey with a relentless focus on student learning. With second-order change, some traditions and practices that might define your school must change if they no longer move a school toward the mission and vision it desires. Do you have sacred traditions? Are you relying on magic bullets? Schools are complex organizations that require deep, focused changes to improve student learning.

Every reader of this book is a leader who affects the leadership, culture, students, curriculum, assessment, instruction, and accountability in the schools where you work. You directly influence the work of improving student learning in a focused and meaningful way. Consider the student lives you touch on a daily basis. You have a moral imperative to look each one of those students in the eye and promise he or she will experience the opportunities that education can afford and have access to the resources the school has devoted to making certain all students learn at high levels. Who are the students you serve? How will you make this promise to each one? The answer lies in the work we have described throughout this text in the context of PLCs and the continuous cycle of improvement.

CONTINUOUS IMPROVEMENT

## Embrace PLCs and Continuous-Improvement Cycles

Collaboration is one key to the work of improving schools. How are administrators, teachers, and other stakeholders working with one another to continually monitor and improve student learning? PLCs focus on student learning, collaboration, and results (DuFour et al., 2016). In collaborative team meetings focused on student learning, teams determine the curriculum (chapter 4, page 55), common assessments (chapter 5, page 79), and instruction (chapter 6, page 113) that will most effectively support student learning.

A second key is working in continuous cycles of improvement. Collaborative teams within PLCs hold themselves accountable for student learning in cycles marked by common assessment data that they gather, analyze, and respond to collectively (chapters 3 on page 41, 5 on page 79, and 7 on page 137). Schools recognize small and large successes and teams set future goals for even higher levels of learning. Together, teachers determine how to target additional learning for students who have learned and those who have not learned *yet*. They embody a mantra of leaving no student behind while teaching all students grade-level standards at high levels.

When addressing urgent school improvement, collaborative teams take many forms. They manifest as a guiding coalition, school site councils, behavior teams, and grade-level or course-alike teams, to name a few (chapter 1, page 7). Schools may create special teams to address shifts in culture (chapter 2, page 27) or other specific issues that arise along the journey to improvement that affect student learning. Identify the role of every adult in the school or district in improving the learning of *all* students. The goal through continual accountability and collaboration is always the relentless drive to have all students learn.

Through collaboration and designated cycles of improvement, teams will learn and grow alongside students. This work is too big for any one teacher. It will take the collective responsibility of administrators, teachers, support staff, parents, and community members to address the necessary second-order change. Along the way, adults must always be learning. Teachers on teams discuss how to improve lessons. They identify the strategies that help students learn, developing their own practice. They learn how to create quality assessments and allocate time to teach standards. Together, they effectively and efficiently focus on student learning.

## Plan to Start Now

While it is often desirable to map out a plan of action for improving schools, it too often takes more than one year before the school actually changes. Can you really afford, for example, to start common assessments two years from now? The students sitting in classrooms now can't wait for another year, another month, or even another week to go by without collaborative teams addressing their learning needs. The time to shrink learning gaps is now, this very moment. This means you will be building the proverbial airplane as you fly it.

Throughout this book, we describe actions for schools to take to fully embrace and improve the learning of all students. Since the time to act is now, how do you best fill that time? To attempt to do everything becomes overwhelming; teachers then strive only to survive, which often means they resort back to their traditional ways of doing things. Leaders and teams will have to determine the most effective next steps.

Each school is in a different place on its journey to continual school improvement. Each chapter details actions for teams to take to move student learning forward. As early as possible and regularly, teams must collect and analyze data. With that in mind, figure E.1 reviews the critical actions for school improvement for all. Use the chart to identify those actions you have already taken and those you wish to address next.

| Action | Current Level 1–4 (With Evidence) | Next Steps | Evidence That You Have Achieved Next Steps |
|---|---|---|---|
| **Leadership** | | | |
| Form a team that is capable of leading change. | | | |
| Develop urgency and a collective vision for the change. | | | |
| Develop collective commitments that lead to action. | | | |
| Clarify and communicate expectations for collaborative teams. | | | |
| **Culture** | | | |
| Assess culture. | | | |
| Transform culture. | | | |
| Recognize symbols and artifacts. | | | |
| Celebrate positive steps. | | | |
| Examine rituals. | | | |
| Get the right people on the bus. | | | |

**Figure E.1: Reflection and action plan for *School Improvement for All*.**

continued →

| Action | Current Level 1–4 (With Evidence) | Next Steps | Evidence That You Have Achieved Next Steps |
|---|---|---|---|
| **21st Century Learners** | | | |
| Address student needs with classroom intervention and remediation. | | | |
| Address student needs with a schoolwide focus on student learning. | | | |
| Empower students. | | | |
| **Guaranteed and Viable Curriculum** | | | |
| Identify priority standards | | | |
| Create a proficiency map. | | | |
| Unpack standards into learning progressions and student learning targets. | | | |
| Create unit plans. | | | |
| Create daily plans. | | | |

| Common Assessments | | | |
|---|---|---|---|
| Determine what to assess using standards and proficiency scales. | | | |
| Determine how to assess using assessment design. | | | |
| Determine how to communicate results and respond to student learning. | | | |
| **Instruction** | | | |
| Design classroom culture. | | | |
| Plan units of instruction. | | | |
| Use first-best instructional practices. | | | |
| Respond to student learning. | | | |
| **Accountability** | | | |
| Promote and embrace collaborative teacher team accountability. | | | |
| Promote and embrace leadership accountability. | | | |
| Promote student accountability. | | | |

*Visit **go.SolutionTree.com/PLCbooks** for a free reproducible version of this figure.*

The students who come to school each day form the center of school improvement. They deserve the best curriculum, instruction, and assessment, and they deserve to be a part of the process of identifying what they have learned and what they have not learned yet. They deserve strong leaders and a culture conducive to learning along with accountability to that learning. To make this happen, collaborative teams must continually monitor and adjust their practice. This is not easy work, yet it is critical to the life of each and every student.

## Know That Everything Matters

In a thriving school focused on student learning, every meeting, every piece of paperwork, every wall decoration, and every minute of the school day matters; each is designed for the purpose of improving student learning. The culture promotes growth mindsets in teachers and students alike, and all are willing to roll up their sleeves and productively struggle along the journey to maximize learning. Leaders define what is tight and loose and celebrate the successes of teams and students (DuFour et al., 2016). Complaints without attempts to problem solve are absent.

Just as all students can learn, so can all schools become a model of school improvement and student achievement. Another school year will come and go. Will that year include a focused journey to school improvement? It is hard work, but doable—and imperative for the lives of the students you serve.

# References and Resources

Ainsworth, L. (2003). *"Unwrapping" the standards: A simple process to make standards manageable.* Englewood, CO: Advanced Learning Press.

Allensworth, E., Ponisciak, S., & Mazzeo, C. (2009). *The schools teachers leave: Teacher mobility in Chicago Public Schools.* Chicago: Consortium on Chicago School Research.

American Psychological Association. (2012). *Facing the school dropout dilemma.* Washington, DC: Author. Accessed at www.apa.org/pi/families/resources/school-droupout-prevention.aspx on May 5, 2016.

Bailey, K., & Jakicic, C. (2012). *Common formative assessment: A toolkit for Professional Learning Communities at Work.* Bloomington, IN: Solution Tree Press.

Bailey, K., Jakicic, C., & Spiller, J. (2014). *Collaborating for success with the Common Core: A toolkit for Professional Learning Communities at Work.* Bloomington, IN: Solution Tree Press.

Barth, R. (2001). *Learning by heart.* San Francisco: Jossey-Bass.

BERC Group. (n.d.). *1st and 2nd order change.* Accessed at www.bercgroup.com/1st-and-2nd-order-change.html on July 10, 2016.

Bergland, C. (2014, February 16). *Tackling the "vocabulary gap" between rich and poor children* [Blog post]. Accessed at www.psychologytoday.com/blog/the-athletes-way/201402/tackling-the-vocabulary-gap-between-rich-and-poor -children on July 18, 2016.

Black, P., & Wiliam, D. (1998). Inside the black box: Raising standards through classroom assessment. *Phi Delta Kappan, 80*(2), 139–148.

Bloom, B., Anderson, L., & Krathwohl, D. (2001). *A taxonomy for learning, teaching, and assessing: A revision of Bloom's taxonomy of educational objectives.* New York: Longman.

Boaler, J. (2015). *Mathematical mindsets: Unleashing students' potential through creative math, inspiring messages and innovative teaching.* San Francisco: Jossey-Bass.

Branch, G. F., Hanushek, E., & Rivkin, S. (2013). School leaders matter. *Education Next, 12*(1), 63–69.

Breslow, J. M. (2012, September 12). By the numbers: Dropping out of high school. *Dropout Nation.* Accessed at www.pbs .org/wgbh/pages/frontline/education/dropout-nation/by-the-numbers-dropping-out-of-high-school on May 5, 2016.

Brown, E. (2016, November 29). U.S. students still lag many Asian peers on international math and science exam. *Washington Post.* Accessed at www.washingtonpost.com/local/education/us-students-still-lag-many-asian-peers-on -international-math-and-science-exam/2016/11/28/cdf2e1d2-b588-11e6-959c-172c82123976_story.html?utm _term=.ec15d3216d97 on March 13, 2017.

Buffum, A., & Mattos, M. (Eds.). (2014). *It's about time: Planning interventions and extensions in elementary school.* Bloomington, IN: Solution Tree Press.

Buffum, A., Mattos, M., & Weber, C. (2012). *Simplifying response to intervention: Four essential guiding principles.* Bloomington, IN: Solution Tree Press.

Burris, C. C., & Welner, K. G. (2005). Closing the achievement gap by detracking. *Phi Delta Kappan, 86*(8), 594–598.

College Board. (2014, February 11). *The 10th annual AP report to the nation.* New York: Author.

Collins, J. (2001). *Good to great: Why some companies make the leap . . . and others don't.* New York: HarperCollins.

Conzemius, A., & O'Neill, J. (2013). *Handbook for SMART school teams: Revitalizing best practices for collaboration* (2nd ed.). Bloomington, IN: Solution Tree Press.

Daggett, W. R. (2014). *Rigor/relevance framework: A guide to focusing resources to increase student performance.* Rexford, NY: International Center for Leadership in Education.

David, J. L., & Talbert, J. E. (2013). *Turning around a high-poverty district: Learning from Sanger.* San Francisco: S. H. Cowell Foundation.

Deal, T. E., & Peterson, K. D. (2016). *Shaping school culture* (3rd ed.). San Francisco: Jossey-Bass.

Dean, C. B., Hubbell, E. R., Pitler, H., & Stone, B. (2012). *Classroom instruction that works: Research-based strategies for increasing student achievement* (2nd ed.). Alexandria, VA: Association for Supervision and Curriculum Development.

Depka, E. (2017). *Raising the rigor: Effective questioning strategies and techniques for the classroom.* Bloomington, IN: Solution Tree Press.

Dickens, C. (1859). *A tale of two cities.* London: Chapman and Hall.

DuFour, R. (2015). *In praise of American educators: And how they can become even better.* Bloomington, IN: Solution Tree Press.

DuFour, R. (2016). *Keynote presentation.* Professional Learning Communities at Work™ Institutes.

DuFour, R., DuFour, R., Eaker, R., & Many, T. (2010). *Learning by doing: A handbook for Professional Learning Communities at Work* (2nd ed.). Bloomington, IN: Solution Tree Press.

DuFour, R., DuFour, R., Eaker, R., Many, T. W., & Mattos, M. (2016). *Learning by doing: A handbook for Professional Learning Communities at Work* (3rd ed.). Bloomington, IN: Solution Tree Press.

DuFour, R., & Marzano, R. J. (2011). *Leaders of learning: How district, school, and classroom leaders improve student achievement.* Bloomington, IN: Solution Tree Press.

Dweck, C. S. (2006). *Mindset: The new psychology of success.* New York: Ballantine.

Eaker, R., & Keating, J. (2012). *Every school, every team, every classroom: District leadership for growing Professional Learning Communities at Work.* Bloomington, IN: Solution Tree Press.

Eaker, R., & Keating, J. (2015). *Kid by kid, skill by skill: Teaching in a Professional Learning Community at Work.* Bloomington, IN: Solution Tree Press.

Effective School Research. (2003). Accessed at www.lakeforest.edu on March 13, 2017.

Elmore, R. F. (2004). *School reform from the inside out: Policy, practice, and performance.* Cambridge, MA: Harvard Education Press.

Erkens, C., Schimmer, T., & Vagle, N. D. (2017). *Essential assessment: Six tenets for bringing hope, efficacy, and achievement to the classroom.* Bloomington, IN: Solution Tree Press.

Fouts, J. T. (2003). *A decade of reform: A summary of research findings on classroom, school, and district effectiveness in Washington State.* Seattle: Washington School Research Center, Seattle Pacific University.

Fuller, E. J., & Young, M. D. (2009, April). *Retention of newly hired principals in Texas.* Austin, TX: University Council for Educational Administration.

Greenstone, M., Looney, A., Patashnik, J., & Yu, M. (2013). Thirteen economic facts about social mobility and the role of education. *Hamilton Project Policy Memo.* Washington, DC: The Brookings Institute. Accessed at www.brookings.edu /research/reports/2013/06/13-facts-higher-education on November 9, 2016.

Gregory, G., & Kaufeldt, M. (2012). *Think big, start small: How to differentiate instruction in a brain-friendly classroom.* Bloomington, IN: Solution Tree Press.

Guskey, T. R. (2015). *On your mark: Challenging the conventions of grading and reporting.* Bloomington, IN: Solution Tree Press.

Hall, P., & Simeral, A. (2015). *Teach reflect learn: Building your capacity for success in the classroom.* Alexandria, VA: Association for Supervision and Curriculum Development.

Hargreaves, A., & Fullan, M. (2012). *Professional capital: Transforming teaching in every school.* New York: Teachers College Press.

Hattie, J. (2009). *Visible learning: A synthesis of over 800 meta-analyses relating to achievement.* New York: Routledge.

Hattie, J. (2012). *Visible learning for teachers: Maximizing impact on learning.* New York: Routledge.

Hattie, J., & Yates, G. (2014). *Visible learning and the science of how we learn.* New York: Routledge.

Hess, K. K. (2004, August). *Applying Webb's Depth-of-Knowledge (DOK) levels in reading.* Accessed at www.nciea.org /publication_PDFs/DOKreading_KH08.pdf on May 20, 2016.

Hess, K. K. (2005a). *Applying Webb's Depth-of-Knowledge (DOK) levels in social studies.* Accessed at www.nciea.org /publication_PDFs/DOKsocialstudies_KH08.pdf on May 20, 2016.

Hess, K. K. (2005b). *Applying Webb's Depth-of-Knowledge (DOK) levels in writing.* Accessed at www.nciea.org/publication _PDFs/DOKwriting_KH08.pdf on May 20, 2016.

Hess, K. K. (2010). *Applying Webb's Depth-of-Knowledge (DOK) levels in science.* Accessed at www.nciea.org/publication _PDFs/DOKscience_KH11.pdf on May 20, 2016.

International Association for the Evaluation of Educational Achievement. (2015a). *TIMSS 2015 international results in mathematics.* Accessed at http://timssandpirls.bc.edu/timss2015/international-results/timss-2015/mathematics/student -achievement/trends-in-mathematics-achievement on March 19, 2017.

International Association for the Evaluation of Educational Achievement. (2015b). *TIMSS 2015 international results in science.* Accessed at http://timssandpirls.bc.edu/timss2015/international-results/timss-2015/science/student -achievement/trends-in-science-achievement on Marcy 19, 2017.

Johnson, D. W., & Johnson, R. T. (1999). *Learning together and alone* (5th ed.). Upper Saddle River, NJ: Pearson.

Johnson, D. W., Johnson, R. T., & Holubec, E. J. (2008). *Cooperation in the classroom* (Rev. ed.). Edina, MN: Interaction.

Kagan, S. (1994). *Cooperative learning.* San Clemente, CA: Kagan.

Kagan, S., & Kagan, M. (2009). *Kagan cooperative learning.* San Clemente, CA: Kagan.

Kanold, T. D., & Larson, M. R. (2015). *Beyond the Common Core: A handbook for mathematics in a PLC at Work, leader's guide.* T. D. Kanold (Ed.). Bloomington, IN: Solution Tree Press.

Kotter, J. P. (1996). *Leading change.* Boston: Harvard Business School Press.

Kramer, S. V. (2015). *How to leverage PLCs for school improvement.* Bloomington, IN: Solution Tree Press.

Kutash, J., Nico, E., Gorin, E., Rahmatullah, S., & Tallant, K. (2010, September). *The school turnaround field guide.* Boston: Foundation Strategy Group.

Lawyers' Committee for Civil Rights of the San Francisco Bay Area. (2013, January). *Held back: Addressing misplacement of 9th grade students in Bay Area school math classes.* Accessed at http://lccr.com/wp-content/uploads/HELD-BACK-9th -Grade-Math-Misplacement.pdf on July 23, 2016.

Le Floch, K., Garcia, A. N., & Barbour, C. (2016, March). *Want to improve low-performing schools? Focus on the adults.* Washington, DC: Education Policy Center.

Leithwood, K., Louis, K. S., Anderson, S., & Wahlstrom, K. (2004). *How leadership influences student learning.* New York: Wallace Foundation.

Lezotte, L. W., & Snyder, K. M. (2011). *What effective schools do: Re-envisioning the correlates.* Bloomington, IN: Solution Tree Press.

Many, T. W. (2016, Summer). Is it R.E.A.L. or not? *AllThingsPLC Magazine*, pp. 34–35.

Marzano, R. J. (2003). *What works in schools: Translating research into action.* Alexandria, VA: Association for Supervision and Curriculum Development.

Marzano, R. J. (2006). *Classroom assessment and grading that work.* Alexandria, VA: Association for Supervision and Curriculum Development.

Marzano, R. J. (2010). *Formative assessment and standards-based grading.* Bloomington, IN: Marzano Research.

Marzano, R. J., & Pickering, D. J. (2011). *The highly engaged classroom.* Bloomington, IN: Marzano Research.

Marzano, R., & Pickering, D., & Heflebower, T. (2011). *The highly engaged classroom.* Bloomington, IN: Marzano Research.

Marzano, R. J., Pickering, D. J., & Pollock, J. E. (2001). *Classroom instruction that works: Research-based strategies for increasing student achievement.* Alexandria, VA: Association for Supervision and Curriculum Development.

Marzano, R. J., & Simms, J. A. (2013). *Vocabulary for the Common Core.* Bloomington, IN: Solution Tree Press.

Marzano, R. J., Waters, T., & McNulty, B. A. (2005). *School leadership that works: From research to results.* Alexandria, VA: Association for Supervision and Curriculum Development.

Mattos, M., DuFour, R., DuFour, R., Eaker, R., & Many, T. (2016). *Concise answers to frequently asked questions about Professional Learning Communities at Work.* Bloomington, IN: Solution Tree Press.

McKenzie, K. B., & Skrla, L. (2011). *Using equity audits in the classroom to reach and teach all students.* Thousand Oaks, CA: Corwin Press.

Melsa, J. L. (2007, September). The forces driving change. *ASEE Prism, 17*(1). Accessed at www.prism-magazine.org /sept07/asee_today.cfm on July 29, 2016.

Muhammad, A. (2009). *Transforming school culture: How to overcome staff division.* Bloomington, IN: Solution Tree Press.

Muhammad, A. (2015). *Overcoming the achievement gap trap: Liberating mindsets to effect change.* Bloomington, IN: Solution Tree Press.

Muhammad, A., & Hollie, S. (2011). *The will to lead, the skill to teach: Transforming schools at every level.* Bloomington, IN: Solution Tree Press.

Muhammad, A., & Peterson, K. D. (2012). *Sample school culture audit.* Accessed at www.newfrontier21.com on March 13, 2017.

Mullis, I. V. S., Martin, M. O., Foy, P., & Arora, A. (2012). *TIMSS 2011 international results in mathematics.* Chestnut Hill, MA: Trends in International Mathematics and Science Study and Progress in International Reading Literacy Study Center. Accessed at http://timssandpirls.bc.edu/timss2011/downloads/T11_IR_Mathematics_Fullbook.pdf on November 10, 2016.

National Center for Education Statistics. (2015). Table 219.75: Percentage of high school dropouts among persons 16 to 24 years old (status dropout rate), by income level, and percentage distribution of status dropouts, by labor force status and years of school completed: 1970 through 2014. *Digest of Education Statistics.* Accessed at https://nces.ed.gov /programs/digest/d15/tables/dt15_219.75.asp on March 19, 2017.

National Center for Education Statistics. (2016a, April). *2015 results: Mathematics and reading, grade 12.* Accessed at www.nationsreportcard.gov/reading_math_g12_2015/files/infographic_2015_g12_math_reading.pdf on November 8, 2016.

National Center for Education Statistics. (2016b, May). *Immediate college enrollment rate.* Accessed at http://nces.ed.gov /programs/coe/indicator_cpa.asp on July 28, 2016.

National Center for Education Statistics. (2016c). *Program for International Student Assessment (PISA) data.* Accessed at https://nces.ed.gov/surveys/pisa/pisa2015/pisa2015highlights_9.asp on March 19, 2017.

National Center for Education Statistics. (2016d, May). *Public high school graduation rates.* Accessed at http://nces.ed.gov /programs/coe/indicator_coi.asp on July 28, 2016.

National Education Association. (n.d.). *Preparing 21st century students for a global society: An educator's guide to the "four Cs."* Accessed at www.nea.org/assets/docs/A-Guide-to-Four-Cs.pdf on July 20, 2016.

National Governors Association Center for Best Practices & Council of Chief State School Officers. (2010a). *Common Core State Standards for English language arts and literacy in history/social studies, science, and technical subjects.* Washington, DC: Authors. Accessed at www.corestandards.org/assets/CCSSI_ELA%20Standards.pdf on January 3, 2017.

National Governors Association Center for Best Practices & Council of Chief State School Officers. (2010b). *Common Core State Standards for mathematics.* Washington, DC: Authors. Accessed at www.corestandards.org/assets/CCSSI_Math %20Standards.pdf on January 3, 2017.

Nation's Report Card. (2015). *Mathematics and reading assessments.* Accessed at www.nationsreportcard.gov/reading _math_2015/#mathematics/scores?grade=4 on March 19, 2017.

Oklahoma State Department of Education. (2016, January). *Oklahoma academic standards: Mathematics.* Accessed at http:// sde.ok.gov/sde/sites/ok.gov.sde/files/documents/files/OAS-Math-Final%20Version_2.pdf on Mary 18, 2017.

Organisation for Economic Co-operation and Development. (2011). *Fifty years of change in education.* Accessed at www.oecd.org/dataoecd/37/45/48642586.pdf on May 5, 2016.

Partnership for 21st Century Learning. (2007). *Framework for 21st century learning.* Accessed at www.p21.org/our-work /p21-framework accessed on July 23, 2016.

Patterson, K., Grenny, J., Maxfield, D., McMillan, R., & Switzler, A. (2008). *Influencer: The power to change anything.* New York: McGraw-Hill.

Payne, R. K. (2005). *A framework for understanding poverty* (4th rev. ed.). Highlands, TX: aha! Process.

Peterson, K. D. (2002). Positive or negative? *Journal of Staff Development, 23*(3), 10–15.

Peterson, K. D., & Deal, T. E. (1998). How leaders influence the culture of schools. *Educational Leadership, 56*(1), 28–30.

Popham, W. J. (2003). *Test better, teach better: The instructional role of assessment.* Alexandria, VA: Association for Supervision and Curriculum Development.

Ravitch, D. (2016). *Network for Public Education state report card 2016.* Accessed at https://networkforpubliceducation.org /tomswisher/current_map.html on March 18, 2017.

Reardon, S. (2011). The widening academic achievement gap between the rich and the poor: New evidence and possible explanations. In R. Murnane & G. Duncan (Eds.), *Whither opportunity? Rising inequality and the uncertain life chances of low-income children.* New York: Russell Sage Foundation.

Reeves, D. B. (2002). *The leader's guide to standards: A blueprint for educational equity and excellence.* San Francisco: Jossey-Bass.

Rowe, C. (2016, July 9). Some Seattle schools end "tracking" in push for equity and success. *Seattle Times.* Accessed at www.seattletimes.com/education-lab/an-effort-to-raise-achievement-by-dismantling-de-facto-segregation/?utm _source=email&utm_medium=email&utm_campaign=article_title_1.1 on July 19, 2016.

Schlechty, P. C. (2001). *Shaking up the schoolhouse: How to support and sustain educational innovation*. San Francisco: Jossey-Bass.

Schuhl, S. (2016, April 27). *Doing it or doing it well? Using data for learning* [Blog post]. Accessed at www.allthingsplc.info /blog/view/325/doing-it-or-doing-it-well-using-data-for-learning on July 31, 2016.

Sheninger, E. C. (2016). *Uncommon learning: Creating schools that work for kids*. Thousand Oaks, CA: Corwin Press.

Smith, H. (2014, January 21). *What the Common Core Standards mean for special education students* [Blog post]. Accessed at www .scilearn.com/blog/what-the-common-core-standards-mean-for-special-education-students on March 13, 2017.

Sousa, D. A., & Tomlinson, C. A. (2011). *Differentiation and the brain: How neuroscience supports the learner-friendly classroom*. Bloomington, IN: Solution Tree Press.

Sparks, S. D. (2013, July 29). Dropout indicators found for 1st graders. *Education Week*. Accessed at www.edweek.org /ew/articles/2013/07/29/37firstgrade.h32.html?tkn=YRXFxf2U7fneiqZz7tQQsojrJgXCEYZRzZxk&cmp=ENL-EU -NEWS1 on May 5, 2016.

Sprenger, M. (2005). *How to teach so students remember*. Alexandria, VA: Association for Supervision and Curriculum Development.

Stephens, T. L. (2015, August 21). *Encouraging positive student engagement and motivation: Tips for teachers* [Blog post]. Accessed at www.pearsoned.com/education-blog/encouraging-positive-student-engagement-and-motivation-tips-for-teachers on March 21, 2017.

Stiggins, R., Arter, J., Chappuis, J., & Chappuis, S. (2006). *Classroom assessment for student learning: Doing it right—Using it well*. Princeton, NJ: Educational Testing Service.

Strong, R., Silver, H. F., & Robinson, A. (1995). Strengthening student engagement: What do students want (and what really motivates them)? *Educational Leadership*, *53*(1), 8–12.

Tavernise, S. (2012, February 9). Education gap grows between rich and poor, studies say. *New York Times*. Accessed at www.nytimes.com/2012/02/10/education/education-gap-grows-between-rich-and-poor-studies-show.html ?pagewanted=all on May 5, 2016.

Texas Essential Knowledge and Skills. (2011). *Chapter 113: Texas Essential Knowledge and Skills for social studies, subchapter C—High school*. Accessed at http://ritter.tea.state.tx.us/rules/tac/chapter113/ch113c.html on May 19, 2016.

Toncheff, M., & Kanold, T. D. (2015). *Beyond the Common Core: A handbook for mathematics in a PLC at Work, high school*. T. D. Kanold (Ed.). Bloomington, IN: Solution Tree Press.

U.S. Census Bureau. (2006). *Current population survey: Educational attainment in the United States*. Washington, DC: U.S. Department of Commerce.

Vagle, N. D. (2015). *Design in five: Essential phases to create engaging assessment practice*. Bloomington, IN: Solution Tree Press.

Waterman, S. (2010). *Pathways report: Dead ends and wrong turns on the path through algebra*. Accessed on January 10, 2017 at www.noycefdn.org/documents/Pathways_Report.pdf.

Webb, N. L. (1999, August). *Alignment of science and mathematics standards and assessments in four states* (Research monograph no. 18). Washington, DC: Council of Chief State School Officers. Accessed at http://facstaff.wcer.wisc .edu/normw/WEBBMonograph%2018AlignmentPaper.pdf on May 20, 2016.

Webb, N. L. (2002, March 28). *Depth-of-knowledge levels for four content areas*. Accessed at www.hed.state.nm.us/uploads /files/ABE/Policies/depth_of_knowledge_guide_for_all_subject_areas.pdf on May 20, 2016.

Zubrzycki, J. (2016, May 17). *Girls outperform boys on first NAEP technology, engineering test* [Blog post]. Accessed at http:// blogs.eduweek.org/edweek/curriculum/2016/05/naep_engineering_test_embargoe.html on November 8, 2016.

# Index

# Wait! Your professional development journey doesn't have to end with the last pages of this book.

We realize improving student learning doesn't happen overnight. And your school or district shouldn't be left to puzzle out all the details of this process alone.

**No matter where you are on the journey, we're committed to helping you get to the next stage.**

Take advantage of everything from **custom workshops** to **keynote presentations** and **interactive web and video conferencing**. We can even help you develop an action plan tailored to fit your specific needs.

## *Let's get the conversation started.*

Call 888.763.9045 today.

 SolutionTree.com

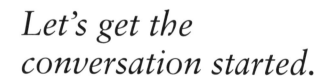

### How to Leverage PLCs for School Improvement
**Sharon V. Kramer**

Discover how to build a professional learning community that fosters collaboration and collective responsibility to create lasting change and improve student learning schoolwide. Read a true account of a school that experienced reform, reversed its culture of failure, and reaped lasting results.

**BKF668**

### Essential Assessment
**Cassandra Erkens, Tom Schimmer, and Nicole Dimich Vagle**

Discover how to use the power of assessment to instill hope, efficacy, and achievement in your students. Explore six essential tenets of assessment that will help deepen your understanding of assessment to not only meet standards but also enhance students' academic success.

**BKF752**

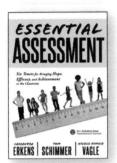

### Engage in the Mathematical Practices
**Kit Norris and Sarah Schuhl**

Discover more than forty strategies for ensuring students learn critical reasoning skills and retain understanding. Each chapter is devoted to a different Standard for Mathematical Practice and offers an in-depth look at why the standard is important for students' understanding of mathematics.

**BKF670**

### Learning by Doing
**Richard DuFour, Rebecca DuFour, Robert Eaker, Thomas W. Many, and Mike Mattos**

Discover how to transform your school or district into a high-performing PLC. The third edition of this comprehensive action guide offers new strategies for addressing critical PLC topics, including hiring and retaining new staff, creating team-developed common formative assessments, and more.

**BKF746**

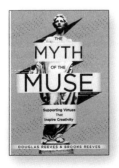

### The Myth of the Muse
**Douglas Reeves and Brooks Reeves**

The authors argue that creativity is not spontaneous or inborn but a process that can be cultivated. Ideal for team study and discussion, the book outlines seven "virtues" that inspire creativity and includes activities and guidelines to encourage and facilitate creativity.

**BKF655**

## Solution Tree | Press

a division of

Solution Tree

Visit SolutionTree.com or call 800.733.6786 to order.